LINDA JOHNSON-BELL

GOOD FOOD
FINE WINE

THE ESSENTIAL GUIDE TO MATCHING FOOD AND WINE

CASSELL

For Michael and Benjamin

First published in the United Kingdom in 1999 by Cassell

A CIP catalogue record for this book is available from the British Library

ISBN 0-304-35149-0

Designed by Chris Bell
Illustrations by Sarah Symonds
Diagram by Richard Garratt
Printed and bound in Great Britain by Mackays of Chatham

Chart on page 77 from Le Conseil Interprofessionnel du Vin de
Bordeaux, 1 cours du XXX Juillet, 33075 Bordeaux France,
Tel: 33.56.00.22.66; Fax: 33.56.00.22.82

Cassell
Illustrated Division
The Orion Publishing Group
Wellington House
125 Strand
London WC2R 0BB

Contents

Introduction

I VERY immodestly consider myself a wine expert, and a purist at that. At first, I never paid very much attention to food. It was simply what came with my wine. I cringed when waiters in restaurants brought the food menu first, treating the wine selection as an afterthought. Anyone who didn't consider wine as first and foremost, and who didn't insist that the food bow to the superior power of the· grape, was a heathen, in my book. But no more. I no longer ridicule food writers or those attention-hungry chefs who become pop stars (well, not as much as I used to). For I have married the enemy: a 'foodie'.

Do not get me wrong, I am not a stranger to good food. I come from one of those rare American households where fast food and cola drinks were *verboten*, where dinner was a formal ritual, and where every meal was fresh and original. In addition, for over ten years, I wallowed in gastronomic excess while living in France, scouring the daily markets for the freshest produce, making hundreds of pots of home-made *confiture* and attending almost every Michelin-star restaurant opening. I even prepared and ate things that still wriggle in your dish when served. I *did* the French thing – wholly and completely. But I did it from a wine drinker's perspective. With the benefit of hindsight, however, I realize that a love of good food was slowly infusing into my subconscious, without my knowledge or consent.

My 'foodie' owns a wonderful restaurant in London's Portobello Road. I found myself surrounded. I had no choice but to convert. Now, all day long, magnificent odours waft about me. I find myself engrossed in conversation with the chefs over how long squid should be marinated for the ceviche, which spices would best liven up the vegetarian dishes, and which wines would best complement the new menus.

Suddenly, I found myself speaking another language. I was force-fed a diet of freshly picked wild raspberries, duck egg omelettes, home-grown salads filled with nasturtium leaves, rose petals, chives, rocket, three different varieties of mint, lavender and rosemary, not to mention fresh oysters with horseradish and lime, sashimi of salmon with wasabi and fresh ginger, sweet potato with peanut and coriander pesto, roast pork with crackling, and banoffee pie. My 'foodie' had introduced me to the other side of the equation – my tastebuds couldn't keep up. It worked. I was seduced. He didn't get me drunk, he just got me properly fed – something I was told would never happen to me in England!

It is fun. It is interesting. And, suddenly, it all makes sense. We can only really know and understand wine and the taste of it, if we know and understand the same about food. They are mated for life.

The tradition of enjoying food and wine together has become so much a part of our daily routine that it is practically involuntary: food on table, wine in glass. What could be more natural? We whip up a creamy *fettucini Alfredo*, deftly uncork a bottle of cool, crisp Chianti, throw on some Pavarotti and light some candles *et voilà*! We've usually mastered this scenario (and what follows!) by the time we leave university. But why does this classic combination work so well? How did we know that the fresh Parmesan and nutmeg, the dominant flavours of the pasta, would go so nicely with the Sangiovese grape that dominates the wine? We are all familiar with the golden rules of wine service, passed to us through years of Sunday lunches with the family or gleaned from the jacket flaps of recipe books: rules such as 'white meat takes white wine, and red meat, red wine', and 'white wine before red', and so on. But did you ever stop to think why? Why do food and wine taste the way they do and why are these tastes so varied?

With today's plethora of international foods and wines available, the choices can become overwhelming. If you are confused as to how to match wine with food, put away your beer and despair no more. It is easier than you think. For, despite the apparent complexity of matches, you have been deceived. Most information available to us takes a generic and simplistic approach: lamb goes well with red wine, for example. Or, they go to the other extreme and are overly specific: Icelandic lamb of a specific age with a curry and coconut milk sauce with a dash of coriander and parsley goes well with 'so-and-so's wine of one or two particular vintages of the last decade, unattainable in Britain, made of an obscure grape variety, served at 15° Celsius'.

Actually, it is not the lamb you should be worrying about. Here is the secret: marry the dominant flavour of the dish (usually found in the sauce) to the dominant grape variety of the wine. This is the crux of the situation. Basic ingredient meets basic ingredient (worry about texture and weight later). An Indian lamb curry dish may be better with a spicy, acidic white such as a Gewürztraminer, whereas a classic lamb roast in gravy with roast potatoes and mint sauce would prefer a rich Pomerol or New World Cabernet Sauvignon. (Note that Cabernet Sauvignon is the dominant grape variety used in the Cabernet Sauvignon, Cabernet Franc and Merlot Bordeaux blend in Pomerol.)

But we can make things even easier. It is not just about Indian food going best with spicy whites and Chinese with tannic reds – but about the sweet, sour, salty or spicy flavour of the food going with the sweetness, acidity, bitterness or astringency of the wine. Nowhere does there exist a complete compilation of dishes with an explanation of *why* things taste the way they taste, and therefore match or don't match. This guide will provide that information.

In addition to listing specific dishes, you will also be given an explanation from the specific to the general. Illogical you might say, but working first with specific flavours, then their groups, then the dishes, does make sense.

Furthermore, you will discover the reasons why some pairings work and others don't, how the classic marriages developed, how to vary taste themes without disastrous results, and the industry secrets and remedies when dealing with wine's sworn enemies.

It is interesting to note is that all this used to be very easy – that is, if you lived in Rome or Peking or Delhi. If you were a local inhabitant of any of these places – so recognizable as the origins of our regular take-aways – you wouldn't have to think twice about your accompanying brew. Having to worry about what goes with what is a relatively modern dilemma.

Every country or region that is known for a particular speciality produces a wine or other alcoholic beverage intended to strike the perfect accord with its food. Usually it is also a home-grown product created from pretty much the same ingredients that are in the food. The Romans drink Frascati Superiore Secco with their *spaghetti alla carbonara*, the Swiss enjoy Chasselas with their cheese fondue, the North Africans choose fig alcohol and mint tea with their couscous, the Russians serve vodka with their bortsch, and the Scandinavians appreciate aquavit with their gravad lax.

These rich food and drink pairings are often regional. Nowhere is this clearer than in Italy or France. In France, one drinks Riesling with *choucroute garnie à l'alsacïenne*, Sancerre with Chavignol cheese, and Sauternes with foie gras. None of this has come about by accident, but by design – nature's design. Wine is simply made from grapes, and grapes are fruit, which are grown just like any other fruit or crop. Fruit born of the same soil, in the same climate and of the same environment, very naturally make perfect bedfellows.

This gets a little more difficult in countries that have brought everything with them, so to speak! The USA is a perfect example. Theoretically, the staples of the Native American – corn, potatoes, beans, squash, pumpkin, tomatoes and fried bread – were married to whatever they drank locally: cactus juice, whiskey given to them by the cavalry? The Mexicans used beans, chillies and corn, adapted to their tastes, and soothed their burning tongues with Tequila, while the European settlers of the West relied heavily on sourdough bread and pinto beans. Until, that is, they moved in completely and imposed their preferences from home, with hybrids such as clam chowder and pumpkin pie being the results. American cuisine today is a complete fusion of local and regional crops mixed with the recipes and foodstuffs imported and planted by the immigrants. Hence you'll find Dutch dishes in Pennsylvania, French dishes in Louisiana and, of course, Italian, Jewish, Polish, German and more, in New York, where the original immigrants first landed.

In the United Kingdom, there is a similar situation. We have the most amazing choice of both food and wine at our disposal – a truly international selection of imports. We even have our own wines, although local wines are not sufficiently appreciated as yet and most of the wine-drinking population turns to the imports.

What is happening is that we are, in a way, re-inventing the wheel. We are having to analyse and work at something that has always been second nature to us. Before we were so spoiled for choice, we drank mead, beer or home-made wines and that was the end of the story.

Today we are so concerned about food and wine pairings that we have even coined the term 'food wines' to denote wines that are easily matched to foods. This is both a good and a bad thing. It is true that in an effort to persuade consumers to consider wine an everyday beverage, essential to a healthy diet, it has to be associated with food. Heavy marketing of wine as an accompaniment to food was the only direction to take, using the European culture as a model. Unfortunately it has almost gone too far, and consumers now don't expect anything more from a wine than that it costs less than £5 and that it goes with an entire meal. Heaven forbid it overshadows the Thai sauce on the prawns.

But perhaps we are overlooking the vital importance of a wine's personality. Some wine producers have gone as far as deliberately to make easy, light, noncommittal wines for this reason: they are marketable and consumer friendly and are getting the job done. But these are probably not wines you would always want on your table. Yes, if we are feeling lazy, it is easy to grab a non-committal companion who will agree with everything we say. But isn't it far more interesting and agreeable to have a companion with a personality and opinion of their own?

This lack of originality may have come about because although ethnic foods have been successfully imported, the corresponding beverages have not, so for many countries, the wine/food equation has been lost.

Luckily, more and more regional wines from Europe are becoming accessible. We not only have more wines from new countries being imported, but a more varied selection from countries we already know. For example, the French imports are no longer restricted to Burgundy and Bordeaux but now include all their lovely satellite regions.

The problem with some of the typical local wines we only see while on vacation in Europe is that they are produced in such small quantities that there is not enough to export. For example, Hungary's goulash has been duplicated, copied and Westernized for ages, whereas

their wines, such as Tokaji or Kékfrankos, are relatively unknown. Thus we have little choice but to drink Burgundy with our goulash, which might well work, but was not what the plains' cowboys in Hungary enjoyed. (Actually, I doubt that they sat around the camp fire commenting on the steely mineral backbone of a Tokaji, but you know what I mean!)

Some would argue that the reason these wines never left home is because they are undrinkable or subject to low technical and even lower hygiene standards. This is hardly a problem any more (I personally like a little dirt in my wine). But I would argue that if they had the international recognition needed to provide the funds and regenerate the industry, then these problems would be corrected and a regional style could be preserved, within traditional parameters yet on a larger scale. And this is what is happening. Countries like Portugal, Romania and Hungary are receiving investment and are refusing to enter the international market by riding on the fame and reputation of the ubiquitous, well-known European grape varieties. They argue that if they are obliged to re-market their wine's reputation, why not use that as an opportunity to educate wine drinkers and to market their own grape varieties and wine styles?

This is a brave step, especially in a market where the simple word 'Chardonnay' on a bottle label can triple profits. But the market, as well as the consumer, is changing. The first step was to get us drinking wines from countries we could not even point to on a map. The next is to introduce us to grape varieties and styles that, while traditional in their own right, are presented as 'new and different' to the international consumer.

So with more food and wine choices available than ever before, where does one begin? If you understand the workings of flavour groups, then you will easily master the game of food and wine matches. This guide will put you in control of your palate and your imagination. Part 1 explains what gives wine its taste, and we go much further than simply the grape variety – we go to its true origins and examine everything about its composition. In Part 2, we do the same with food, thus making very clear the analogous relationship of food and wine. In Part 3, the extensive cross-reference should cover every imaginable match you could conceive. If you find any oversights or omissions, please do not hesitate to let me know!

When you understand why food and wine taste as they do, you can then understand why and how the classic rules have developed, which then gives you the freedom and confidence to break or adapt them in clever and personal ways. Take sweet white wines, for example. We call them 'dessert' wines – how short-sighted! A good sweet white can be served alone as an aperitif, with a first course of foie gras or quiche, with a main course of roast pork stuffed with prunes or apricots, with a fruit salad or a green salad made with walnuts, and is sublime with blue cheese, Roquefort, mild and strong goats' cheeses (but not the sweet, creamy kind), and Epoisses or Beaufort cheeses. And all of this before you even get to dessert! Another surprise is Champagne. We forget that Champagne is a wine that can take a meal from beginning to end – nothing beats ending a meal with a light and digestible Champagne.

So break all the rules. The essential is that both personalities of food and wine are respected and complemented, and that neither one is dominated. If a wine has brought forward an aspect of the food, and the food has reinforced an element of the wine, then a successful match has been made.

Let pleasure be your guide.

PART ONE

THE TASTE OF WINE

The taste of wine

WHEN I first started learning about wine, I was twenty years old and studying in Paris. The French family with whom I was living was a noble old family which, like many others, had little more than their titles and the crumbled remains of a château as reminders of their glorious past. My baroness had a heart of gold. Her dear husband, although I adored him for it, was a clever, quite frugal conniver, who had turned cheating the system into his livelihood. (This is a very French thing, by the way.) One evening, early in the year, they organized a dinner party for all the family to view the new American arrival. For this auspicious occasion, they brought out a bottle of wine which, I was proudly told, was produced by one of their family members in Bordeaux. As prior gustatory forays at my Californian girls' school had only introduced me to the delights of California coolers and strawberry daiquiris, I was very intimidated and was trying desperately to keep my virgin palate in the closet.

The wine was presented with what I thought then was great style and tradition. With hindsight, I can assure you it was pure blundering pomp. I tasted it. They all looked at me. What was I supposed to say? That it tasted good? Did it? How was I supposed to know? I had nothing with which to compare it. Because I appreciated that it had a little more 'umph' than my last gallon of Gallo

Burgundy, I said so – but not in so many words, of course. The rest of the family was served the wine and very soon we had duly drained the last drop from the bottle. Yet it sat there, empty, until one of the cousins pointed out that we were in need of more refreshment. Baron de Plouc scowled at the cousin, picked up the bottle and took it back to the kitchen. He reappeared a few minutes later with a fresh bottle, this time served without any of the previous hullabaloo. I noticed that he had uncorked it in the kitchen. Glasses were happily refilled and we drank on.

But wait a minute. Something was definitely very strange. This glass of wine tasted distinctly unlike our first glass. I discreetly looked at the bottle that was still proudly on display in the middle of the table and confirmed that, yes indeed, it was the same wine as the first. Actually, it was even the same bottle as the first! It had the same little water stain on top of the 'm' in 'mis en bouteille'. Being an inexperienced young Yank, I said nothing and kept drinking, deciding that there must be more to this wine game than I thought. I looked around the room and no one else seemed even to bat a tastebud. This went on all evening; the bottle kept disappearing and coming back to the table full.

The party became quite gay. Baron de Plouc now only needed a cursory glance from the cousin before performing his hostly duties. After five more bottles of decidedly inferior red brew had been served, I decided to investigate. I followed

Baron de Plouc into the kitchen on the pretext that I was going to help clean up. And what did I spy? The Baron bending over the family's precious heritage, pouring the contents of a two-litre container of Felix Potin's 12F a litre, generic red wine through the funnel I saw him use to fill up the Renault Cinq the previous week. He saw me and my aghast expression, and shot me a conspiratorial smile accompanied by a hissing *'dites-rien, d'accord?'* I agreed, and morosely went back out to join the other guests.

Voilà. One of my very first interludes with French wine. Believe it or not, that very same bottle appeared on the table every time we had important guests for dinner – and I never said a word.

Learning about Wine

I continued my wine education on my own by soaking off and saving the bottle labels of every wine I tasted, even bothering wine waiters in restaurants. I would then glue the labels into my wine notebook and write down the date, the place, the meal and my companions, and then note my impressions. At the beginning, I could usually only muster an 'I like this' or 'I do not like this'. Not a very encouraging start but it did actually work because, before too long, I could look at all the wines I did like and find their common denominator, thereby determining my first preferences. Eventually, I was able to detect differences between the wines and then was able to put names to these tastes.

You may be asking why go to all this bother? Today, wine labels are increasingly informative, telling you what sort of foods the wine will match, and often even including information on the region's climate or soils. But not having to rely on commercial copy scripted by the wineries' PR teams, and learning the ground rules about what goes into the taste of wine – which you will learn from this section of the book – will help you to assess and taste wines, better understanding your preferences and better matching your food and wine. The first lesson we learn when tasting wines is what we like and do not like. This is half the battle. The other half is learning why you like them or do not like them. If you can then find the common denominators: grape variety, wine style, regional preference, and so on, you have come a long way and the rewards will be many!

What Is Taste?

So what is taste? We tend to take our sense of taste for granted. Do you realize that – just as with our senses of hearing, sight and touch – we constantly taste things even when we are not eating? For the senses of smell and taste are so closely linked that we always taste what we smell and vice versa. The two work in conjunction with one another. Furthermore, our sense of sight also aids our sense of taste. Our whole sensorial repertoire tells us what a piece of burnt toast is going to taste like even before we put it into our mouth.

In the same way that different people have different strengths of eyesight or hearing, so people are born with different abilities in the areas of taste and smell, which are further influenced by our cultural and sensorial past. So every individual has uniquely tuned physiological mechanisms that release or stimulate a reaction and therefore a personal minimum and maximum threshold of taste and smell perception. Like the other senses, smell and taste serve as a source of information for our brains. Our sensorial logic then discriminates and identifies those different sensations.

When we taste something, we experience a sensation in special parts of the mouth: the tastebuds. These are dispersed throughout the mouth, and some have specific sensors: sourness is recognized with the tip of the tongue; sweetness with the flat of the tongue; bitterness under the tongue; tartness on the inner surface of the cheeks.

We have tried endlessly to create a finite classification of flavours, but as each individual will interpret a substance differently, a standard of measurement can only be vague and subjective. However, we do know that we can classify the larger taste groups of sweetness, acidity, saltiness, sourness and bitterness. But even with these groups, the boundaries are far from precise as it is difficult to establish a clear demarcation between one type and another because the taste of individual foods or wines comes, in fact, from a combination of these basic flavours. Also, our ability to perceive the flavours themselves is influenced by other factors such as temperature and flavour combinations.

How a Good Upbringing Ensures Good Taste

What influences a wine's taste? First of all, what is wine? Wine is simply the result of the partial or entire alcoholic fermentation of fresh grapes or the juice of fresh grapes. It tastes like the things it contains, therefore the predominant flavours of wine come from the skin, or just beneath the skin, of the grapes used to make it.

In the simplest terms, wine is composed of: water (between 75 and 90 per cent), alcohols, acids, polyphenols (or colouring agents), sugars (fructose and glucose), carbon dioxide and aromatic components (chemical). In addition to these, there are also all the components of wine that we cannot see, smell or taste, such as vitamins, proteins, amino acids, and so on. Each of these plays an important role in the taste of a wine.

Like human beings, a wine's taste is going to depend a great deal on both its origins and its upbringing. In fact, the French use this very word 'upbringing', or '*élevage*', when describing a wine's early life.

The taste of a wine is therefore the result of the combination of many factors, starting with the unique characteristics of the grape variety, or varieties, used to make it. The next factors are how the vines were planted, grown, pruned and treated; the soil and subsoil; the general climate of the vineyard's region; and sometimes even the climate of the surrounding areas. Were the vines grown on a fertile valley floor or clinging to a steep slope? Did they have to fight for food or were they over-fertilized and watered? Did they get too much sunshine or just what they needed? Were they allowed to produce all the fruit they wanted (the French call this '*pissing*' the vines) or were they pruned and obliged to produce fewer but better-quality grapes? The vintage year will also affect the taste of a wine as the weather and growing conditions are never the same from one year to the next.

The vinification method, how the wine was treated before being bottled, and how long it has been left to mature in the bottle, all add to its unique flavour combination. Will it be a flash-in-the-pan sort of wine or will it mature nicely and develop even more character as it grows old? All in all, has it been disciplined or spoiled rotten? A spoiled wine, like a spoiled child, will be lazy, brash and superficial. A wine with character will behave more subtly and will reveal its strength and personality as you get to know it.

What Does Wine Taste Like?

The taste elements of both wine and food are the same: sweetness, acidity, bitterness and astringency.

The sweetness in the taste of wine comes from the fructose and glucose, types of sugar, in the grape and from the alcohol produced during the fermentation. The alcohol is not sweet in itself, it just underlines those components that are, and helps to counteract the acidity and tannins, making the wine appear sweeter.

The acidity comes from the tartaric and malic acids in the grapes. Malic acid is green-tasting and can make wine very bitter, which is why the fermentation processes chosen by the winemaker are so important in achieving a balance as they will affect the malic acid levels in the wine.

Bitterness and astringency come from the tannins in the grapes. There are very few tannins in white wines, so most discussion of tannins is reserved for the red wines.

The Taste of Acidity

The sour-tasting substances in wine are the acids: tartaric, malic and citric are in the grape; succinic, lactic and acetic result from fermentation. The total acidity of a wine depends upon whether the growing season was cold – in which case the grapes are too acidic and under-ripe – or hot – in which case the grapes become over-ripe and lack acids. White wines generally have more acidity than reds. It is the amount of acid that is important: too little and the wine is bland and flabby, too much and it is vinegary. The right amount of acid, in balance with the wine's other components, makes the wine look and taste crisp, clean and lively, as well as ensuring its longevity.

Tartaric acid is unique to grapes and to wine and represents one-third to one-quarter of the total acid composition of wine. It is the strongest acid and it strongly influences the pH of a wine. The pH measures the concentration of hydrogen ions, which for wine means its dryness. The lower the pH, the safer the wine is from diseases and from oxidation, and therefore the greater its ageing potential. The tartaric acid content decreases as the grape ripens, then varies depending upon the harvest weather conditions.

Malic acid is found in every part of the grape vine. It is the most fragile of the acids, which allows for its easy transformation into lactic acids (called malolactic fermentation), which diminishes considerably the overall acidity of a wine. The hotter the year's weather, the faster the acid decreases during the ripening process, which is why there is more of it when the weather has been cooler. All red wines are allowed to go through a complete malolactic fermentation. White wines can either go without, go partially, or go entirely through this second fermentation. It depends upon the juice's initial acid and sugar levels and the style of wine desired. If a winemaker wants a crisp and 'green' white wine, then the malolactic fermentation is halted or not even allowed to begin. For a 'buttery', smooth white, the malolactic fermentation is permitted for longer or until its completion.

Acids give a wine its shine or brilliance, especially the tartaric acids which renew the wine's colour. It is the presence of malic acid which often gives a wine an apple smell, and in the mouth we can sense the amount of acids by the irritation of our gums and the inside of the mouth.

The Taste of Tannins: Bitterness and Astringency

The most important of the three types of polyphenols, or colouring agents, tannins give a wine texture rather than taste. Tannins that are 'condensed' are present in the grape, and those that are 'exogene' are procured from the wood during barrel ageing. In the stalks, skins and pips there are tannins that are released during fermentation and pressing, giving the wine its specific character and contributing to its ageing capacity. Storing, or ageing, the wine in new oak introduces additional tannins, which are transferred from the wood's fibres. These are more common in red wine than in white. Tannins obtained from the oak barrels can improve a wine's ageing potential, complement its texture and fill it out, but only if the wine itself has a solid backbone of acids, fruit extracts and condensed tannins. Oak ageing cannot replace the raw materials that are lacking in the first place.

The wine's red colour fades as the anthocyanins, another tannin, diminish with age. The more mature a wine, the more yellow or brown the 'disk', or surface, becomes. The combination of these colouring agents can give the wine a sour taste and a drying sensation in the mouth. This is called 'astringency'. Different tannins from different-aged wines and wines from various regions will have distinct sorts of astringency. For example, young Bordeaux will have tough, astringent tannins, while old Bordeaux will have velvet-soft tannins. The more tannin present in a wine's youth, the more it makes the sides of your mouth pucker and the longer it will take to mature. Don't buy a recent vintage Bordeaux Premier Cru and expect it to go down like velvet; it is meant to age and mature in the bottle. This is why bottle-ageing is so important, as we will see later.

The Taste of Sweetness

There are three major sweet-tasting substances in wine: the sugars and poly-alcohols, both originating in the grape, and alcohols from fermentation.

Each style of wine has a different level of sugar depending upon the grape's maturation when harvested. Sweet wines contain several dozen grams of sugar per litre, while a dry white wine normally contains less than two grams per litre. The sugars, along with the alcohols, give the wine body and are visible because of the 'legs' formed on the side of the glass. The sugars don't really have any odour but could eventually contribute to the overall expression of the wine. And it is the sugar that gives the wine its sweet taste, its fatness and its unctuousness.

Alcohol is an important element in wine – it gives it great looking 'legs'. It is produced during fermentation when enzymes created by the yeasts change the sugar of the grape juice into alcohol, carbon dioxide and heat. It is the proportion of alcohol to glycerine which determines the limpidity, or the 'body', of a wine, which we observe as 'legs' or 'tears'. More alcohol and the wine is thinner, thus the 'legs' run down the side of the glass more quickly. The more glycerine present, the thicker the wine will be and thus the more slowly the legs will drip down the side of the glass. It is also primarily the amount of ethyl alcohol that will determine the sweetness of the wine.

The Taste of Bubbles

Carbon dioxide is the principle product, along with ethyl alcohol, of the alcoholic fermentation. It is present in both still wines and effervescent wines. If the wine is effervescent, carbon dioxide manifests itself as bubbles. Like tannin, bubbles do not have an odour or taste as such, but the bubbles help to release the wine's perfumes and definitely alter its texture. If anything, you can detect an acidic taste edge while it pricks and tickles the tongue.

For a Fragrant Smell

Aromatic components (chemical substances) exist in minuscule quantities in wine and are issued from various chemical groups: alcohols, acid, ethers, and so on. For example, the presence of ethyl acetate might smell like vinegar, phenylethyl acetate like rose, ethyl caproate like soap, menthol like mint and vanillin like vanilla.

What is important to note is that these are all visual, olfactive and gustative results born of the wine itself, its contents. In addition to these, there are other man-made manipulations, such as adding fabricated yeasts to the grape juice to jump-start fermentation, and other measures which are taken to rectify nature's flaws of low sugars and high acidity, which also alter the smell and taste of wine. We'll discuss these later.

The Grapes

All the factors we have looked at are important in telling you about the taste of a wine, but the single most important factor is the grape variety or varieties from which the wine is made. In winemaking, just as in cooking, if you use inferior raw materials and do not adjust the proportions of the ingredients correctly, your final dish will fall short of the mark.

Do not forget that the grape is a fruit or a crop like any other, and crops come from different regions for a reason. Bananas come from the tropics, figs from the Mediterranean, apples from temperate areas like Britain or the American northwest. It would be foolhardy to try to grow these fruits in places other than their indigenous habitat or where the growing conditions are totally different. They might survive, but they would probably not be as good. So why do we do it with the noble European grape varieties? The Chardonnay grape is at its optimum in Burgundy, as is the Cabernet Sauvignon in Médoc and Graves, the Merlot in St-Emilion or Pomerol, the Kékfrankos in Sopron, Hungary, the Nebbiolo in Piedmont, and the Tempranillo in Rioja. There are even indigenous grape varieties in some of the New World countries. However, there is debate that even these have European roots. For example, California's Zinfandel, although considered indigenous if not old and settled, is of Italian origin from the Primitivo grape. South Africa's Pinotage is a hybrid of France's Cinsault and Pinot Noir varieties, and Australia's Shiraz is the Rhône Valley's Syrah. In any event, they are grapes that have been there long enough to have taken on a personality which reflects the region's soil and climate. They all make delicious and unique wines.

THE SMELLS AND TASTES OF WINE

The following is an exhaustive list of the various smells and aromas a wine can have. A wine's smell can tell us a lot about how it was made, where it is from, how old it is, and whether or not it is of good quality. Identifying a wine's smell also develops your taste memory, which is indispensable when trying to establish what kind of wine you prefer and when matching food and wine. Do not forget that smell and taste remain subjective senses and not everybody will taste the same odour, or will identify it as the same thing. Also remember that despite the general rules and guidelines of winemaking, there are always exceptions.

Family of smells	Examples	Comments
FLORAL	Acacia Carnation Hawthorn/May blossom Honeysuckle Narcissus Vine Wild flowers	These are considered to be good odours and are found in young, dry white wines and sparkling wines.
	Broom Jasmine Lime blossom Rose Violet	These are more present and heavy and are found in serious white wines that will age and in some red wines. Look for rose in a Gewürztraminer or Muscat.
	Geranium	A very strong presence of this flower usually indicates a misuse of ascorbic acid.
FRUIT		You may have noticed that in a good white wine, especially in a sweet one, the fruit aromas evolve as the wine matures. They become almost jammy and take on the smells of compote, dried and stewed fruit.
	Lemon	An elegant perfume which lightens the bouquet and gives the wine a freshness.
	Apricot Peach	You are likely to find these odours in top white wines of considerable strength meant for ageing, and in sweet wines.
	Blackcurrant Raspberry Summer fruit	The typical and easily recognizable principal smells found in red wines meant for early drinking and in those red wines meant for ageing that are drunk when young.

FRUIT *(continued)*	Blackberry Mulberry	The original odour associated with quality in reds.
	Quince Strawberry	Depending on the grape variety and the soil type, these perfumes can be evident in a wine maturing or on the decline.
	Bergamot Lemon Orange Tangerine	These are powerful and elegant smells and are very characteristic of Muscatel-like fortified wines. Also found in Australian Rieslings and in the Sémillon grape.
	Cherry Redcurrants	A subtle perfume which is considered favourable. Think Cabernet Sauvignon or Pinot Noir.
	Apple	Can be either a good or bad thing. If it smells like an over-ripe apple or beet, it is a sign of oxidation or problematic malolactic fermentation. If it smells like a golden or green apple in a young, dry white wine, then it is good.
	Banana Pear	When there is too much of this smell it almost resembles nail polish. It is a very simple odour usually found in white wines of little originality, whose fermentations were jump-started with industrial flavoured yeasts, in Primeur red wines, and in 'technological' rosés.
	Plum Raisin	These are pretty rare in wines. Might detect them in some young, simple reds.
	Guava Kiwi Lychee Papaya Passion fruit	Considered to be original and agreeable smells, if not too strong, in certain white wines (Gewürztraminer, for example).
NUTS AND **DRIED FRUIT**	Hazelnut Grilled almond	These are considered to be aromas of great class, especially when present in the tertiary bouquet of the top, well-built and solid white wines of a mature white Burgundy.
	Dried fig Walnut	Very classic aromas found in aged, fortified wines as well as in top wines at their peak of maturity.
	Prunes	A bad sign. This usually means that a red wine that has faded or died, or is an indication that there was a problem with oxidation, probably due to bad storage or conservation conditions.

VEGETABLE	Cut grass Herbaceous Stalks or stems	Considered a bad thing, these smells are usually the result of bad harvesting practices: grapes that are too crushed or not de-stalked well. You also find these odours in 'technological' wines that are past their prime.
	Fern	A very distinguished odour that is found in white and red wines meant for long-term ageing.
	Cut hay	A nice odour present in certain red wines.
	Juniper Incense Pine Resin Turpentine	These are powerful perfumes that are found in red wines from regions of southern or meridian climates of pine forests.
	Humus Lichen Marsh Mushroom Undergrowth Wet straw	Considered to be desirable odours, they are linked to the phenonenon of reduction in the bottle and so are found in top red wines that have undergone a number of years of bottle ageing.
	Dry leaves Herbal infusion Tea Tisane or herbal tea Tobacco	Smells that usually indicate a certain amount of ageing and evolution. Found in both red and white wines meant for ageing.
	Mint Eucalyptus	Characteristic smells of Cabernet Sauvignon grown in Australia, South Africa or California.
	Dust Earth	Not considered desirable, these odours usually disappear with a little airing.
	Green pepper	The dominant odour usually associated with the Cabernet Sauvignon grape. If too strong, it means that the grapes were harvested while under-ripe.
SPICES AND HERBS	Basil Bay Cinnamon Lavender Nutmeg Thyme	Power odours found in red wines and certain mature white wines issued from vintages of substantial warmth and sunshine.

SPICES AND HERBS *(continued)*	Liquorice Pepper	Considered very elegant and noble, these aromas are often present in the best reds from the best *terroirs*.
	Aniseed Cloves Fennel	In small amounts, these are acceptable smells.
	Garlic Onions	Not so good. Usually means that the wine suffered reduction in the bottle.
	Vanilla	A very pleasant perfume which can bring balance and harmony to the wine if not overpowering. Usually found in wines that have been aged in new oak barrels.
	Truffle	A very strong odour which can sometimes resemble aspects of the vegetable family (undergrowth and humus), or even the animal family (sweat, urine). If present in old wines, it is an expression of quality but definitely needs aeration in order to appreciate it fully.
ANIMAL	Amber Civet (cat) Musk	All these three are powerful and surprising odours which are usually appreciated if they are found in well-developed, aged and evolved red wines.
	Game	A very powerful aroma usually found in very old red wines – Pommards can definitely smell a bit gamey.
	Cat urine	Found in Sauvignon Blanc grapes that were picked while under-ripe, or yields were too high.
	Fur Game Leather Sweat Wet dog	A very particular odour appreciated by those who go in for this sort of thing. Found in great red wines after a long and perfect maturation.
	Chicken gut Fox	Bad smells associated with wines that have been poorly vinified or are from hybrid grape varieties.
ROASTED	Burnt Grilled Smoke Toast	Can be lovely when found in some white wines of distinction. Aged white Burgundies often have these notes.

ROASTED *(continued)*	Cacao Chocolate Coffee	Very desirable aromas found in the top red wines when at their apogee.
	Burnt wood Creosote Rubber Smoke Tar	A characteristic of certain red wines while in the process of maturation. They often disappear once the wine is fully mature.
	Caramel	A heady, heavy perfume, like the quince, usually indicates that the wine is maturing too quickly or that it was vinified at too high a temperature.
	Flint Gunpowder	Typical of dry white wines of the Loire Valley. A very pleasing smell and taste which is said to be due to the flinty soil.
DIVERSE	Honey Wax	Lovely perfumes that develop in mature white wines of great class.
	Acetate Nail polish	Disagreeable smells found in poorly made young red wines or 'technological' rosés.
	Beer Cheese Cider Dirty dishcloth Milk Sauerkraut Yeast Yoghurt	A whole pack of not-so-lovely odours which are all caused by poorly managed fermentations.
	Cattle shed Mould Pigsty Soap Stagnation	Again, odours considered to be not so good and which are linked to poor quality.
ALCOHOL	Eau de vie Kirsch Old marc	Perfumes present in very heady wines rich in alcohol.
	Graphite Iodine	Rarely found in wine and not considered to be good signs.

Translated and adapted from *La Dégustation*, pp. 48–53, G. Gribourg/C. Sarfati, Edisud, France 1989.

When noble European grape varieties are grown in new, adopted soils they produce different tastes and styles, usually as a result of the warmer climate. Once I would have argued that not only were these new models different, but also that they were inferior. I would not say so today. It is simply that it is too soon to know how these varieties will settle into their new environment. It is unfair to compare a vineyard that has been producing fruit for hundreds of years, such as Chablis (100 per cent Chardonnay grape by law) with one that has only been doing so for a couple of decades. It will take ages for nature to sort out the myriad of variables that are best suited: which grapes with which soil, which climate, and so on.

You also have to decide whether or not you accept a new and different perception of the classic model. Should we accept that the Chardonnay grape could have a Chablis (Burgundy) taste, a Carneros (California) taste, or a Maipo (Chile) taste? And even more to the point, is there a significant difference between a Californian and a Chilean Chardonnay? Or are all Chardonnays of the New World subject to, and thus products of, the same technical and climatic treatments? For you to decide!

Not All Grapes Can Go It Alone

Some grape varieties – despite occasional flirtations – do very well on their own: Pinot Noir, Sauvignon Blanc, Riesling, Chardonnay. Others are best when blended with other grape varieties: Merlot, Cabernet Sauvignon, Cabernet Franc.

Why? Take Bordeaux wines as an example, where Cabernet Sauvignon is the main ingredient of the recipe. Merlot, because it is a sweeter and softer grape than the Cabernet Sauvignon, has traditionally been used to soften the tannins of the Cabernet Sauvignon. Cabernet Franc is also added as the 'spice' of the recipe, giving its own special character, plus there are minute doses of Petit Verdot and/or Malbec. Combining the taste elements of all the varieties gives each Bordeaux appellation its unique flavour.

Each appellation has a designated 'recipe' according to which grape varieties do better in that area because of the soil and microclimate. And within this recipe, each winemaker makes their own variations according to which grapes did better than another in any particular year, and according to the personal tastes of the château owner and winemaker. In the same way, when cooking, we follow a basic recipe yet we will vary the proportion of ingredients (meat, vegetables, spices and flavourings) according to our personal taste, the seasonal availability of ingredients and perhaps our financial resources.

The Style Parameters of the Grape Varieties

Every grape variety produces grapes which have a specific chemical constitution and therefore possess a particular aromatic potential in varying degrees of intensity and quality. Some varieties are considered to have no interest at all; these are usually hybrids. The varieties considered rich in primary aromas, such as Muscat, Gewürztraminer or Riesling, produce wines that taste as though you've just bitten into a grape. These are the varieties that are vinified in such a way as to preserve or amplify these aromas.

Then there are the varieties suscept-ible to an aromatic potential of interesting secondary aromas: Gamay, Pinot Noir, Marsanne, Cabernet Sauvignon, Grenache, Chardonnay, Syrah and Chenin. Only vinification can reveal the hidden aro-matic potential of these grapes.

Finally we have those varieties that develop through vinification and con-tinue to evolve with ageing: Pinot Noir, Cabernet Sauvignon and Syrah, for exam-ple. Take a Gamay from Beaujolais and a Pinot Noir from Burgundy, and it will be the Pinot Noir that will still taste amazing after sitting in your cellar for five or ten years, not the Gamay, no matter what a winemaker does to it. Each grape variety has a finite aromatic and taste potential.

A grape variety, from the start, is either meant for ageing or is not. There are varieties which produce wines with a balance of sugar, acid and tannin which gives them the structure needed to sus-tain ageing. Then there are varieties that produce wines that are meant to be drunk while young, as they reveal themselves best while still youthful, and whose sugar, acid, tannin balance is relatively light.

Winemakers can try to squeeze as much as they like out of grapes by letting them overproduce and by extracting as much flavour during the vinification as possible. For example, to get the most out of a variety that does not have much aroma, such as the Ugni Blanc, a wine-maker can vinify the must, or grape juice, with little or no oxidation and at very low temperatures, thus eking out a little more flavour. But this will only be a superficial result. Nature has provided built-in limits.

To make a grape happy, all you need to do is to provide a perfect environment. In its optimal site of acclimation – the place where the soil, climate and growing conditions are all perfect – each variety will find its optimum individual and spec-ific sugar, acid and tannin balance. For example, in Alsace, the Gewürztraminer will always be sweeter than the Riesling. In the Côtes du Rhône, Carignan will always be more acidic than Grenache, and in Burgundy, Pinot Noir will always be more tannic than Gamay. In the right region and conditions, each grape variety is reaching its own taste potential.

The White Grapes

To help you identify grape varieties, here is a list of the major white grapes and their characteristics.

White wine grape varieties generally smell and taste like citrus and other tree fruit, like lemon, orange, grapefruit or apple. In mature white wines, or in sweet white wines, we often taste more exotic or tropical fruit, like pineapple, mango, apricot, pear, melon and lychees.

Both red and white wines can have odours and tastes such as mineral, spice, herbs, tobacco, hay, yeast, honey, caramel and nuts. The tastes come from either the grape variety, the yeasts (if indigenous yeasts are not used to start fermentation), the fermentation period, or the oak used for ageing.

Chardonnay

An easy-going kind of grape, the Chardonnay seems to want to please everyone. It does its best to adapt to every soil, every climate of every country, and every winemaking style. Who would believe that the same grape could give us a wine that is steely, mineral and salty to one that is fat, buttery, oaky and lightly sweet? But the Chardonnay does just that. And nowhere are its many personalities better illustrated than in the *marno-calcaires* soils of Burgundy. Indeed, Burgundy is the perfect region in which to observe varietal variations and provides a strong defence for the unique variable of soil type. From the cool climate and *calcaire* soil of Chablis to the warmer Mâcon, the Chardonnay adapts perfectly, becoming more aromatic and supple as it moves further south. Take it out of its native Burgundy altogether and it quickly becomes attuned to its adopted land's climate and environment.

Chardonnays from northern Italy and southern France are both light and fruity; those from Chile are vibrant with fruit and light oak; from New Zealand's cooler regions, the wines become intense with balanced fruit; and from California, they are tropical, oaky wines.

Chenin Blanc

Good Chenin Blanc is one of the world's most underrated grape varieties. It is true that Chenin Blanc from a very cold year can produce a sour wine, but with a little sunshine, its true colours are revealed and this happens best in its home, the Loire Valley. The Chenin Blanc has several very distinct sides to it. When harvested at optimum maturity, it produces a dry, firm, elegantly floral wine, such as a Savennières. It also produces sparkling wines of good quality in Saumur and Vouvray. When harvested late so that noble rot (*selection de grains nobles*) is successfully achieved – when the grapes are deliberately allowed to shrivel and intensify on the vine before harvesting – then the most succulent and famous sweet wines are the result: Coteaux du Layon, Bonnezeaux and Quarts de Chaume, all apples and apricots with nutty, honey tones and underlined by a high acidity that helps to carry it all along. These are long-lived, but not as fat or ageless as a Sauternes.

Outside the Loire Valley and into warmer climates, Chenin Blanc unfortunately becomes a fairly innocuous thing. New World versions are at best fruity, but lacking any of its crucial steeliness or complexity. Nor does this grape lend itself to high yields: overproduction is truly merciless. Having realized this, the South Africans and others are starting to nurture older vines in an attempt to get more concentrated and complex fruit (older plants give fewer, more concentrated grapes, while younger plants produce higher yields of lighter fruit).

Gewürztraminer

There is no more distinctive or aromatic grape than the Gewürztraminer. Alsace is its home and there it produces, if yields are kept reasonably low, a rich tapestry of fruity, floral and spicy tastes. Its texture in the mouth is round, rich and smooth. Like the Riesling, it can be harvested late (*vendanges tardives*) to produce a very classy wine and in certain years, when the weather is perfect and noble rot is attained, the results are amazing. Although often described as 'spicy', the first impression is frequently of roses and lychees. When made in the dry style, it is still opulent but it does not fare well in warm years or warm climates, where the heat lets its acid levels plummet, leaving it overly sweet, oily and flabby.

Germany's Pfalz and Baden regions run a close second to Alsace, and lighter versions come from Austria and Italy's Sudtirol. Outside Europe, the wines are usually off-dry, easy and without much character. But growers who take it seriously in cooler climates such as

Washington State, Oregon, are producing some great results.

Marsanne

Native of the mid Rhône Valley, this variety is one of the Rhône Valley Hermitage staples, and when coupled with Roussanne produces Hermitage, Crozes-Hermitage and St-Joseph. It has also been planted farther south in France and in Australia. When young, it is a discreet wine that becomes more floral as it ages, moving towards notes of wax, honey and nuts. On the palate, the wines are supple, fat and round.

Müller-Thurgau

A cross between Riesling and Silvaner, its creator, German Dr Hermann Müller, was trying to combine the quality of the Riesling grape with the reliability of the Silvaner. Since Silvaner is an early-maturing grape, it is very popular in cold vine-growing regions as it matures before the worst weather arrives. But Müller-Thurgau turned out to make a rather flabby, mediocre wine, especially when a product of Germany's high yields. It does much better in New Zealand, Washington State, some parts of Italy, and is the most common variety grown in England. At its best, it charms us with its floral scents of privet and flowering currant leaves.

Muscat

You may have noticed that most grapes taste of everything but grapes as we have always thought of them. Muscat is a 'grape'-tasting grape and is also one of the oldest grape varieties in the world. Alsatian Muscats are elegant, dry, rose-scented wines, usually drunk as an aperitif. The very sweet, fortified Muscats of the south of France and the Rhône (Frontignan, Lunel, Rivesaltes and Beaumes-de-Venise) are drunk with desserts. Australia produces darker, heavier liqueur Muscats of high quality. Italy's fizzy, low-alcohol, sweet Moscatos, such as Asti Spumante, are refreshing and versatile, and who can ignore the delectable Moscatel de Setúbal from Portugal?

Pinot Blanc

You may think that the Pinot Blanc is an innocuous little grape, but it has quite a lot to say for itself, which is difficult for a grape that is a mutation of a mutation. The Pinot Blanc, originally from Burgundy, is a white mutation of the Pinot Gris, which is a mutation of the Pinot Noir! The Germans, French and Italians have long appreciated its startling resemblance to light, unoaked Chardonnay. Indeed, this resemblance is physical as well as gustative, as it is very difficult to tell the plant vines apart. A well-made Pinot Blanc will remind you of apples, butter and warm, sweet sap. The Alsatian version contributes something to almost every meal, its delicacy present yet discreet.

Pinot Gris

Pinot Gris, as we have just mentioned, is a mutation of the Pinot Noir grape, and comes in many packages and under several names, but it finds its full expression in Alsace, where it is known as Tokay Pinot Gris, although the Hungarians are insisting that Tokay be dropped from the name so there is no confusion with their famous Tokaji. It skirts seductively between the steeliness of the Riesling and the spicy voluptuousness of the Gewürztraminer, never making up its mind. It is smoky, spicy, nougaty. At the other extreme, it produces a light, dry wine, the Pinot Grigio, in Italy.

Riesling

The true Riesling of German origin is one of the world's great grape varieties. Like Sauvignon Blanc, it has both a strong personality – one that is better off without the influence of oak – and high acidity, but it is far more adaptable. It thrives in the cool climates of Europe, especially in Germany and Alsace and, to some extent, the warmer climates of Australia, although high yields in such a climate can render it 'soapy'. It is very susceptible to noble rot, which means that it can produce wines in many styles, from the dry to the intensely sweet. Because of the high acidity and sugar levels, Rieslings can age for many years. Wherever it is grown, whether it is old or young, and no matter which wine style it has produced, you should always be able to detect a vivid fruitiness and a lively acidity. If too sweet, it loses its personality and becomes heavy and cloying. It should sing to you of honeysuckle, crunchy green apples, spiced baked apples, quince and orange, and of that famous 'tarry' aroma.

Sauvignon Blanc

This grape is responsible for many of France's great white wines: from the gorgeously noble Sauternes and its many sisters (Barsac, Cadillac, Ste-Croix-du-Mont, Loupiac) and the dry white Bordeaux, to the crisp, elegant and delicate Sancerre with its steely, stony, white-flower aromas typical of the Loire Valley's flint soils. Transported to other soils, it is quite transformed, perhaps that is why it is rarely recognized. New Zealand's refreshing version is an explosion of gooseberries, freshly cut grass and tropical fruit. Be careful if you detect the lingering odour of tinned asparagus, green beans or an exaggerated herbaceousness – almost a steminess – as these are considered, not surprisingly, to be undesirable and are certainly due to too-high yields.

Sémillon

One member of the trio of the famous white Bordeaux blend (Sauvignon Blanc, Muscadelle and Sémillon), Sémillon makes an unforgettable sweet white wine – Sauternes, Barsac, Cadillac, and so on – and, of course, the dry white Bordeaux, the Graves and Pessac-Léognan. There is a good reason that it is usually part of a blend, as on its own it creates a dry white wine that is at best lightly citrus-fruity, slightly herbaceous like the Sauvignon Blanc, but usually lacking originality. Heavily oaked, as in the Barossa Valley, it produces a fat, vanilla, lemony wine. It has won great acclaim for its results in an unusual dry white from Australia's Hunter Valley. Other New World countries have married it to Chardonnay to pad out the yield shortages of the extremely popular Chardonnay grape.

Ugni Blanc

A grape possessing many names and roles – surprisingly, considering its lack of distinction and originality. Or perhaps, this is just what makes it the perfect candidate for ubiquitousness. Known as Ugni Blanc, Clairette Ronde and Muscadet in Aigre in France, and as Trebbiano in Italy, whence it originates, legend has it that Ugni Blanc was brought to southern France during the fourteenth century, probably via Avignon, the seat of the papal court. It is the most planted variety in both France and Italy, stealing its way into all of our favourite Provençal, Rhône and Bordeaux blends – not to mention its importance in brandy. This is because it will grow vigorously, providing high yields, in almost any warm-climate conditions, withstanding both disease and rot. At best, as a varietal, it makes a light, white and crisp wine, low in alcohol and high in acidity. At worst, it is boring and tasteless.

Viognier

Native to the Condrieu region of the Rhône Valley, this grape is the stuff of heady, perfumed, yet dry, full-bodied opulence. It is all lime blossoms, musk, apricots and peaches. On the palate, it is well rounded and mellow, despite its high acidity and alcohol content, making it a wine of great class. However, it is considered unreliable and needs to reach a perfect maturity in order to express itself fully. This is best assured when it is planted on the south-facing slopes of the Rhône Valley. Still, if the weather is not right there is no crop at all – and even when all goes to plan, the yields are low, which means high prices. Also grown in Languedoc-Roussillon and California with excellent results, where it has been designated a trendy new grape.

The Red Grapes

Now let's look at the characteristics of the major red grape varieties.

Red wine grape varieties generally taste like the red fruit family: black and red cherry, redcurrant and blackcurrant, raspberry, strawberry and plum.

As we have seen, both red and white wines can have odours and tastes such as minerals, spices, herbs, tobacco, hay, yeast, honey, caramel and nuts. The tastes come from either the grape variety, the yeasts (if indigenous yeasts are not used to start fermentation), the fermentation period, or the oak used for ageing.

Barbera

Usually part of a blend, the most valuable contribution of the Barbera grape is its naturally high acidity. Hailing originally from Piedmont, it is best matched with grapes of higher tannin content and body (such as its nemesis Nebbiolo), as it produces red wines lighter in style and earlier maturing than Barolo, with pronounced astringency. Because of its high acidity, it does well in warm and hot climates. It has been very successfully grown in Argentina, where it produces a warm, juicy and intense wine with strong undertones of its typical sour-cherry notes. It is also very popular in California's hot Central Valley because of this high acidity.

Cabernet Franc

Another blending grape, this variety adds a touch of spice and reliability (it matures easily in all weathers) to the formidable Bordeaux blend (usually no more than 20–25 per cent), along with Cabernet Sauvignon and Merlot (and traces of Petit Verdot and Malbec). Although it would not stand a chance as a single variety in Bordeaux (although we should not forget the Château Cheval Blanc, 66 per cent Cabernet Franc, 33 per cent Merlot, 1 per Malbec), it totally holds its own in the Loire Valley, where it offers us the aromatic, tannic, red-fruity Saumur-Champigny, Bourgueil and Chinon. It does well in cool, inland climates, and produces fabulous results in Argentina, Long Island New York, and New Zealand. One place it is not really suited for is the overly warm Napa Valley, where it was planted in order to obtain the Californian 'Bordeaux' blend Meritage. I also must add that I have enjoyed several spicy, personable and intense bottles from Hungary.

Cabernet Sauvignon

The Cabernet Sauvignon grape, like the Chardonnay, has become one of those over-transported, over-planted, abused grape varieties victimized by the trend-setters of the New World. The result is that there are so many versions of this grape that we forget what it does best: a trio act, in Bordeaux. Yes, it is adaptable, but it shouldn't be made to perform every trick under the sun. Under ideal climatic conditions, it produces an aromatic, tannic wine that ages and evolves elegantly yet powerfully. If harvested when under-ripe or with enormous yields, the results can be truly mediocre: the wine too tannic and light-bodied with very violent green pepper and herbaceous odours. If the climate is too warm and the grapes are over-ripe, the resulting wines can have very jammy, baked, fortified flavours and will lack structure. A perfectly balanced Bordeaux is what we are after and, if achieved, it will have notes of blackcurrants, cedar, cigars, lead pencils, green pepper, mint and dark chocolate. Sounds delicious.

Gamay

Gamay is a native of the granite soils of Beaujolais, and if you truly know how this grape variety works, you will understand why Beaujolais Nouveau is best drunk immediately – and I mean within a few days! It was the grape variety deemed too 'common' by the medieval king, Philip the Bold, who demanded that all the Gamay on the Côte d'Or be uprooted in favour of the 'nobler' Pinot Noir of Burgundy. But the peasants working the vineyards insisted on keeping a few plantings, as that was what they relied upon to give them sustenance. Because it was considered inferior and because it was not treated seriously, it was drunk before it could even be bottled. It is true that when Gamay is given a very short *cuvaison* (the time spent in the vat) and is of a high yield, it produces Primeur wines that are light but fresh and very aromatic with notes of red fruit and bananas. However, I am always reminded of an aftertaste of a copper coin. When allowed to macerate longer, as with the Crus of Beaujolais – wines from ten specially designated villages – the wine can be very well rounded, elegant and enjoyable.

Grenache

Although originally from Spain, this grape is best known for its great works in France's Rhône Valley: Châteauneuf-du-Pape, AOC or *Appellation d'Origine Contrôlée* Côtes du Rhône, Gigondas, and so on. Again, here is a grape variety that is best used as a blend (with Syrah, Cinsault and Mourvèdre), but is often used as a single variety in southern France and in the New World. When not of high yields, the wine has a dark robe, is rather aromatic, with notes of pepper, raspberries and herbs, with supple acids, a round, fat texture, generous alcohols and a rustic edge. When yields are too high, the wine is light-coloured and tastes a bit oxidized, or like cheap cherry bonbons. It is very popular in South Africa, Australia and California because it is very susceptible to rot and mildew and thus is better suited to dry climates.

Malbec

Again, a grape variety that is used in the red Bordeaux blend, where the Cabernet Sauvignon, Cabernet Franc and Merlot dominate its personality. However, this dark, tannic grape (also called Auxerrois) comes into its own in south-western France where it can be a major component in the lushly rustic, dark and brooding

Cahors, Buzet, Bergerac, Côtes de Duras, Côtes du Frontonnais, Côtes du Marmandais and Pécharmant. In Argentina, it produces the best reds: velvety, vigorous, aromatic and worthy of cellar ageing. In Chile, it tends to be blended with the softer Merlot and is gorgeous. Almost anywhere it is grown, Malbec seems to retain its lovely tastes of blackberries, blackcurrants, lavender and spices.

Merlot

In the red Bordeaux blend, I like to think of the Merlot as the sugar in the recipe, the Cabernet Sauvignon as the flour, and the Cabernet Franc as the spices. Merlot gives softer, plumper and juicy, early-maturing wines that are sweeter; a perfect complement to the tannic Cabernet Sauvignon and the spicy Cabernet Franc. The Merlot tastes of plums, roses, blackcurrants and rich fruit cake. There are appellations in Bordeaux where the bulk of the blend is Merlot-based, such as Pomerol and St-Emilion. As an unblended varietal wine it does well in California, as the warmer climate accentuates is natural sweet suppleness and thus has a commercial appeal. However, I find most of the Merlots grown in warm climates and served up as single varieties lack structure, acid and character. It needs the company of other grapes to show off its potential, as hotter climates do bring out its spicier, plummier side, but the allure is a superficial one. It produces light, grassy wines in northern Italy, and if blended does well in New Zealand and South Africa. Chile also seems to get it to stand rather well on its own.

Mourvèdre

Originally a Spanish grape, known there as Monastrelli, its robust aromas are better known in Provence's Bandol region and in the Rhône Valley, where it is often blended with Syrah and Grenache. The south of France has embraced it as one of its trendy varietals. It does best in hot climates, where its tastes of blackberries, game and leather can be appreciated. Because it is a rather tannic, highly coloured and robust grape, its wines need ageing, which will further enhance its wild, gamey character. South Australia and California (as a 'Rhône Ranger') are both doing good things with it.

Nebbiolo

The small, thick-skinned Nebbiolo grape produces some of the driest, biggest and toughest of intense red wines, capable of long bottle ageing. When well made and matured, it is a magical confusion of prunes, tar, liquorice, violets, roses, chocolate and spicy fruit cake. Its stronghold is Piedmont and thereabouts in north-west Italy, where its two most famous wines are Barolo and Barbaresco. It is rare outside Italy and this is probably a very good thing, as other versions tend to be uninteresting and harsh.

Periquita

This is a very versatile grape variety native to southern Portugal. It has five or six other names, all of them unpronounceable and impossible to spell. It was named Periquita (small parrot) by José Maria da Fonseca after his small farm where he stared his winemaking operation. I guess he too found the other names too difficult to spell! It is often dismissed as very ordinary, but when aged in wood, I think it makes a most original wine. It has a silky texture and full-bodied sweetness, yet is powerful with a pleasant bite. If you want a taste of Portugal, try the indigenous grape varieties, not the ubiquitous Chardonnays and Cabernet Sauvignons. There are hundreds more grape varieties in Portugal, all capable of creating the most characterful brews.

Pinot Noir

When asked if I prefer Bordeaux or Burgundy, I quickly jump at the chance to enthuse passionately about the seductive superiority of the Pinot Noir. When grown correctly (cool climate, small yields), a Burgundy reaches the pinnacle of sophistication and elegance so often associated with the Bordeaux, but then surpasses it, flaunting its sexy, animal-like charm. The Burgundy seems to overflow exuberantly, while the Bordeaux, however moving, always seems a bit restrained in comparison. It is the mature Pinot Noir's complex flavours of raspberries, strawberries, cranberries, violets, game, compost, allspice, tobacco and hay, coupled with its silky, velvety texture, that is so captivating. Pinot Noir is the most precocious of the fine-wine grapes to grow and vinify. Relatively low in tannin and acidity, it needs a cool climate. Too little sun leads to pallid, thin-tasting wine. With too much warmth, Pinot Noir can develop jammy, baked flavours, losing its elegance and silkiness. Even the best New World Pinot Noirs lack the magical complexity of the greatest Burgundies, where it is perfectly at home in the *argilo-calcaire soils* and cool climate.

Pinotage

Considered an indigenous grape variety of South Africa, this is actually a cross between Pinot Noir and Cinsault (since 1926). It produces everything from light, fruity wines to robust, distinctive and hearty reds with strong tannic backbones,

and flavours of plums, brambles, flambéed bananas and smoky oak. One of the best offerings from South Africa, it is a lovely, original-tasting grape variety.

Sangiovese

Taste a Sangiovese (blood of Jove) and you will immediately conjure images of Italy. As the major component of the famous Chianti wine (along with Cannaiolo Nero, Trebbiano and Malvasia del Chianti), it is actually grown all over Italy. Naturally tannic, it is best used in a blend, usually with Cabernet Sauvignon as a Super Tuscan, although on its own it shines as the delicious Rosso di Montalcino and Rosso di Montepulciano. As with the other late-maturing grape varieties we have seen (Grenache and Mourvèdre), it needs a hot climate in order to produce the richness and alcohol content required for bottle ageing. In cooler climates, it tends to have sharp acids and bitter tannins. It is a very rich, robust wine that will do well with long bottle ageing. Styles vary from light, astringent and ordinary to a full-bodied, firm, slightly spicy, red (with bitter cherry, tobacco and herb flavours). It is becoming very popular in the New World, especially in California, where it is often blended with Cabernet Sauvignon.

Syrah

Called Shiraz in Australia and South Africa, Syrah is the magic varietal behind the Rhône Valley's famous Hermitage, Côte-Rôtie, Cornas, St-Joseph and Crozes-Hermitage. At home in the valley's granite soils, it produces wines that are deep in colour and aroma. When young, they display floral and fruity (raspberry) notes. Once matured, this evolves into notes of black pepper, leather, spices and game.

Syrah is a very versatile grape and can be grown in almost any climate, although yields need to be kept down and over-ripeness must be avoided or the wine can become heavy, flabby and too tannic. Some winemakers then fall into the trap of harvesting when the grapes are not at all mature, which gives equally mediocre results. Outside France, in Australia and California, Syrah is used both as a single variety and in blends with good results.

Tempranillo

Often labelled as Spain's Cabernet Sauvignon, Tempranillo is the mainstay of most of its reds. It does well in its native Rioja because it is not too high in alcohol or acidity, despite the hot climate. These are rich, dark grapes that make wine capable of bottle ageing. We know it best as an oaky (often over-oaked!), mellow, sultry, vanilla-rich red. Without oak, its fruity notes are more evident.

Zinfandel

Considered to be the indigenous grape variety of California, it has finally been established that Zinfandel is indeed the same as the Primitivo of southern Italy, which means that it is one of many varieties that made it to the New World via an immigrant's suitcase. In California, it became best known back in the 1970s and 1980s as a White Zinfandel. So much so that most consumers assumed that it was a white grape and not red! After the 'blush' trend faded, winemakers started producing more red Zinfandel. A good Zinfandel is robust, spicy, blackberry-ish, interesting and, in my opinion, by far the most individual variety coming out of California. If yields are respected and the grapes are grown in cooler hillside regions, the results are worth cellaring for many years.

WHY ARE THE NEW WORLD WINES MOSTLY VARIETAL WINES?

Have you noticed how most of the New World regions produce and market mainly single grape variety wines, while European wines are identified by geographical region? This is usually what puts us off the Old World wines. Other than sitting down and memorizing, how are we supposed to know that Sancerre is made from 100 per cent Sauvignon Blanc and Vouvray from Chenin Blanc?

Most credit for the fact that New World wines are identified by the grape variety and not the region goes to Robert Mondavi. In California in 1966, he started the single-variety craze, using the dominant grape in the wine as its name as opposed to its geographical origins. This is probably because California had no specific geographical qualities for grape growing and so winemakers had no choice but to put the influence on the grape or producer; it was an unavoidable move. It was also a very astute marketing ploy.

As the single varieties were the first to attract a new consumer – ones accustomed to the consistent tastes of Coca-Cola and beer – this was not only an easy way to label the wine, but the wine itself was easier to appreciate, being made from a single variety. A sweet Merlot is easier to sell than a complex Bordeaux blend containing three, four or maybe even five grape varieties. It was thought that only a sophisticated palate could appreciate the range of flavours in such a wine.

However, the Californians then realized that they could only take their brand names to a certain level. Selling wine like one would a line of clothing had its drawbacks. By going back to the idea of *terroir*, or soil – a concept they were scathing about only a decade earlier – they are now all clamouring to have their specific piece of soil designated as special vine-growing areas, or AVAs (American Viticultural Areas). This allows them to sell their wine at a higher price.

Napa Valley was the first appellation designated by the Bureau of Alcohol, Tobacco and Firearms (BATF) in 1981. Today there are over 60 designated AVAs in California and over 100 in the US. This means that wines labelled with one county or vineyard as the appellation need only use 75 per cent of the grapes from that county or vineyard, whereas wines from AVAs are required to have 85 per cent. To establish an AVA, the grower or winery must petition to the BATF and provide evidence that their area possesses a unique character for grape growing. It is difficult to dispute that there exists a difference between a Chardonnay from Carneros and one from the Russian River Valley. But for now, whether this difference is due to 'unique character' or not, is debatable.

Many question the rigour with which these areas were created. Tim Mondavi once told me that 'the AVAs are only meant to be a statement of

origin and not a guarantee of quality'. This is a valid point. But the opposition – people who happen to own land outside the AVAs – contend that to market specific vineyards such as Stag's Leap (made famous by such wineries as Clos du Val, Pine Ridge and Silverado) detracts from the reputation of the larger appellation of Napa Valley, upon which they rely so heavily.

So how large a role did geographical features play as opposed to that of local politics? The bickering continues. Also questioned is why there should be such a system. Is it truly a move towards quality or is it surrendering to the irresistible lure of the higher prices that could be gained for AVA-controlled wines? At least everyone is clear on the importance of one point: finding a system that is standardized yet not stifling.

This is also happening in southern France, in the Midi – now even nicknamed France's 'New World' region – where the wine laws are less strict than in the more traditional wine-growing regions. Single-variety marketing was and still is the marketing game plan. But now they have seen how a place name gives notoriety – whether that notoriety is deserved or not. The sceptics say it is all about marketing and not about wine, while supporters explain that it is part of a natural learning curve, a necessary and inevitable evolution of the consumers' palates and lifestyles. As the grape varieties settle into the area, natural marriages begin to emerge and are then identified as appellations.

WHICH GRAPES MAKE WHICH WINES?

What follows is a list of geographically named wines. It is not necessary to be exhaustive here, as the topic of grape varieties could fill another book, and indeed if you turn to the works of Jancis Robinson, you will be in very good hands! This list contains some of the more well-known wine names, including those referred to in the cross-reference of Part 3.

When learning about the wines of a particular region, it is often simpler to start with the grape varieties grown in each appellation (regulated by law) than to memorize the wine names, not knowing of what they are comprised. Why? Because it will help you to find wines you like. A grape variety often has different names in different countries and you might be surprised to see a grape you know from the south of France in a far-flung corner of Italy. Also, if you consistently prefer a Blanc de Blancs to a Blanc de Noirs Champagne, this means that you prefer Champagne issued from the Chardonnay grape rather than the Pinot Noir or Pinot Meunier. Then you can choose sparkling wines from other countries or, as the grapes truly produce different tastes, you will be better able to match them to food.

The grape varieties for each wine are listed in order of proportion, often the first being 50 per cent or more of the blend. I listed all the varieties where space permitted – even if only traces of a grape are used – but where there were too many to list, I resorted to using '+'.

Name	Region, country	Colour/style	Grape varieties
Ajaccio	Corsica, France	Red	Sciaccarello, Grenache, Cinsault, Carignan
		Rosé	Barbarossa, Neilluccio, Sciacerello, Vermentio Blanc, Carignan, Cinsault, Grenache
		White	Ugni Blanc, Vermentino Blanc
Alenquer	Portugal	Red	Camarate, Mortagua, Periquita, Preto Martinho, Tinta Miuda
		White	Vital, Jampal, Arinto, Fernao Pires
Almeirim	Portugal	Red	Castelao Nacional, Poeirinha, Periquita, Trincadeira Preta
		White	Fernao Pires, Arinto, Rabo de Ovelha, Talia, Trincadeira das Pratas, Vital
Aloxe-Corton	Burgundy, France	Red	Pinot Noir
Amarone della Valpolicella	Veneto, Italy	Red	Corvina, Rondinella, Molinara
Anjou	Loire, France	Red	Cabernet Franc, Cabernet Sauvignon, Pineau d'Aunis (Chenin Noir)
		Rosé	Cabernet Franc, Cabernet Sauvignon, Gamay, Cot, Groslot
		White	Chenin Blanc, Chardonnay, Sauvignon Blanc

Crémant de Bourgogne	Burgundy, France	Sparkling	Pinot Noir, Chardonnay, Pinot Gris, Pinot Blanc, Gamay, Aligoté
Crémant de Loire	Loire, France	Sparkling	Chenin Blanc, Cabernet Franc, Cabernet Sauvignon, Pineau d'Aunis, Pinot Noir, Chardonnay, Menu Pineau +
Crépy	Savoie, France	White	Chasselas
Crozes-Hermitage	Rhone	Red	Syrah
Dão	Portugal	Red	Alfrocheiro Preto, Bastardo, Jaen, Tinta Pinheira, Tinta Barroca +
		White	Encruzado, Assario Branco, Barcelo, Borrado das Moscas
Dolcetto d'Alba	Piedmont, Italy	Red	Barbera
Echezeaux	Burgundy, France	Red	Pinot Noir
Entre-deux-mers	Bordeaux, France	White	Sémillon, Sauvignon Blanc, Muscadelle
L'Etoile	Jura, France	White	Chardonnay, Poulsard, Sauvignon Blanc
Falerno del Massico	Campania, Italy	Red	Aglianico, Piedirosso
		White	Falanghina
Fitou	Languedoc, France	Red	Carignan, Lladoner Pelut, Grenache +
Fleurie	Beaujolais, France	Red	Gamay
Frascati	Latium, Italy	White	Malvasia, Trebbiano
Fronsac	Bordeaux, France	Red	Merlot, Cabernet Franc, Cabernet Sauvignon, Malbec
Gaillac	South-west France	Red/Rosé	Duras, Fer, Sevadou, Gamay, Syrah, Cabs, Merlot +
		White	Len de l'El, Mauzac, Sémillon, Sauvignon Blanc +
Gavi	Piedmont, Italy	White	Cortese
Gevry-Chambertin	Burgundy, France	Red	Pinot Noir
Gigondas	Rhône, France	Red	Grenache Noir, Syrah, Mourvèdre
Grave del Friuli	Friuli-Venezia Giulia, Italy	Red	Cabernet Franc, Cabernet Sauvignon
		White	Chardonnay, Pinot Bianco
Graves	Bordeaux, France	Red	Cabernet Sauvignon, Cabernet Franc, Merlot
		White	Sémillon, Sauvignon Blanc, Muscadelle

Greco di Tuffo	Campania, Italy	White	Greco, Falanghina, Biancolella
Hermitage	Rhône, France	Red	Syrah
		White	Marsanne, Roussanne
Irouléguy	South-west France	Red/Rosé	Cabernet Sauvignon, Cabernet Franc, Tannat
		White	Courbu, Manseng
Lambrusco di Sorbara	Emilia-Romagna, Italy	Red	Lambrusco di Sorbara, Lambrusco Salamino
Limnos	Greece	White	Muscat of Alexandria
Lirac	Rhône, France	Red/Rosé	Grenache Noir, Cinsault, Mourvèdre, Syrah, Carignan
		White	Clairette Blanc, Grenache Blanc, Bourboulenc, Ugni Blanc, Picpoul +
Loupiac	Bordeaux, France	Sweet white	Sémillon, Sauvignon Blanc, Muscadelle
Lugana	Lombardy, Italy	White	Trebbiano di Lugana
Mâcon	Burgundy, France	White	Chardonnay
Madiran	South-west France	Red	Tannat, Cabernet Sauvignon, Cabernet Franc
Margaux	Bordeaux, France	Red	Cabernet Sauvignon, Cabernet Franc, Merlot, Carmenère, Malbec, Petit Verdot
Marino	Latium, Italy	White	Malvasia, Trebbiano
Marsala	Sicily, Italy	White	Grillo, Catarratto, Pignatello, Calabrese, Nerello, Mascalese, Inzolia, Nero d'Avola
Mercurey	Burgundy, France	Red	Pinot Noir
		White	Chardonnay
Meursault	Burgundy, France	White	Chardonnay
Minervois	Languedoc, France	Red/Rosé	Grenache, Syrah, Mourvèdre, Carignan, Lladoner Pelut Noir +
		White	Grenache Blanc, Bourboulenc Blanc, Maccabeu Blanc, Marsanne Blanche +
Monbazillac	Bordeaux, France	Sweet white	Sémillon, Sauvignon Blanc, Muscadelle
Morgon	Beaujolais, France	Red	Gamay
Moulin-à-Vent	Beaujolais, France	Red	Gamay
Muscadet	Loire, France	White	Melon
Naoussa	Greece	Red	Xynomavro

Navarra	Spain	Red	Tempranillo, Garnacha Tinta, Cabernet Sauvignon, Merlot +
		White	Viura, Moscatel de Grano Menudo, Chardonnay, Garnacha Blanc +
Nemea	Greece	Red	Aghiorghitiko
Orvieto Abbocado	Umbria, Italy	White	Trebbiano Toscano, Verdello, Grechetto, Canailo Bianco, Malvasia Toscana
Pacherenc du Vic-Bilh	South-west France	White	Arrufiac, Courbu, Gros, Petit Manseng
Palette	Provence, France	Red/Rosé	Mourvèdre, Grenache, Cinsault +
		White	Clairette, Gros Grains, Petits Grains, Ugni Blanc +
Patrimonio	Corsica, France	Red/Rosé	Nielluccio, Grenache, Sciacarello, Vermentino Blanc
		White	Vermentino Blanc, Ugni Blanc
Pauillac	Bordeaux, France	Red	Cabernet Sauvignon, Merlot, Cabernet Franc, Malbec, Petit Verdot
Penedès	Spain	Red	Tempranillo, Garnacha Tinta, Cabernet Franc, Merlot, Pinot Noir, Cabernet Sauvignon +
Pomerol	Bordeaux, France	Red	Cabernet Franc, Merlot, Cabernet Sauvignon
Pommard	Burgundy, France	Red	Pinot Noir
Port	Portugal	Fortified red	Touriga Francesa, Touriga Nacianal, Bastardo, Mourisco, Tinto Cao +
		Fortified white	Gouveio, Malvasia Fina, Rabigato, Viosinho, Donzelinho
Pouilly-Fumé	Loire, France	White	Sauvignon Blanc
Pouilly-Fuissé	Burgundy, France	White	Chardonnay
Pouilly-sur-Loire	Loire, France	White	Chasselas, Sauvignon
Puligny-Montrachet	Burgundy, France	White	Chardonnay
Quarts de Chaume	Loire, France	White	Chenin Blanc
Quincy	Loire, France	White	Sauvignon Blanc
Reguengos	Portugal	Red	Aragonez, Moreto, Périquita, Trincadeira

Reguengos *(continued)*		White	Manteudo, Perrum, Rabo de Ovelha, Roupeiro
Ribeiro	Spain	Red	Caino, Garnacha, Ferron, Souson, Mencia, Tempranillo +
		White	Treixadura, Loureira, Albarino, Jerez +
Richebourg	Burgundy, France	Red	Pinot Noir
Rioja	Spain	Red	Tempranillo, Garnacho
		White	Viura, Malvasia Riojana
Rueda	Spain	White	Verdejo, Viura, Sauvignon Blanc, Palomino Fino
Rosato di Salento, Rosso Conero, Rosso Piceno, Rosso di Montalcino	Tuscany, Italy	Red	Sangiovese
Rosso di Montepulciano	Tuscany, Italy	Red	Sangiovese, Canaiolo Nero
Rully	Burgundy, France	White	Chardonnay
St-Amour	Beaujolais, France	Red	Gamay
St-Emilion	Bordeaux, France	Red	Merlot, Cabernet Sauvignon, Cabernet Franc, Malbec
St-Estèphe	Bordeaux, France	Red	Cabernet Sauvignon, Merlot, Cabernet Franc, Malbec, Petit Verdot
St-Joseph	Rhône, France	Red	Syrah
		White	Marsanne, Roussanne
St-Julien	Bordeaux, France	Red	Cabernet Sauvignon, Merlot, Cabernet Franc, Malbec, Petit Verdot
St-Véran	Burgundy, France	White	Chardonnay
Ste-Croix-du-Mont	Bordeaux, France	Sweet white	Sémillon, Sauvignon Blanc, Muscadelle
Samos	Greece	White	Muscat Blanc à Petits Grains
Sancerre	Loire, France	White	Sauvignon Blanc
Saumur-Champigny	Loire, France	Red	Cabernet Franc, Cabernet Sauvignon, Pineau d'Aunis
		Rosé	Cabernet Franc, Cabernet Sauvignon, Pineau d'Aunis, Gamay, Côt, Groslot
		White	Chenin Blanc, Chardonnay, Sauvignon Blanc

Sauternes	Bordeaux, France	Sweet white	Sémillon, Sauvignon Blanc, Muscadelle
Savennières	Loire, France	White	Chenin Blanc
Savigny-lès-Beaune	Burgundy, France	Red	Pinot Noir
		White	Chardonnay
Soave	Veneto, Italy	White	Garganega, Pinot Bianco, Chardonnay, Trebbiano
Tavel	Rhône, France	Rosé	Grenache Noir, Cinsault, Clairette Blanche, Clairette Picpoul, Calitor, Syrah, Carignan
Tokaji	Hungary	White	Furmint, Harslevelu
Vacqueyras	Rhône, France	Red	Grenache Noir, Syrah, Mourvèdre
		Rosé	Grenache Noir, Mourvèdre, Cinsault
		White	Grenache Blanc, Clairette Blanc, Bourboulenc, Marsanne Blanc, Roussanne Blanc, Viognier
Valdepeñas	Spain	Red	Cencibel
		White	Airén
Valpolicella	Veneto, Italy	Red	Corvina Veronese, Rondinella, Molinara
Vin de Corse	Corsica, France	Red/Rosé	Nielluccio, Sciacarello, Grenache, Cinsault, Mourvèdre +
		White	Vermentino, Ugni Blanc
Vin Jaune (Côtes de Jura)	Jura, France	Sweet white	Sauvignon Blanc
Vesuvio	Campania, Italy	Red	Piedirosso, Sciascinoso
		White	Coda di Volpe, Verdeca
Vinho Verde	Portugal	Red	Vinhao, Espadeiro, Azal Tinto, Borraçal, Brancelho, Pedral
		White	Loureiro, Trajadura, Paderna, Azal, Avesso, Alvarinho
Vino Nobile di Montepulciano	Tuscany, Italy	Red	Sangiovese, Canaiolo Nero
Volnay	Burgundy, France	Red	Pinot Noir
Vosne-Romanée	Burgundy, France	Red	Pinot Noir
Vouvray	Loire, France	Dry/sweet white	Chenin Blanc
Zitsa	Greece	White	Debina

Major Influences on the Taste of Wine

We have already seen that there are a number of influences on the taste of a particular wine and have talked about the taste of wine in the context of its grape variety. In the descriptions of the grape varieties, I have referred to climate, soil, yields and winemaking techniques. These all have direct influences on the grape's taste. Let's find out exactly how.

How Does Soil-type Affect a Wine's Taste?

Soil is defined by its richness in fertilizing elements (which affects the plants' vigour); its structure (whether it is compact, rocky or muddy); its mineral composition (granite, chalk or limestone); its colour (red soils warm up faster in springtime than lighter-coloured soils); and its topographical situation (on a hill, in a valley or on a plain).

Soil – in combination with its exposure to the sun and other climatic elements — creates *terroir*, essentially the French word for dirt! *Terroir* is not a place but a happening, a combination of circumstances. *Terroir* defies description and cannot be reproduced or fabricated. Either it happens or it doesn't, and either a place has it or it doesn't. And a *terroir* can be wasted if the right grape variety is not married to it. Furthermore, designating a particular parcel of soil as an appellation does not automatically bestow upon it the title of *terroir*. Clearly *terroir* affects the taste of the wine to a considerable degree and it is, in fact, probably the major difference between a good wine and a great one.

Different grape varieties prefer certain soil types to others, and there is a good reason why some grapes match some soils better. Vines need soils that will store moisture reserves for droughts, drain excess water during heavy rains and force the vine to grow deep roots to search for its nourishment, thereby developing character and strength. Vines on hillsides are going to need different soils from vines planted in valleys, which are vulnerable to stagnation and poor draining pockets, thereby producing diluted, diseased fruit. As James Wilson, author of the book *Terroir*, so eloquently explains: 'Vine roots are predatory in their search for lenses of fine-grained material and pounce on them ravenously. Roots are

Below This 'slice' of the Bordeaux vineyards shows how each château can vary enormously in soil type and thus taste. The nuances are in the earth's geological history. Based on an illustration from *Terroir* by James E. Wilson (Mitchell Beasley, 1998).

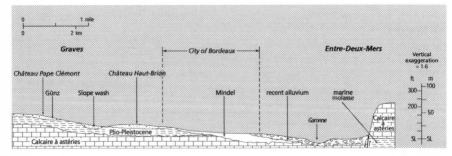

almost human in their perseverance to penetrate the barren layers and hardpan, passing through them without branching, in search of nourishing lenses.' The characteristics of the vine must therefore complement the characteristics of the soil on which it is cultivated, and the balance between the variables is a delicate one.

For example, Syrahs from the Rhône Valley's top *terroir* Les Bessards (which has an entirely granite soil) in the same year, in the same vineyard, of the same estate, will have a leather and spicy smell on the nose and the mouth will be very tannic. These wines will age very well. On the other hand, the same grapes from Meal (a *terroir* of stony soils on hills and terraces) have very fruity and delicate aromas, an elegant mouth with nice round tannins.

Take Bordeaux. In an oversimplification, the various proportions of grape varieties used in the blends are based on how suited each of the varieties are to the *terroir* in question. St-Emilion wines are a majority of Merlot, then Cabernet Franc, with Cabernet Sauvignon and Malbec in smaller doses because St-Emilion's soils welcome the Merlot more than the soils of, say, Pauillac or Pomerol, which are Cabernet-Sauvignon-dominated plantings.

Another example is the Gamay grape. Philip the Bold was right. In the granite terrain of Beaujolais with its thin, sandy soils, it produces a fine and agreeable wine. Though when planted on the rich limestone soils found just a few miles towards the north on the Côte d'Or, the variety produces a wine that is light, thin and not very pleasant. This observation can also be made with other varieties and other *terroirs*. The only conclusion is clear: that each variety has a soil that best expresses its originality.

How Does Climate Affect a Wine's Taste?

A grape needs to mature on a vine before it is picked. If the weather is too cold, the grapes will not mature and will thus taste 'green' and acidic. If it is too hot, they will reach maturity too quickly – but it will be a superficial maturity and not complete. White wines from a hot climate will lack acidity and therefore taste flabby and too sweet, while red wines will have too much alcohol and will have a very forward 'first attack' before seeming to evaporate on the tongue and completely disappear before the wine gets down your throat. The correct climate is needed to ensure that the growing period, or the ripening period, is long and slow.

Furthermore, the warmer and sunnier the climate, the less distinction there will be between grape varieties and the less the varietal character will develop. This is because in cool climate areas, the lesser amounts of sunshine produce high levels of odour-active compounds. Higher levels are produced because the cooler weather permits a longer, slower fruit maturation. We can smell these compounds (aromatic esters and aldehydes) as the familiar primary aromas of a grape variety. This is why climates that are too warm are really not conducive to quality grape-growing. There will also be less variation from year to year, and vintage will therefore be less of an issue.

Believe it or not, with a trained palate, you can detect the climatic origin of a wine. You can taste whether or not it came from a hot climate or a cool climate – they taste quite different. You have probably tasted the difference yourself before but may or may not have realized what was making this difference. To put it simply, wines from a hotter climate will taste almost cooked or boiled, whereas wines from a cooler climate will taste fresher and cooler. Why?

To each grape variety there is a specific climatic area where it best expresses its quality potential. For example, Riesling is perfectly adapted to the continental climate of Alsace, and the Pinot Noir to the continental climate of Burgundy. The Syrah is used to a temperate climate like that of the Rhône Valley, the Mourvèdre to a southern climate, and the Cabernet Sauvignon to the oceanic climate of the Bordeaux region. This is why there is such a difference between the way grape varieties taste in different countries. Chardonnay in Chablis is crisp and acidic, whereas in the Napa Valley it tastes oaky and tropical.

If a variety meant for a warm climate is grown in a cooler climate, its character is refined. For example, if the Grenache, of Spanish origin, is planted in the Côtes du Rhône, it produces finer, more delicate wines. And the inverse is true. If a variety is planted in a more southerly climate than its original home, then it will make a heavier wine, with heavier aromas and also with a higher alcohol content. Californians and other New World winemakers sometimes add acidity to a flabby wine grown in a too-warm location rather than take the risk of planting a variety in a place where it may not ripen every year.

Sunlight permits and encourages the accumulation of sugars, but not sunlight alone. It cannot get the job done unless it is accompanied by the right temperatures – and more importantly, the sum of temperatures throughout the growing period of the vine. This is what people are referring to when they talk about 'growing days' or 'heat summation'. The general rule is that the warmer it is during the period directly preceding the harvesting of the grapes, the higher the sugar levels will be and the lower the acidity. Inversely, the cooler the temperatures at this time, the lower the grape's sugar content will be, and the richer its acidity levels.

The synthesis of the polyphenols (colouring agents) is also in direct relation to the temperature. The warmer it is during the period just before harvest time, the more colour and tannins the red grapes will have when harvested.

The relationship between the sugar, acid and polyphenols is a crucial one and is additionally influenced by the precipitation the vines receive during the maturation period. The best balance between them is achieved when the vines have a humid vegetative cycle (but not too wet) until the *veraison* (when the grape ripens from green to white or red-black) to permit an optimal growth, and finally, a rather dry period just before harvesting, so the sugars have reached their optimal levels.

To each type of climate, there is a corresponding type of wine, the character of which will be defined by the balance of alcohol/acid and tannin.

Grapes grown in a warm and dry climate, such as the Mediterranean, will produce a wine that is rich in sugars, has relatively few acids, but is rich in polyphenols. An oceanic climate has fairly even temperatures with average sunshine, and produces grapes with average sugar and acid levels but which are rather rich in polyphenols. A continental climate is one that produces grapes average in sugars, relatively acidic and lacking a bit in polyphenols.

The majority of the world's vineyards are in areas which enjoy a Mediterranean climate, such as Italy, Greece, Spain, Portugal, North Africa, Asia, South Africa, Australia, California and Chile. In this type of climate, the white wines won't have very much aroma and will lack acidity. To fix this, winemakers use technological advances such as fermenting at low temperatures and blocking the malolactic fermentation to obtain a fresh and aromatic white wine. This is fine, but one must be conscious of the fact that white wines of great quality should reflect and be typical of not only their vinification method, but also their climate, soil and grape variety. In other words, yes, we can fix things, but in doing so we've changed them and inevitably altered their quality.

How Does Yield Affect Wine's Taste?

One of the first issues that will greatly affect a wine's quality and taste can be influenced even before the grapes get into the winery. This is the vineyard's yields, or the volume of grapes the vineyard is allowed to grow. Every year, the minimum and maximum yields are fixed in the various appellations of Europe, depending upon weather and crop conditions.

Very much like rose bushes or other plants in our gardens, grape vines need to be treated in such as way that they do not go wild. A plant that is over-nourished will actually produce more foliage than fruit. Too much of either leaves or fruit is bad. For every grape variety, an augmentation of yields will dilute all its characteristics: colour, sugar, acids and tannins. Inversely, small yields will best show off the grape's character. The variation of yields depends upon several things: whether or not a prolific rootstock was chosen, the planting density of the vines, their fertilization and watering programme, and the pruning techniques employed.

Planting Density As we have seen, too many clusters on a branch or too many branches on a vine both allow a plant to produce too much fruit. However, another factor to consider is the number of plants, or vines, allowed to grow in any one area, such as a hectare of vines. The French call this the '*pieds de vignes*', or the 'feet of vines' planted. Vines that are planted very close together will have to fight for survival. They will have to struggle and compete with each other for the nutrients and water in the soil. Thus their roots will be forced to run deeper into the ground, unlike plants that are planted far apart, the roots of which tend to spread out horizontally and superficially and thus become lazy, as all they need is easily accessible to them. So, like a spoiled child, they will lack character. Stressing vines, whether by planting them closer together on hillsides or by heavy pruning, builds character and therefore allows a higher level of quality.

Why are plants sometimes planted further apart? For monetary reasons usually. Fewer plants planted means less cost in terms of buying the plants and tending the parcel. When plants are close together, machine harvesters cannot fit between the rows to pick the fruit – it has to be done by hand, which is slower and more expensive.

It is also interesting to note that planting density is, or should be, tied to climate. In cooler climates, the density is traditionally about 8,000–10,000 plants per hectare, while in warmer climates, 4,000–5,000 is more the norm. Any less than this and the quality can be compromised. So to obtain richer grapes, it is best to permit as few clusters as possible on the plant, which is achieved by planting the plants very close together. Before

45

the Phylloxera crisis – when the fungal infection spread like wildfire through the vineyards and decimated many wine-producing areas – there were some plantings in Champagne and Burgundy that were as dense as 20,000 plants per hectare!

Pruning   If a vine were not pruned, it would develop terrifically during the first few years, exhausting its growth and shortening its life. It would bear less fruit and the quality of the grapes would not be as good. It is necessary to control the growth of a young vine in proportion to its strength and the depth of its root system, therefore pruning is individual to every vine. Pruning can be performed at two stages during the year: in the December or January after the harvest when the vines are in hibernation, and in July or August, called 'green pruning' because the vine plants are in their vegetative cycle.

The Age of the Plants   Another factor affecting yields is the age of the vines. Older vines that have been well pruned and not squeezed to maximum production will slowly yield fewer, more concentrated grapes as they get older. Vines are just getting interesting when they hit thirty years or more. So it is best if they arrive at that ripe age in a sober fashion. Vines that are '*pissent*', a very elegant French term for being over-worked, are drained and worn out by the time they are twenty.

Even the age at which a winemaker allows a plant to start producing fruit is an important factor in a wine's overall taste and quality. On average, a new plant is pruned very severely and not allowed to produce any fruit until it is three or four years old. At either end of the spectrum, there are extremes. Those winemakers who are particularly commercially driven, will sometimes let two-year-old plants produce fruit, and lots of it, while I know of a young winemaker who runs a family business in Germany who won't let the plants produce one grape until they are seven years old! Which would make the better wine in your opinion?

Determining Yield   So when determining yield, it is not enough to ask how many hectolitres per hectare have been produced, but other questions are equally important. How much pruning was done and how often? Are heavy fertilizers used? Is irrigation allowed? Which rootstock was chosen? How many plants per hectare are there? How old are the plants? When were they first allowed to produce fruit? And so forth. These are all variables in the final equation of quantity and therefore quality.

How Does the Winemaking Technique Affect the Wine's Taste?

Having looked at the magic trilogy of soil, climate and grape variety, there are those who would say there is a fourth element that is even more important (I wouldn't). Is that person a magician who makes it all possible, whose gentle hand leads the juice on the path of a greater beverage – or are the winemakers the ultimate intruders, manipulators who permanently imprint their personal style and interpretation of the grape on to each bottle? The answers are all of the above. It depends on the winemaker's politics and methodology.

Some winemakers claim that they are simply standing back and letting the fruit express itself, although meanwhile, they maximise the extraction of colour and

WHEN TO PICK A GRAPE AND HOW THIS AFFECTS ITS TASTE

As each grape variety has a specific taste and aroma potential; it also has a window of time in which it has reached its maturity and should be picked. This is very important and is probably the hardest task a winemaker has, for nature doesn't always keep to schedule.

To put it simply, there are grapes that mature in the first period, those that mature in the second, and those in the third. Within those three categories, there are also grapes that are more precocious than others. So there exists a harvesting order corresponding to the time each grape variety matures. If a winemaker has a vineyard of Chardonnay (first), Cabernet Sauvignon (second), and Grenache (third), the grapes are 'brought in' in that order. Further, if the vineyard has Merlot (early second), Cabernet Franc (middle to late second), and Cabernet Sauvignon (late second) plantings, then although they are all second-period varieties, they will be harvested in that order because they mature in that order.

This order is for the noble European grape varieties and their native climate. Take a grape out of its native environment and a little jiggery pokery has to go on. For example, the Chardonnay is a late first period, or *première epoque tardive*, grape. When grown in a warmer climate, it often reaches over-maturation (and so would taste flabby and too sweet) as it is so warm, so the grower is obliged to pick the grapes earlier, sometimes before they are mature. To vinify this type of grape will not give it a chance to express itself fully. The resulting taste will be one-dimensional, overtly fruity and short on the finish.

The chart below lists the major grape varieties and their comparative maturation periods in France. It is not totally exhaustive, but it provides an interesting comparison and should give you some insight into the correlation between climate, maturity and taste. Notice that those grape varieties that mature in the first period are found in the northern or cooler climates of France. Those that mature in the second period are found in the more central climates, and those that are late maturing are in the south, where the climate is Mediterranean.

FIRST PERIOD

Gewürztraminer	North-east
Pinot Noir	
Pinot Meunier	
Gamay	
Chardonnay	
Sylvaner	

SECOND PERIOD

Sauvignon Blanc	West and south-west
Colombard	South-west
Chenin Blanc	West
Viognier	South-east
Sémillon	South-west
Marsanne	South-east
Roussanne	South-east
Syrah	South-east
Cinsault	South-east
Merlot	South-west
Cabernet Franc	South-west
Cabernet Sauvignon	South-west

THIRD PERIOD

Clairette	Mediterranean
Ugni Blanc	
Grenache	
Carignan	
Mourvèdre	

flavour when fermenting. Others might say they prefer to allow the soil to speak for itself and opt for winemaking methods which are more hands-off.

These two different philosophies can be illustrated rather well in Burgundy. It is interesting to take a particular domain and try to determine whether each of its wines from different villages or vineyards reflect their variety and where they are grown, or if the common denominator of each wine is the style in which it has been made. I have tested this. I studied in great detail a particular winemaking family which has parcels in four or five of the well-known appellations in Burgundy. Up and down Burgundy, in all the blind tastings, you could actually pick out their wines – the style of the wine was definitely stamped with their technique rather than with the different wine parcels. You could barely tell the difference between the Pommard, the Volnay or the Mercurey! All their wines were delicious, mind you, and the wine style was very elegant, but it became boring and completely counteracted the beauty and the point of Burgundy.

Another aspect of winemaking, and a rather modern one, is the advent of the flying winemaker. These are freelance winemakers who make wine for any number of clients anywhere in the world. Again, there are bad and good things in this. The original idea was supposed to have had something to do with spreading and communicating badly needed viticultural information to certain wine regions. Frenchmen were flying to Australia and California, Australians to Portugal, all of them to Hungary and Bulgaria. Top flying winemakers have become celebrities in the wine world. They have up to a couple of dozen clients

around the world. But at what point does information and knowledge stop being shared and personal style preferences take hold, creating homogeneity?

Choices for the Winemaker

There are many choices a winemaker has to make – and they will *all* affect the final taste of the wine.

Hand or Machine Harvesting?

If hand-picked, the grapes will arrive at the winery in better condition. Those that are ripest, least bruised and healthy will be distinguished from those that are unripe, bruised and rotten. Also, any unwanted debris can be avoided. This means a cleaner wine, less vulnerable later to unwanted flavours. However, hand-picking is labour-intensive and therefore very expensive. Most of the traditional vineyards continue this practice, while modern ones plant their vines further apart on purpose so that harvesting machines can fit between the rows and do the picking. Despite any hand-sorting later in the winery, this means more bruised grapes and debris.

To Partially or Fully Separate Stems and Stalks?

Before maceration and fermentation, the winemaker has to decide how much, if any, of the stalks are going to be separated from the grapes. If they are allowed to remain in contact with the must (the unfermented grape juice) and the must is rather delicate or light (either due to the grape variety, the style of wine or dilution caused by rain), then they can turn the wine sour and astringent. The wine could even taste of sticks and branches. If the must has the strength to take it (an intense red variety in a good year), then leaving some stalks and stems in with the rest of the grape can give it more structure, as these parts of the grape contain tannins, acids and some minerals.

How Long to Macerate the Wine

The length of time the skins remain in contact with must is only relevant when making red wines. This is what gives the must its colour, flavour and structure. A long maceration is used for the noble grape varieties such as Cabernet Sauvignon, Pinot Noir, Nebbiolo and Syrah because they have better-quality skins. Other red grape varieties will need less time in the vat. If they are macerated for too long, the skin extracts will make the wine taste bitter, green and hard.

How to Start and at What Temperature to Ferment the Must

The first fermentation that grape juice undergoes is the alcoholic fermentation. This is simply allowing the yeasts to convert the juice's sugars to alcohol. The only problem is that sometimes the yeasts do not get going on their own and need a jump-start. Ideally, a winemaker can use indigenous yeasts from that vineyard, but if this is not possible, they can buy commercial yeasts and use them to initiate fermentation. Yeasts of this sort can be bought in different flavours, such as apricot, banana or peach, to give an otherwise light raw material more appeal. So sometimes, this is what you taste!

Assuming things get off naturally, red wines are allowed to ferment at a higher temperature than whites to extract more colour and flavour. But beware; if allowed to ferment at too high a temperature, the yeasts will become inactive and the fermentation will come to a halt or the wine will taste cooked or boiled.

Whether to Allow a Partial or Full Malolactic Fermentation

This is the second fermentation, and is when the malic acids (which taste like green apples) are transformed into lactic acids (which taste like yoghurt), making the wine more supple. It is usually only applied to white wines as they can be more acidic. A winemaker can allow a partial or full malolactic fermentation, and this greatly alters a wine's taste.

As a matter of fact, one can usually tell if the wine has undergone such a fermentation or not. Typically, a wine from a cool climate, like Champagne or Alsace, might need a partial or full fermentation to soften some of the acids without loosing their crisp, apple-like tastes and smells. In wines made from grapes in a warmer climate, on the other hand, the winemaker might not let malolactic fermentation occur or the wine would be too flabby and sweet.

The Length of Barrel Ageing and the Sort of Wood 'Programme'

After fermentation, the wine is usually put into containers of various sizes for ageing. The container chosen is most often an oak barrel. Red wines, depending on their quality and structure, will usually be aged for anywhere between six months and two years. White wines are usually aged for less than six months, or not at all.

Of all the decisions a winemaker has to make about oak, whether to use it during fermentation, ageing, or both; to use new oak, used oak or both; how long to use it; or to choose light, medium or heavy toast – one of the most important (toasting is also crucial) will be the selection of its origins, but not for the reasons that most of us would assume. The question is not Alliers, Nevers or Limousin (all French oak forests), and the argument should not be French versus American or even Slovenian, Hungarian or Russian, for there are variations in quality and confusion of hybrids in all these places. The primary factor in the selection of oak quality is tight-grain versus wide-grain, and only secondly, how much oak is actually used; too much of even the best oak is too much.

Even oak trees have their problems of soil, site and climate, and forests in cooler climates produce trees that have tight grains. This permits a more subtle transfer of vanillin and less extraction of the aggressive oak flavours.

Over-oaking is a big problem in modern winemaking. It started with the late 1970s California trend of showing off your new and expensive, imported French oak barrels. But today, there is still the even worse offence of hoping that the oak barrels will provide the tannins, flavour and complexity that the fruit is lacking. The problem is often not that there is too much oak, but that there is not enough good fruit. When used as the key ingredient, oak can mask many faults and deficiencies. Oak should be the spice of the recipe, not the flour!

A competent winemaker will evaluate the structure of the wine and decide how much oak it can take. They may put only one-third of the wine in new oak, one-third in two-year old oak, and the last third in stainless steel. This is what one refers to as a 'wood programme', and again, it is all about balance and getting the best recipe to fit the raw material. Red wine that has spent too long in new oak will taste dry and harsh, while white wine that has spent too long in new oak often ends up tasting bitter and resiny.

What Effect Does Ageing Have on Wine?

It is a known fact that a wine is a living entity that improves with age and changes with its evolution – that is, if it is made from a grape variety that is physiologically intended to improve with age, if this grape variety is grown in the most suitable climate and if the appropriate winemaking techniques have been applied. If that is the case, there will be a definite difference between what we call the primary aromas of a wine, or its grape variety while young, and the more developed smells that come from oak and bottle ageing, what is called the wine's bouquet.

What Is Maturation?

Assuming that everything goes all right until bottling, wine will continue to mature. In very simple terms, the maturation of a wine is the function of its composition, its origin (*terroir*) and its vintage. No two bottles from the same Bordeaux château, of two different years, will develop and mature in the same number of years.

When we say we are letting a wine mature, we are waiting for all its components to fall into balance with each other. A good wine is one that is balanced and harmonious. The acids, alcohols, tannins and fruits have all blended into one, creating a personality, a character. A less good wine will never fall into place because the fruits will die; or the tannins will fade away into nothing instead of softening and holding the wine together; or the acids, the backbone and life of the wine, may become flabby or disappear. When tasting a young wine, we look for all of these elements and try to determine how well the wine is made and how it will mature. We can be rather certain of a wine's character, but we never really know whether that character will endure until we test it years later.

During bottle ageing, red wines deposit little plaques and grains of colouring agents and other molecules which bond and fall to the bottom of the bottle. The heavier clusters settle faster than the smaller ones, which need years to settle. As these colouring agents settle in the bottles, the intensity of the wine's colour diminishes, becoming more and more reddish-brick, and finally yellowish, as the anthocyanins, or colouring agents, in the tannins soften and diminish as the tannins do. When we say that the tannins 'soften', we mean that the wine has reached a point of balance in its development curve. The harsh edge is taken off the wine and the wine's texture is smoother and less drying.

Polymerization progresses continually as the wine ages so that tannic wines for long ageing become gradually harder and more tannic before reaching a peak where they are more tannic then when they were in barrel. Then the slope starts a gradual decline. The extra-large molecules lose their ability to combine with other proteins and their astringency diminishes. At the same time they are combining with other components in the wine, becoming insoluble and precipitating to form the characteristic deposit. At this point the wine is in its mature, mellow phase and is softer, richer and rounder: this is maturity.

If kept too long, the increasingly large polymers gather strength once more, a sort of final wind, and become dry and astringent once again. This is compounded by the fact that the wine is also losing its fruit and gaining volatile acidity. It is

drying out, or dying. Knowing at which moment at which to open a wine is a skill acquired, happily, through much practice!

Certain wines will reach maturity sooner than others and not every wine will have the same length of maturity. In general, the duration of a wine's ideal maturation period is the length it needed to reach it. If a 1990 Latour will reach its apogee in 2010, then we can hope to be able to enjoy our bottles for twenty years.

What Does a Mature Wine Taste Like?

To best describe how a mature wine tastes, imagine the following analogies:

Young	Mature
Fresh cherries	Black cherry jam
Citrus fruit	Tropical fruit
Fresh red fruit	Cooked warm red fruit
Fresh fig	Dried fig
Green pepper	Black pepper
Honeysuckle	Honey or caramel
Green apples	Apple crumble
Orange juice	Orange liqueur
Peanuts	Grilled almonds
Freshly cut grass	Wet straw or hay
Cinnamon gum	Mulled wine

Does this give you an idea? Proper ageing adds depth and complexity to an odour. Plus there are some odours that are not even apparent until some oak ageing or bottle ageing has taken place, such as cigar and tobacco smells, and the smell of mushrooms and undergrowth. There is no 'young' smell analogy for these.

How to Taste Wine

There are many techniques developed by wine professionals that help you to maximise the taste experience.

When we taste a wine we are looking out for many things, because whether or not we like the wine will depend on many factors. We are tasting for balance between the acids, tannins, alcohol and fruit – acids for the backbone, tannins for preservation and longevity, alcohol for its structure and fruit for its taste. The better a wine is made, the more balanced it will be and the longer it will last.

Tasting a wine is merely breaking down the different components of taste and analysing them. Anyone can do it, but it does take concentration and practice. The more you taste, the more 'memory' you will have and the more information you will collect with which to create your own standards. As your skill increases, you will be able to blind-taste the difference between a red and white wine, recognize a Cabernet Sauvignon grape or a Pinot Noir, know whether the wine is from France, the USA or Australia, determine if a wine was made in a hot or cool climate, and be able to tell a young wine from an older one.

The process of tasting a wine is basically broken into three categories: sight, smell and taste. Fill the glass no more than one-third full when tasting and never more than half full when at table.

Sight

With the glass held vertically, look down on it from directly above. This will allow you to view the wine's surface, clearness and depth of colour, and any carbon dioxide (bubbles) that may be present.

With the glass tilted almost in a horizontal position against a white tablecloth, look at the wine (red) at its centre as well as its rim. The centre, or the 'eye' of the wine, will determine its hue and help you to know its age. The lighter, or rubier, red a red wine is, the younger it is. Once it is in the red-brick, orange tones,

you know it is older. By looking at its rim, you can also determine its age. The younger the wine, the thinner the watery rim will be; the older the wine, the thicker this watery rim will be.

Now look at the wine horizontally with your eyes directly at its 'disc' level. This enables you to observe the wine's 'robe', its colour which, as described above, will help to determine the wine's age. With white wines, the colour will tell you a lot about its weight and taste intensity. A very light, watery colour will almost always mean a light, watery wine. You will also be looking for deposits. In an older red, this would be normal; even if decanted well there may be bits that escaped. And with whites, deposits used to mean that it was a wine with good extracts and was considered perfectly natural and desirable. However, in today's world, most people prefer wines to be as stable and (in my opinion) as sterile as possible so as to better survive the conditions imposed by international transport and storage. Apparently, Americans get a bit squeamish if there are bits of pulp or fining material in their Pouilly-Fuissé!

Next, tilt the glass so a little wine covers the sides. Look at it again horizontally at eye level, but look for the little 'tears' or 'legs' which are running down the side of the glass. Are they slow and languorous or thin and rapid? The slower the legs run the more glucose (sugar) is present in the wine, and the more watery or fast the legs run, the more alcohol is present in the wine. This will already give you a first idea of how the wine may taste.

Smell

Before swirling, smell the wine. This will permit you to smell any varietal qualities or characteristics.

CAN YOU TASTE WINE FAULTS?

Improper harvesting and production techniques, handling and storage can all cause wine faults. Here are a few you might discover when tasting wine.

What it tastes like	What happened	When it happened
Rot and a bitter herbaceousness like crushed green leaves	The grapes were damaged by hail or were rotten, or there were leaves and other foreign objects with the grapes.	During harvest
Herbaceous (in excess)	The grapes were roughly treated and poorly de-stemmed, de-stalked and crushed, or the grapes were immature at harvest.	Arrival at winery
Bitter; stalks, stems and branches	The grapes were pressed too violently, which bruises the skin.	Pressing of white grapes
Dry, sour and astringent tannins	The *cuvaison* (vatting time) was too long.	Fermentation
Thin and light	The *cuvaison* was too short.	Fermentation
Taste of cooked caramel	The temperature was too high.	Fermentation
Lacks colour and structure	The temperature was too low.	Fermentation
Earthy, manure-type smells	Brettanomyces (Brett), a strain of yeast, is liked by some but disliked by many Californians. In small amounts it adds character, in large amounts it is considered offensive.	Fermentation
Flavour of fresh dirt or cement	Dekkera is another wild yeast of the genus Brett. Liked by some in France, it can also come from contaminated equipment and barrels.	Fermentation
Taste of the lees	There was no racking or not enough.	Racking
Taste of oxidation (flat and aldehydic)	There was too much racking.	Racking
Tastes oxidized, musty, stale and dirty	The container was opened and re-closed.	*Elevage*

Tastes of a mouldy *cuve* or tank	The container is dirty or mouldy.	*Elevage*
Smell of rotten eggs	Too much hydrogen sulphide from bacterial contamination. Can some-times be cured by airing.	*Elevage*
Smell of burnt matches	Too much sulphur dioxide was used. Can sometimes be cured by airing.	Preparation and cleaning of oak barrels
Taste of sulphur	Too much sulphur was used.	Preparation for bottling and bottling
Heavy deposits	Poor filtering.	Preparation for bottling and bottling
Taste of rotten cork	Bad cork.	Preparation for bottling and bottling
Smells like musty cardboard or a damp basement	The wine is corked. This is caused by trichloranisol (TCA), a compound released by moulds that can infest the bark from which corks are made. One theory is that you cannot get TCA without chlorine, which is used to bleach corks, so if corks aren't properly rinsed and dried after bleaching, this problem can occur.	Preparation for bottling and bottling
No fruit flavour left, off colour	Wine is maderized, or subjected to oxygen or heat through poor storage. It ends up tasting like Madeira or Sherry.	Storage
Sharp, tart, green, thin, like an unripe grape	Excessive acidity, excessive fixed or volatile acids, a high proportion of tannins, or too much ethyl acetate.	Fermentation
Smell of rotten eggs, garlic, onion or even skunk	Reduction of a wine results in a smell of mercaptans, which are formed by yeast reacting with sulphur in the lees.	During primary alcoholic fermenta-tion
Vinegar smell	Volatile acidity. This indicates the presence of acetic acid caused by bacteria. Airing can help.	Fermentation

Then swirl the glass and smell again. Either use one or both nostrils. It sounds odd, but experiment with each nostril; you might be surprised at the differences. You should be looking for major faults and remarking the differences from when the wine was still. Here you'll find more intense aromas for young wines and a bouquet for mature wines.

If you think you've detected a fault, or if you can't seem to 'wake-up' the nose, continue swirling, or cover the glass and shake it violently once or twice.

Taste

Some people advise taking a small sip, but I tend to take large mouthfuls as it helps me to feel or 'chew' the wine's texture. Or I take a small first sip, go through my analysis, and then take a second, much larger, sip and rinse it through the mouth like mouthwash either to confirm or discount my first impressions. It's up to you to decide what works best. This first taste is meant to judge the *première bouche* or 'first attack'. Is it soft or firm, smooth or sharp? How soon afterwards do you feel the tannins, the acids, the texture?

Swish the wine around in your mouth. Go ahead and make that gurgling, airy noise between your teeth to aerate the wine. Swallow a tiny bit. Concentrate on what is happening on your tongue and on the sides of your mouth. Are you experiencing a puckering, drying sensation? Young, tannic wines will do this. Is it velvety smooth, with softened tannins indicating an older wine, correctly aged? Is it like butter, all creamy and almost thick? This is where the 'mouth' is determined. Is it ample or thin? Here also, you can fully analyse the wine's flavours, its intensity and its texture.

Spit the wine, breathe out through the nose and palate and concentrate on the back of your mouth. Here we analyse the 'finale', or finish, of the wine. The better the wine, the longer it will linger in the back of the palate. Here also the balance of the tastes and aromas is important. A wine which has a delicious up-front and fruity attack, and an ample, warm mouth may often disappoint us once it gets to the finish. An overly alcoholic wine with lots of heavy fruit, spice and oak flavours up-front will fool us until the finish, where it is short or even non-existent, a certitude that the wine is unbalanced. Even an immature wine will show some signs of the shape of its future; and a complete lack of finish, at any stage, is a bad one.

How Does the Wine's Temperature Effect Its Taste?

If ever you are served a wine, either red, rosé or white, that is really chilled, be wary. When a wine is super cold, you can no longer taste it, and therefore any attributes or faults it may have are masked. Often inexpensive rosés or Primeur reds are served like this for that very reason! And drinking wines that are too warm has the opposite effect. Every aspect of the wine is laid bare before us and to its worst advantage. And beware: contrary to popular belief, 'room temperature' can often be too hot.

Last summer, I ordered a bottle of red Burgundy in a restaurant, and as I had noticed that the wine rack was directly over the hot, vibrating stereo system next to the kitchen door, I asked for an ice bucket. The waitress looked a bit confused, went away, and then came back to the table, smugly announcing that the Burgundy I ordered was indeed ´a red wine, madam, and is served at room temperature'. I replied, even more smugly, that 'room temperature' in that particular room, at that particular moment, was near, or over, 25°C and that the Burgundy I had ordered was meant to be enjoyed at 15–17°C so could she please bring an ice bucket? She didn't look convinced, but grudgingly complied. This happens to me all the time. And I am not particularly fond of boiled Pinot Noir.

Remember that the word '*chambré*' is the adjectival form of '*chambre*', or room. When château walls were feet thick and there was no central heating, room temperature was between 16–18°C at most (if they were lucky!). Serving a red at 20–25°C often alters the taste of the wine. When serving a red wine that is warm, one should not refer to this as chilling the wine because you are not, you are simply bringing it back to the temperature at which it should be served. A red wine served too warm is too heavy, alcoholic and flat tasting. At the correct temperature it will be lively and more flavourful – too cold and it will have no taste at all.

Serving Temperatures

Sparkling wines
Simple sparkling (Cava, Crémant, Saumur, non-vintage Champagne) 5–7°C/41–45°F

Sweet sparkling 4–7°C/39–45°F

Finest sparkling and vintage
Champagne 6–9°C/43–48°F

White wines
Simple, sweet whites (Anjou Blanc, Muscat, German QbA) 4–8°C/39–46°F

Simple, crisp, dry whites (Muscadet, Sancerre, Sauvignon Blanc, Pinot Blanc) 6–8°C/43–46°F

Complex dry whites (Burgundy,
Graves, Rioja) 9–11°C/48–52°F

Medium sweet whites (German Spätlese, Auslese, New World Riesling) 10–12°C/50–54°F

Finest sweet whites (Classed-growth Sauternes, top German wines,
late-harvest wines) 5–9°C/41–48°F

Finest dry whites (Mature white Burgundy, Graves, top New World Chardonnay) 10–12°C/50–54°F

Rosé wines
Simplest should be most
chilled 6–8°C/43–46°F

Red wines
Early drinking reds (Loire, simple Beaujolais, Côtes du Rhône,
vins de pays) 10–12°C/50–54°F

Simple reds (Young Bordeaux and Burgundies, New World reds) 14–15°C/57–59°F

Complex, mature reds, notably Pinot Noirs (Burgundy, New World Pinot Noir, Italian and Spanish reds) 16–17°C/61–63°F

Mature fine reds, notably Cabernet Sauvignons (Classed-growth Bordeaux, serious New World Cabernet,
Côtes du Rhône) 17–18°C/63–64°F

Fortified wines
Dry (Fino Sherry) 9–11°C/48–52°F

Medium (Amontillado Sherry, Madeira, white Port) 10–12°C/50–54°F

Sweet (Cream Sherry, tawny Port,
vintage Port) 15–16°C/59–61°F

Getting It All Together
These are just some of the decisions that affect the final product – the wine you drink – but they give you a pretty good idea of why wines taste as they do. And as all this information on wine has probably made you hungry, let's move on to the tastes of food.

PART TWO

THE TASTE
OF FOOD

The taste of food

THE first sign that I was to have a special relationship with food was at birth. My mother delights in recounting the fact that I was the first baby in the history of Scott and White Hospital in Temple, Texas, to finish my first bottle and ask for more. The affair continued well throughout my childhood and is marked by another memorable anecdote – my personal favourite. At the gustatorily naive age of twelve, our Girl Guide group, of which my mother was the leader, embarked on a backpacking adventure near the Grand Canyon. This was to be a foray into the true wild. We were all outfitted with special backpacks, space blankets and lightweight cooking gear. To top it off, my mother made a noble attempt to keep the trip authentically austere by spending a fortune on powdered food of the type used by astronauts. She half-heartedly planned our daily menus entirely from a selection of aluminium foil packets.

But I would not have it. Carry a thirty-pound pack – yes; piddle in the middle of the woods with no loo paper – yes; run the risk of meeting a coyote – yes; but eat powdered scrambled eggs – NO! So as the rest of the troop was outside loading the camper, I quickly raided the kitchen, taking three eggs, bacon, a frozen sirloin steak and a large potato with fresh butter and chives. Tucking these safely into my pack, I smugly set off with the rest of the girls.

I waited, sadistically, until we had suffered a day and a half of powered meals. Then early one morning, as everyone was tucking into their cornflakes in powdered milk, I buttered my miniature frying pan (also borrowed from my mother's pantry) and broke open the eggs. I threw on the bacon and sat back, sipping my hot tea, imagining the feast to come. The odour very soon wafted over to my mother's tent and very soon a furry cap emerged. 'I smell eggs, *real* eggs!' The next instant, the entire troop was sitting round my fire trying to figure out how to divide three eggs into fifteen portions. I left them to it, as they didn't know what I had up my sleeve for dinner that night! Needless to say, I didn't earn any badges on that trip.

From Wine to Food

We are now moving, in a sense, from one food group to another because most of the principles we established in Part 1 can be applied to food. We know a lot more about wine than we think we do, just by being food lovers. In fact, learning about wine is probably easier than learning about food as there are an even greater number of variables affecting a food's taste as there are that of a wine.

The things that are important to a grape's quality – and therefore the quality of the wine – are the same things that we look for when choosing our food. We all prefer fresh food to stale, colourful to pale or insipid, tasty to bland, and purity of taste to ambiguity.

The only problem with today's food industry is that we cannot count on any of the home-grown ingredients that were taken for granted by all country dwellers until the 1940s. Unlike wine, we have no idea where our food comes from. There are no appellation restrictions for tomatoes or potatoes, for example; we know only that our eggs are 'free range' or that our meat is Scottish or English; and other than the rare markets of local fresh produce that some of us are lucky enough to have in our villages, we have to rely on the large supermarkets who can ship their goods from anywhere in the world. So, where good farming used to be directly responsible for good cooking and good eating, it seems that 'good shopping' is the modern equivalent.

Nature has a reason for everything. Interestingly, the more I learn about food and wine, the more I find myself referring to gardening encyclopedias! I think that is the beauty of the industry. It marries so many disciplines: history, geography, chemistry, climatology, geology, ecology and agriculture.

Food's Natural Influences

The analogies between food and wine are endless. Food, like wine, needs to be grown in good soils with enough sunlight and rain, to be produced in small yields and with careful harvesting and preparation techniques. Just as there are different grape varieties, there are different varieties of tomato, of mushroom, of potato, of apple. Then, just like wine, each variety is further differentiated by its origins. The same things that provide a country or region with its variances in wine (the landscape, the vegetation, the soil and the climate) are all things that lend a food

its diversity. And just as there is a grape variety suited to a set of geographical conditions, so is there a geographical set of conditions which are ideal for a food item: figs are at their best when from the Mediterranean, apples from north-eastern USA, salmon from Norway, butter from Normandy, beef from Scotland, truffles from the Perigord, goats' cheese from the Loire Valley, Parma ham and Parmesan cheese from Tuscany, and so on.

Even in blending, there are similarities between food and wine. Just as a fine Bordeaux is blended from the very best of a winemaker's *cuvées*, so is the fine, sweet, corn cereal, polenta. There are four types of polenta grain, for example, and an authentic way to make polenta. The finest producers strive for smaller yields to maintain quality. Then they mix the four grains each year according to their flavour and quality and to the secret recipe or blend of the individual producer. Doesn't that sound familiar?

The Manipulation of Food and Wine

Cooking methods, as with winemaking techniques, can change the original flavours and therefore greatly vary the choice of a suitable wine pairing. We know that winemaking techniques (apart from the other factors of climate, soil, and so on) can change the taste of the grape. Take Chardonnay, for example. If you ferment and age it in oak barrels rather than stainless steel, it will taste oakier. If full malolactic fermentation is allowed, then it will taste more buttery. This means that we can't say that Chardonnay always goes with such-and-such a dish; we need to identify a particular style of Chardonnay, such as a steely, mineral-complex Chablis, or a buttery, oaky, sweet Napa Valley.

The same scenario is true for food. Take a hamburger. What kind of mince are you going to use for the patty? Do you buy organic, lean, fatty or grain-fed? The origin of the meat will already be a factor in the resulting texture and taste. Then, how are you going to cook it? Are you going to opt for an outdoor barbecue, sauté it in a frying pan, grill it, or roast it in the oven? Four different cooking methods produce four distinctly different tastes.

Now, add the condiments. Will you use onions, garlic, Tabasco sauce or ketchup? Will you top it with Cheddar, Swiss or blue cheese? Perhaps you'll add some bacon and avocado? Finally, are you going to put it on a sesame seed bun or on a toasted and buttered bap? The final taste results are infinite. And each one of these choices could vary the final choice of wine. If your hamburger were barbecued, you might try a spicy Zinfandel, especially if the coals were mesquite. With a pan-fried hamburger, perhaps a Merlot; with blue cheese, a Cabernet-dominated Bordeaux or a heavy, oaky, slightly sweet Chardonnay.

Cooking and Preparation Methods

The way in which a food is cooked has an enormous impact on the way it will taste. Just imagine the difference between a hard-boiled egg and a fried one; a raw carrot and a boiled one; or a grilled steak and a beef stew. Two things define all cooking methods: the variations of heat; and the variations of the amount of liquid used. The more liquid used and the less heat applied, the more the food's texture is

softened and the more the flavour is reduced yet complex. The less liquid and more heat applied, the more the food's flavour is intensified, while its colour and flavour are preserved or increased and its texture becomes crispy. To put it simply, 'fast, hot and dry' preserves taste, while 'slow, moderate and moist' intensifies flavours. And when it comes to matching wines, a general guideline is that foods prepared with a light method of cooking (poaching or steaming, for example) usually require a fruity, lightly acidic wine rather than a heavy tannic one, even if the poached food has a spicy or heavy sauce to accompany it.

Steaming

A delicate cooking method which helps foods all their freshness, flavour and texture by using no liquid at all, just tenderizing the food in steam. Steamed foods, such as vegetables or oriental dishes, usually need slightly acidic, fruity white wines.

Poaching

Poaching is a very gentle simmer in liquid (try fresh oysters poached in Champagne with julienne carrots and leeks as a potage). The amount of water, stock or wine in which the food is poached depends on the food itself. Once the food is cooked, the cooking liquid can be boiled until it has reduced, then used as the base for a sauce. Poaching is usually used for foods with delicate textures and tastes, as this method tends to preserve both. As with steaming, it will result in a very delicate dish, regardless of flavourings, and would do well with a fruity, light to medium-bodied wine – probably a white as you don't see much 'poached steak' on menus!

Boiling

As boiling does not add flavour to foods, this method has more to do with texture than taste. It is used for tenderizing tough pieces of meat which are submerged in water or stock at a high temperature. The flavours of the food also tend to be toned down, especially if the food is salty (think of that Christmas ham). The texture of boiled meat needs a medium to heavy red.

Shallow-frying

This method is most successful if performed quickly and at a very high temperature. There are many variables in this method, including the kind of fat that is used and the depth of the pan (from a deep pan to a wok). Frying is primarily meant to preserve a food's colour and flavour, although it does intensify the taste a little. It will produce a dish with a relatively light texture and simple flavour, compared to the heaviness and flavour complexity of a stew, for example. As the sauce is often created in the frying process, its taste will also influence the choice of wine. Usually, a light, fruity, acidic red or white is best – nothing too oaky, too tannic or too sweet.

Deep-frying

Despite what we might think, when we immerse foods in a large, deep pan of boiling fat, it is better to use more fat, not less. According to my *Larousse Gastronomique*, food fried in plenty of hot oil is sealed immediately and therefore does not absorb the fat but becomes crisp, firm and cooked through. When too little fat is used, on the other hand, this sealing process cannot take place so the fat is absorbed into the food and the pieces stick to one another and become soggy.

I learned this while perfecting my *frites* technique in Paris! If cooked correctly, deep-fried foods are surprisingly light and delicate and are best complemented by light, fruity, acidic wines.

Braising, Casseroling and Stewing

Generally used for red meats, such as beef and lamb, these methods can also be applied to veal, pork and venison. The idea is to exchange flavours, so lots of vegetables, spices and herbs are used. Large cuts of meat can be marinated before braising because, as with boiling, this method softens the food's texture. If done slowly, the flavours of the foods are intensified. The results are complex and heavily textured, which means we can match these dishes with full, oaky whites or tannic, rustic reds.

Grilling

A method requiring very intense heat, grilling works by sealing all the nourishing juices into the meat by the crust formed on the surface. Because it is fast and does not allow time for the meat to tenderize, it is usually reserved for the best cuts of meat. Grilling, like roasting, uses dry heat, but it is faster than roasting. It tends to produce more intense and smoky flavours. Grilled meats need mature, full reds with tannins and heavy, dark fruit.

Roasting

Roasting is the complete opposite of steaming, poaching and boiling because it uses dry heat to intensify the taste and add a unique flavour. The flavours are concentrated on the outside, browned layers of the meat where juices have evaporated, which gives a slightly caramelized flavour to the crusty surface –

like crackling, for example. This is how the English like their meats, hence the proverbial Sunday roast. Smooth, elegant and mature reds will best match the juicy, flavourful cuts of meat that are reserved for this most noble of methods.

The Weight of Food

The cooking method employed combines with the food's weight and texture to produce the variables of taste. Faced with a tender fillet of sole, we may decide to preserve its texture and weight by steaming it, or to change its texture and weight by frying it in butter, which will make it heavier and denser. Like wine, we analyse a food's texture, weight and consistency, as well as its basic taste. We use all of these clues to form an opinion and a match.

What we mean by 'weight' is very simply the substance or heaviness of the food or of the dish. Compare a salad to a lamb stew that has been in your crock pot overnight. The salad is the lighter dish in weight, substance and also in its concentration of flavours. The lamb stew is the more substantial, heavy dish. You may have put the same spices in both dishes – say basil and parsley – but that doesn't mean that the two dishes are going to take the same wine, as their respective weights will require different wines.

When matching wines to a dish's taste and weight it is easier to match light wines to light dishes. You can also use a light wine for a heavier dish to cut through it and freshen it, although the more traditional match is a heavier, rustic wine to complement it. Imagine foie gras with a rich and sweet Sauternes, or Indian food with a spicy Gewürztraminer; these two pairings are matching food and wine of similar weights.

The Texture of Food

Texture is quite a different thing to weight. Think about how a wine feels in your mouth. Is it dry and slow to go

---

MATCHING THE CATEGORIES OF TASTE, WEIGHT AND TEXTURE

Food	Wine
Acidic foods	Acidic wines, fruity and aromatic, off-dry
Fatty / oily foods	Acidic wines with a rich, full flavour; rosés not tannic reds
Fishy foods	Fruity, aromatic full-bodied, off-dry whites and rosés
Salty foods	Sweet whites; low-tannin reds
Smoked foods	Oaked, rich and fruity whites; spicy reds
Spicy foods	Fruity, young, low-tannin, moderate alcohol reds; whites with some residual sugar and light acidity
Sweet foods	Sweet wines of equal or greater sweetness
Vinegary foods	Fruity, light and dry or slightly sweet whites, of equal acidity

down, or heavy or smooth? Is it 'puckery' because of its young tannins? Or light and crisp, due to its acidity? Perhaps it tastes round and smooth as a result of the glycerin? Imagine a light, acidic Sancerre (the Sauvignon Blanc grape) with briny, fresh oysters. Imagine a velvety Pauillac or a St-Julien (Cabernet Sauvignon-dominated) with a tender spring lamb roast. In these pairings, the texture of the food and wine match.

However, you can also use contrasting textures. Take our foie gras again but this time marry it with a bubbly, crisp Pinot Noir-based Champagne. Now you have the spicy robustness of this grape contrasting with the sweet smoothness of the foie gras, and the crisp, effervescent texture of the Champagne contrasting with the rich creaminess of the foie gras. A contrasting marriage in this case is just as effective.

The Importance of Sauces

So far we have looked at the cooking method, the weight and the texture of the food. All of these before we even get to the variable of the sauce! Imagine you have before you a poached chicken breast – a fairly innocuous beast that needs a bit of livening-up. Are you going to smother it with a lemon and cream sauce? A mushroom and Marsala sauce? A tomato and onion sauce? And in that lemon and cream sauce, will you use tarragon or parsley? In the mushroom and Marsala sauce, garlic or cloves? And in the tomato and onion, basil or curry? The equation is becoming more complex, isn't it?

Sauces not only change the flavour of the dish but also its texture and weight. A sauce made with butter, olive oil, cream or egg yolks will give the dish more body. Sauces with these bases will also be very rich and will need an acidic wine to cut through the heaviness and provide some balance. Again, there is a wide spectrum even here, with a herb butter sauce being very much lighter than a béarnaise or hollandaise sauce. The former needs fruity, crisp, aromatic wines, like a minerally Chablis or a Sancerre, while the latter needs acidity also, but with more substance, like an oaky Chardonnay or an Alsatian Pinot Gris.

The whole thing could easily become overwhelming but the beauty is that you are in control and can do as you like. Despite all the influences that proceed it, the sauce will contain the magic clues essential for making a good wine match. Think of the sauce as the liquid seasoning for the food. Sauces usually have a base: cream, tomato, red wine, white wine, vegetable stock or meat stock. And to these bases, we can add more layers of flavours or we can stick to the basic ingredients.

Oil-based sauces are actually rather light and in general work well with dry red wines. An olive oil and herb sauce on pasta or roast vegetables will go nicely, not surprisingly, with a medium-weight Italian red such as Barbera. The sesame seed oil you might use in a Chinese stir-fry works with a spicy, sweet white, not only because the oil is light, but because the spices used in the stir-fry are best with a richer, honeyed, fruity wine. Spicy, sweetish whites, such as a Gewürztraminer, will also complement the soy sauce used in Chinese cooking; a wine that had a lot of tannin or is very oaky would become even drier and coarser on the palate with a salty sauce such as soy. Fruity whites and rosés with a touch of sweetness will temper the saltiness in the food and keep the textures balanced. Hazelnut and walnut oils used in salads need oaky, fruity whites like a New World Chardonnay

Barbecued sauces need a sweet, warm-climate red such as a Zinfandel or Shiraz because the warm fruit is sweetish and the tannins can hold up to such a sauce, where a sweetish white would be crushed. Oak-dominated reds would not do so well, however, so stick to the fruit.

Tomato sauces and vegetable purées used as a sauce are usually on the acidic side and so need an acidic yet fruitier counterbalance, such as a Sauvignon Blanc, or a fruity red Italian, or a Merlot if there is meat in the sauce.

You will find specific sauce and wine matches in the sauces listing in Part 3.

After establishing the base of the sauce, the next step is usually adding the herb or spice dimensions. Although they are carefully chosen to match the sauce's base, they often end up with a starring role. Try putting curry with coconut milk. The milk will sweeten it a bit, but there will be no mistaking that the curry is the dominant flavour of the sauce, and of the finished dish.

Spices, Herbs and Condiments

Who can deny the historical, cultural and economic impact the spice trade has had on Britain and indeed the world? Spices have always been more than a simple seasoning. Spices were associated with wealth, exotic travel, the discovery of new continents, sovereignty and power. From the East came sailing ships laden with spices, textiles and perfumes to the great empires of Greece, Rome, Mesopotamia, Arabia and Egypt.

Long before the Christian era, the Greek merchants thronged the markets of southern India. Epicurean Rome spent a fortune on Indian spices, silks and brocades. It is said that Rome fought the Parthian Wars largely to keep open the trade route to India and that there may have been no Crusades and no expeditions to the East without the lure of Indian spices. Spices were such royal luxuries that men were willing to risk their lives for them. This is hard to believe when spices cost so little today.

And what did they use the spices for? To enhance and vary the taste of their foods, certainly, and also to mask the taste of food that was slightly off and would otherwise be thrown away. Some spices were also used for preserving meat and other food without refrigeration. Cloves, for example, were a popular preservative in the sixteenth century. They contain a chemical called eugenol which inhibits the growth of bacteria and are still used to preserve some modern foods like Virginia ham. (When you run out of mints, try sucking on a clove for a few minutes to freshen your breath quickly and make your mouth feel great.) If spices were not available, then food could not be preserved during the winter months and there would be nothing to eat – that is how important they were.

Spices also can be used as antioxidants as they possess antibiotic properties. Spices intensify saliva flow and the secretion of amylase, neuraminic acid and hexosamines. They clean food and bacteria from the mouth and may even help to prevent infection and cavities. They also protect the mucus in the mouth against thermic, mechanical and chemical irritation. Spices increase the secretion of saliva rich in ptyalin, which facilitates starch digestion in the stomach, making carbo-hydrate-rich meals more digestible. Spices may also activate the adreno-cortical function and fortify resistance and physi-cal capacity. Stroke and high blood pressure can be markedly diminished or augmented by means of spices. Indeed, the medicinal uses of herbs and spices would fill another book, but are not the topic under discussion here.

What are Spices?

Spices shape a people's culinary personal-ity. Both are products of a particular place and its environment. The climate will dictate which spices and plants will thrive in the area. A hot climate will produce some pretty fiery-tasting spices and thus infuse the cuisine and entire culture with a similar personality! Subconsciously we associate countries with their family of spices – it suits them. Mention chilli pep-pers and we immediately imagine our-selves lying on a beach in Mexico with a glass of chilled tequila. And before you can say, 'allspice' or 'cinnamon', I am on that French ski slope sipping my mulled wine and brushing up my après-ski skills. (Let's forget the fact that these spices, like most others, are indigenous to tropical climates. We are permitted such day-dreams because they have been in Europe since the ninth and tenth centuries – long enough to allow a bit of poetic licence).

Technically a spice, or condiment, is an aromatic plant with no permanent woody stem above the ground. Spices and condiments are natural plants, vegetable products or mixtures of the two, in whole or ground form, which are used for imparting flavour, aroma and piquancy to foods. Since spices may comprise dif-ferent plant components, we can assume

that herbs are part of spices and condi-ments, and we will group them together here for the sake of clarity and brevity!

There are about 70 known spices grown in different parts of the world. This variety lies in the fact that a spice not only can vary by the plant from which it originates, but also the different parts of the plant – each one having its unique taste. So, where with wine we were concerned with the aromas located in and under the skin, here we are faced with even more infinitessimal choices!

Why such an important discussion on spices? Because they form the basis of our argument. They are the primary ingre-dients used to flavour food and are often the dominant base of a dish to which we are matching a wine. They are indispens-able to the culinary art. Spices are to food what grape varieties are to wine. Basic ingredient meets basic ingredient.

The Components of Spices and Herbs

Even in something as apparently invari-able as a spice or herb, there are qualit-ative requirements and climate, soil and yields are of great importance. Herbs and spices, like vine plants, do not do very well with too many fertilizers or manures. Like the vine, they just need the appro-priate soil, moisture and light, and each one has a natural habitat or climatic ori-gin. If you really want to get carried away, you could use fresh spices imported from their native lands, but most of us are happy enough to grow them on our win-dowsills or to stick with the cultivated variety from in the local supermarket.

We know that spices and herbs, while very healthy for you, are not considered to have any nutritional value. For exam-ple, a dry bay leaf has the following composition: moisture; protein; fat; fibre;

CLASSIFYING SPICES AND HERBS

According the *Larousse Gastronomique*, all condiments (which are of vegetable origin) are classified by their dominant flavour. This is the classification they apply.

Flavour	Spices and herbs
Salty	Sea salt
Acidic	Vinegar, verjuice, lemon juice, capers, sea-fennel, nasturtiums
Bitter	Garlic, shallots, onions, mustard, horseradish
Bitter aromatic	Paprika, dill, anise, basil, coffee, cinnamon, chervil, coriander, cumin, turmeric, tarragon, fennel, juniper, clove, bay, mace, mint, nutmeg, parsley, saffron, sage, thyme, vanilla
Sweet	Sugar, honey
Fat	Oils, butters, fats

---

carbohydrates; ash; calcium; phosphorus; sodium; potassium; iron. It also contains the following vitamins in mg per 100g: 0.10 vitamin B1 (thiamin); 0.42 vitamin B2 (riboflavin); 2.0 vitamin B6 (niacin); 46.6 vitamin C (ascorbic acid); 545 IU of vitamin A. It has 410 calories per 100 grams.

The Spices and Herbs

If you grow herbs at home and wish to use them for cooking, the best time to cut them is when they are in bloom. Some herbs should be cut at the beginning of their blossoming, others towards the end: thyme in May and June, mint in July, sage at the beginning of June, fennel during the end of August and most of September, and marjoram at the beginning of July. Each herb, like each grape variety, has it optimum harvesting or maturity period.

When drying your herbs, tie them loosely in bunches and hang them in a shady and aerated place. To preserve them throughout the year, keep them in a dark, dry container.

Allspice
Pimenta officinalis
Allspice or pimenta is made from the dried, unripe berries of the allspice tree and it is so named because it possesses the combined flavour and aroma of cloves, nutmeg, cinnamon and black pepper.

Uses: ketchup, soups, sauces, pickles, canned meat, gravies, relishes, pies, puddings, mulled wines, curry powders, mincemeat pies, poultry dressing, spicy breads and cakes.

Basil or Sweet Basil
Ocimum basilicum
Native of north-west India and Persia, basil is an annual of the mint family. The flavour is warm, sweet and somewhat pungent. The odour is aromatic, fragrant and sweet. According to *Larousse Gastronomique*, basil was considered a royal plant that could only be picked by the sovereign (*basileus*) with a golden sickle.

Uses: pesto sauce, soups, meat pies, aubergine, courgette, some cheeses, cooked peas and string beans, used with or instead of oregano in tomato-based dishes.

Bay Leaves
Laurus nobilis
Bay leaves grow from an evergreen, hardy tree or bush cultivated since antiquity in Mediterranean countries. The aroma of the crushed leaves is delicate and fragrant. The taste is aromatic and bitter. It is not to be confused with the leaves of the bay rum tree family from Puerto Rico or with the California bay laurel. The taste is warm, slightly spicy and sweetish.

Uses: Spanish, Creole and French soups, sauces, stews, marinades, game, shellfish, tomato sauce and vinegar.

Capers
Capparis spinosa
Capers are the unripe buds of *capparis spinosa*, a low-trailing or prostrate, bushy shrub with dense foliage growing in the south of Europe, North Africa and India. The tiny buds open when the sun rises and close again when it sets. Once cut, they remain closed. The capers are then graded on copper sieves. The smaller the bud, the higher its quality grade. Usually they are cured and prepared in salt. The bitter, vinegary taste is rather pronounced so very few capers are needed when cooking.

Uses: fish and meat sauces, garnish for cold roasts and salads, seasoning for pickles and relishes.

Chillies
Capsicum annum
Chillies, also called red peppers, are the dried, ripe fruit of the capsicum plant, and can be used as a vegetable as well as a condiment. Originating in the American tropics, the plant bears single flowers and its fruit is usually pendant and provides all the forms of red pepper, cayenne, paprika and chillies. The varieties of chilli are broadly divided into two groups: the long, pungent type, including the pickling type used as a spice; and the bell-shaped, non-pungent or mild, thick-fleshed type.

Uses: in all types of curried dishes, roasted and ground with other condiments such as coriander, cumin, turmeric and farinaceous matter to make curry powder. It is also used for seasoning eggs, fish, meat, sauces, chutneys, pickles, frankfurter sausages and Tabasco sauce.

Chervil
Anthriscus cerefolium
Chervil is an annual herb native to Europe, although it does not do well in very hot weather. It can be used both for seasoning salad and as a garnish. It tastes similar to mild parsley and aniseed.

Uses: for garnishing and seasoning, chopped finely and sprinkled over fish, soups, salads, sauces, egg dishes, French dressing, and as part of the *fines herbes* combination.

Chives
Allium schoenoparasum
The chive is a perennial herb belonging to the onion family and is a native of Europe. Chives are completely immune to cold and can also withstand drought. Although the mildest member of the onion family with a light, delicate onion flavour, they can also be a bit tangy or even hot.

Uses: potato salads, green salads, omelettes, cheese bread, soups, stews, with or in cheeses.

Cinnamon
Cinnamomum zeylanicum
A cousin of cassia, cinnamon is a tree spice which consists of layers of dried pieces of the inner bark of branches and young shoots from the evergreen tree. The quality of cinnamon depends, among other factors, upon the region where it is grown. Cinnamon from Sri Lanka and the Seychelle Islands is considered the best. Every part of the tree – the bark (whole or powdered), wood, leaves, buds, flowers, fruit and roots – can be used in one way or another. The taste is warm and spicy with a delicate, musky perfume.

Uses: confectionery, liqueurs, soaps, dental products, chewing gum, sweets, cakes and breads.

Clove
Eugenia caryphyllus
The clove is the air-dried, unripe fruit bud obtained from a medium-sized, evergreen, straight-trunked, tropical tree. Clove is the second most popular spice, being next only to black pepper. The term clove is derived from the French word *clov* and the English clout, both meaning 'nail', due to its likeness to a broad-headed nail. It has been mentioned as far back as the first century BC, usually for its antiseptic properties as it contains eugenol. The Chinese imported it to Europe in 1265. Initially the taste resembles that of allspice but actually has an almost fruity aspect.

Uses: sweet and savoury dishes, baked goods, cakes, chocolate puddings, desserts, sweets, syrups, stews, gravies, ketchup and sauces, especially tomato.

Coriander, Cilantro
Coriandrum sativum
Native of the Mediterranean region, the seed of this umbelliferous plant is one of the richest sources of vitamins C and A. It has a parsley-like aroma with a bold, sage flavour and a tangy, citrus taste.

Uses: with lamb, stuffing, sausages, in curries, in cheeses, for garnishing, in Mexican salsa, chutneys, salad dressing, oriental stir-fry and spicy dishes.

Cumin
Cuminum cynimum
Cumin seeds are long and spindle-shaped, dried yellowish to greyish brown in colour and are either five-sided, smooth or covered in hairs. Believed to be native of Egypt, Syria and the Eastern Mediterranean region, the aromatic seed-like fruit has a peculiar odour that is strong and heavily pleasant to some, but rather disagreeable to others. Its flavour is warm and spicy but slightly bitter. Cumin is one of the oldest spices known since Biblical times, mostly appreciated for its medicinal effect on stomach upset and wind!

Uses: mixed spices, curry powders, soups, pickles, breads, cakes and cheeses.

Dill
Anethum graveolens
Anethum graveolens, rather than Indian dill, is the dill indigenous to Europe and cultivated in England, Germany, Romania, Turkey and the USA. Used whole and ground, the ripe, light brown seeds emit an intense, herbal aroma resembling that of caraway or mild aniseed. The delicate fronds are also used.

Uses: fish, especially salmon, light sauces, butter, carrot soup, breads, devilled eggs, pickles, cucumbers, sauerkraut, dill pickles. Can be used as a substitute for caraway.

Fennel

Foeniculum vulgare

Fennel seed is the dried, ripe seed of this flowering umbelliferous plant, an Italian native cultivated in Mediterranean countries, Romania and India, as it does best in mild climates. It has a sweet aroma resembling aniseed. Fennel seeds are classified for trade purposes according to their place of origin, those from Lucknow in India being considered the best. Its thickened leaf stalks are blanched and used as a vegetable. The leaves, which are reported to have diuretic properties, are also used for flavouring, and the roots are regarded as purgative.

Uses: leaves are used in fish sauce and for garnishing. The dried seeds are used as seasoning in soups, meat dishes, sauces (coquilles St Jacques), liquors, bread rolls.

Garlic

Allium sativum

A member of the onion family, garlic has a stronger flavour than than any of the other members of its family. It grows under much the same conditions as the onion except that it prefers a richer soil in a higher elevation. A well-drained, moderately clayey loam is best suited for its cultivation. Garlic has long been recognized all over the world as a valuable condiment for foods and a popular remedy for various ailments and physiological disorders – such as vampirism! It is used all over the world for seasoning dishes. In America about 50 per cent of the output of fresh garlic is dehydrated and sold to food processors for use in mayonnaise products, salad dressings, tomato products and meat preparations.

Uses: raw garlic can be used in the manufacturing of garlic powder, garlic salt, garlic vinegar and flavoured croûtons. Fresh garlic is used chopped in sauces and salad dressings, in most cooking and even roasted whole as a vegetable.

Ginger

Zingiber officinale

Ginger is the dried underground stem or rhizome of the plant. Ginger, like cinnamon, clove and pepper, is one of the most important and oldest spices and grew originally in Bengal and Malabar. It consists of the prepared and sun-dried rhizomes that are either with the brownish outer cortical layers intact or with the outer peel or coating partially or completely removed. To improve their appearance, some grades of ginger are bleached by liming. According to available historical records, ginger was certainly known to and highly esteemed by the ancient Greeks and Romans, who obtained this spice from Arabian traders via the Red Sea. It was introduced into Germany and France in the ninth century and to England in the tenth. Since the ginger rhizome can be easily transported in a living state for considerable distances, the plant has been introduced to many tropical and sub-tropical countries. It is now cultivated everywhere. It thrives in sandy or clayey loam soils. The aroma is pleasant and spicy and the flavour penetrating and slightly biting, due to antiseptic or pungent compounds it contains.

Uses: ginger bread, confectionery, ginger ale, curry powders, certain curried meats, cordials, soft drinks, bitters.

Horseradish

Cochlearia armoracia / Armoracia rusticana

Horseradish is a near relative of turnip, cabbage and mustard. It is one of the oldest condiments and is a well-known, large-leafed hardy perennial. It is the thick, white, fleshy root of horseradish that is highly prized as an appetizing condiment. A native of the marshy districts of Eastern Europe, it is grown in the USA where about seven million kilograms are processed annually for consumption with food. In England it has become an institution as it balances with the richness of the traditional roast beef. The common type has broad, crinkled leaves and produces roots of high quality. The root contains a pungent, acrid and vesicating volatile oil. The pungency is due to the presence of sinigrin, a sulphur containing glucoside. It is rich in vitamin C.

Uses: cream, sauce or relish.

Juniper
Juniperous communis
Juniper is an evergreen shrub sometimes attaining the height of a small tree. The fleshy berry-like fruit do not ripen until the second year. The plant flowers in March or April and the fruit ripens in August or September of the second year. It is the dried berries that we use. Juniper fruit have a gin-like aroma and a sweet taste with a somewhat bitter aftertaste.

Uses: seasoning gin (commercial), sauces, stuffings, with venison, hare, guinea fowl and game.

Mint
Mentha spicata
Mint is a popular, old household remedy for relieving colds and coughs. It belongs to the genus *Mentha* which consists of about 40 species, *spicata*, *arvensis* and *piperita* being the three most crucial for producing the world's demand for peppermint oil and menthol. Sunny weather with moderate rainfall is conducive to its luxuriant growth and high menthol content. It has a refreshing, sharp and cleansing taste.

Uses: chutneys, meat (lamb), fish, sauces, soups, stews, vinegar, teas, tobacco and cordials. The fresh leaf tops of all the mints are used in beverages, fruit cups, apple sauce, ice cream, jellies, salads, Middle Eastern salads and rice dishes.

Mustard
Brassica nigra (true mustard)
Brassica alba (white mustard)
Brassica juncea (brown mustard)
Table mustard seems always to be a mixture of two or more of these three mustard varieties. Mustard seeds can be brown, black or white. Black and brown seeds are considered to be more aromatic while the white or yellow seeds have more flavour. Once the oil is procured from the seed, it is dried into powder, which is mixed with water to create the mustard we serve as a condiment.

Uses: soups, stews, gravies and sauces with white meats, as a condiment for red meat, in curries, on sandwiches.

Nutmeg
Myristica fragrans
Nutmeg is the dried seed (kernel) of the peach-like ripe fruit of the evergreen tree, *Myristica fragrans*. Nutmeg is used as a condiment and although I promised not to explore the other uses of all of these spices, it is fascinating to know that nutmeg is also a stimulant, carminative, astringent and aphrodisiac. But we most commonly associate it as a main ingredient in our goulash and mulled wine!

Uses: potato and cheese dishes, breads, cakes, cauliflower, milk puddings, sauces.

Onion
Allium cepa

Onions, we know about. They are well known to every country and culture because they can grow practically anywhere and be used in almost anything in various forms. For these reasons the onion has also always been considered a very inexpensive flavouring and has been used for both cooking and as a seasoning. Mild onions are used for cooking or as a salad, while pungent varieties are used as seasoning. Onions are even used as a vegetable dish in onion rings or salad. Onions can be eaten cooked, raw, in powdered form, caramelized, grilled or deep-fried.

Uses: bases of soups and sauces, in salads, seasoning for most meats, fish, poultry, vegetable dishes and in pickles, dressings, chutneys and relishes.

Oregano
Oreganum vulgare

Origanum, oregano or wild marjoram are the dried leaves of an aromatic, branched perennial herb. The colour of the dried herb is light green. The camphor-like aroma is strong and aromatic. Oregano has a pungent aroma, a hot, peppery flavour and a warm, fragrant and hot peppery taste which is slightly bitter. The plant owes its usefulness as a culinary herb to its volatile oil. Botanists and herb growers classify it as the 'pizza herb'. It is also the essential ingredient of chilli sauce and is used in chilli con carne and other Mexican dishes.

Uses: any tomato-based dish, from spaghetti to stewed tomatoes, soups, meat dishes, pork, fish, egg dishes, salads, vegetable soups, courgette and aubergine dishes, marinade for beef or lamb, and breads.

Parsley
Petroselinum crispum

Parsley – a native of Sardinia and widely and extensively cultivated in the Mediterranean and the USA – is a hardy, aromatic, biennial herb, although it can sometimes last up to four years. The colour of the dried herb is green. Its aroma is pleasant, fragrant, spicy and very fresh. In the USA, parsley is always used as a garnish and adorns the side of a plate. Oddly enough, no one dares eat it, probably because it looks limp and lifeless and we are certain that it has made its rounds on several other people's plates that day. But actually it is the best way to cleanse your palate between courses or after a meal. The fresh leaves mask even the heaviest culinary odour. Parsley is a cool-weather crop, growing best in a rich, moist soil, amenable to deep cultivation.

Uses: eaten fresh, as seasoning for grilled, sautéed meats, tomato-based pasta dishes, soups, stews, salads, tabbouleh, butters for seafood, omelettes, relishes and vinaigrette dressings.

Black Pepper, Green and White
Piper nigrum

Black pepper is one of the most popular everyday spices. It is the dried, mature but unripe berries (fruit) of *Piper nigrum*, a branching vine or climbing perennial shrub mostly found in hot and moist parts of southern India. Black, white and green pepper all come from the same plant, and all can be used either ground or whole. The spikes and fruits are ready for harvest when they are fully mature and start yellowing. At this stage, whole spikes are removed from the tall vines. The spikes are either kept for a day or so, then the berries are removed by rubbing or scrubbing, and dried in the sun; or the spikes are dried in the sun for a few days on mats or on clean concrete floors, then turned over and over. Later, the berries are removed by rubbing, threshing or trampling. When completely dry, the outer skin of the berries becomes shrivelled and dark brown to black. Generally 100 kg/220 lb of fresh berries yields about 26–39 kg/57–86 lb of black pepper. Of course, the yield of pepper varies widely in different areas depending upon several factors such as elevation, temperature, distribution of rainfall, soil fertility, cultural practices, variety of pepper and the age of the pepper vine (sound familiar?). In India the yield varies from 110–335 kg per hectare/100–305 lb lb per acre.

Uses: preservative for meats and other perishable foods, and as a seasoning for everything.

Rosemary
Rosemarinus offinalis
Rosemary is an exotic, leafy, evergreen shrub. This is probably why it has a pungent, piney, mint-like taste with a slight ginger undertone. The fresh leaves can be used as a garnish, and when dried and powdered, they are used as a seasoning. It is a very hardy herb that does well on kitchen windowsills as well as in gardens.

Uses: marinade for beef, pork, lamb, hearty soups, tomato and garlic sauces, roast chicken, breads, dressings and stews.

Saffron
Crocus sativus
Saffron is the most expensive spice in the world. It consists of the dried stigmas of *Crocus sativus*, a bulbous perennial native of southern Europe and cultivated in several Mediterranean countries. True

saffron must not be confused with either meadow saffron or safflower, which are occasionally used as adulterants of true saffron. It takes over 200,000 dried stigmas from 75,000 hand-picked flowers, to make 450 g/1 lb of real saffron. The colour is bright yellow-red, the aroma powerful, somewhat bitter and exotic. The principal colouring agent of saffron is the glucoside crocin; the bitter substance is the glucoside picrocrocin.

Uses: in Spanish rice specialities, paella, fish soups, and in Scandinavian breads.

Sage
Salvia officinalis
Sage is the dried leaf of Salvia officinalis, one of the two sage species indigenous to England. It is also a member of the mint family. Native of southern Europe, it is a hardy sub-shrub that grows almost anywhere. Yugoslavian sage is considered by the trade to be the best quality. It has a very distinctive, sophisticated odour, with notes of lemon that, although warm, can be a little bitter.

Uses: in pork sausage, meatloaf, seasoning in meat dishes and in making poultry stuffing, game dishes, liver, sauces, cheese soufflés, vegetables, breads and teas.

Tarragon
Artemisia dracuuculus
Called tarragon, French tarragon or estragon, the dried leaves and flowering tops of this plant are well known for their intriguing flavour. The aroma is warm, aromatic and reminiscent of anise, with a little tang, and it goes very well with cream and cheese-based sauces.

Uses: cream soups, béarnaise sauce, mayonnaise, mustard, salad dressings, roasts, ragouts, butters, shellfish, certain cheeses and vegetables, and olives.

Thyme
Thymus vulgaris
Parsley, sage, rosemary and thyme – a magical combination and a very popular culinary blend. Thyme has a sweet, pleasantly pungent aroma with a faint clove aftertaste. Originally grown in Europe, Australia and northern Asia, it is now cultivated in France, Germany, Spain, Italy and other parts of Europe as well as in England, North Africa, Canada and the USA. The dried leaves and flowering tops are used.

Uses: dressings, sausages, cream cheese, juice, clam chowder, soups, stocks, vegetable dishes, beans and lentils.

Turmeric
Curcuma domestica
Turmeric is the dried, boiled, cleaned and polished rhizome used as whole pieces or ground. A spice greatly appreciated in the Asiatic countries, it is used not only for its important role in curry dishes, but also as a textile dye and in medicines and cosmetics. It is even considered sacred by Hindus.

Uses: meat and fish preparations, in curry powder and cheese, as a colouring for cakes, jellies, and fruit drinks.

Vanilla
Vanilla fragrans
Vanilla pods are the cured seed pod of the vanilla vine, a member of the orchid family. Vanilla originated on the Atlantic coast from Mexico to Brazil and cultivation spread to other countries after the discovery of America. The important vanilla-producing countries are Madagascar, Mexico, Tahiti, Reunion and Indonesia. The world production of cured vanilla is about 1,230 tons. The most important quality attributes of cured vanilla beans for grading purposes are: length of beans, aroma, colour, flexibility, lustre, and freedom from blemishes, mildew and insect infestation not to mention the fact that the very finest quality beans show much less vanillin content. The cost of natural vanilla extract is about 20 times that of the synthetic vanilla seasoning.

Uses: seasoning for many sweetened foods, in the manufacture of chocolates, food products, liquor, ice creams, soft drinks, sweets, tobacco, baked goods, cakes and cookies.

Herbs, Spices and Wines
When my husband, a London restaurateur, was helping to edit this book, he couldn't help but smile at some of the food and wine matches. 'Who sits down to a plate of coriander? Or a bowl of asparagus? According to this, we would need a different wine for each foodstuff and each spice on the plate – which brings Sunday lunch up to a grand total of about fifteen different wines! – a sip with the mash, another sip with the roast and gravy, yet another with the horseradish sauce!'

In case you may have been thinking along the same lines, I'll clarify! The point is that although we may not be eating a dish of bay leaves, we understand that when they are the dominant flavour of the dish, they have a specific effect. And as for the asparagus, my husband's chef just put the most delicious Parmesan and asparagus tarts on the menu – a perfect lunch with a side salad – so we ended up having to know which wine goes with asparagus and Parmesan after all.

MATCHING HERBS, SPICES AND WINES

Spice or herb	Wine type	Wine example
Basil	Fruity, acidic red, or crisp, dry white (no oak)	Chianti, Nebbiolo, Orvieto, Soave
Bay	Young red	Barbera, Chianti
Capers	Dry, acidic, slightly sweet white	Riesling, Sauvignon Blanc
Chillies	Fruity, low tannins and low oak red	Beaujolais, Dolcetto, Merlot
Cinnamon	Spicy, warm, mature red	Merlot, Pomerol, Pinot Noir, Shiraz
Coriander	Fresh, green, crisp white or warm, rustic red	Sauvignon Blanc, Riesling, Syrah
Cumin seed	Fruity, aromatic white	Sauvignon Blanc, Riesling
Dill	Fresh, green, crisp white	Sauvignon Blanc, Soave
Fennel	Full-bodied, warm white or light, acidic red	Viognier, Barbera, St-Véran
Garlic	Dry, herby white or rosé	Côtes du Rhône, Bandol rosé
Ginger	Sweet, young white with good acids	Barsac, Gewürztraminer, Muscat
Horseradish	Fruity, lightly acidic white or light red	Sancerre, Dolcetto, Beaujolais
Juniper	Spicy, full red	Zinfandel, Mourvèdre
Mint	Minty, herby, richly fruity red	Cabernet Sauvignon
Mustard	Solid, acidic white	Sancerre, Moselle, Riesling
Nutmeg	Spicy, mature red	Burgundy, New World Pinot Noir
Oregano	Spicy, earthy red or acidic white	Sauvignon Blanc,
Parsley	Spicy, earthy red or acidic white	Sauvignon Blanc
Pepper	Tannic, rustic red	Cabernet Sauvignon, Côtes du Rhône
Rosemary	Robust, rustic red	Syrah, Bandol, Fitou, Barolo
Saffron	Full or sweet white or fruity red	Merlot, Barsac, Vouvray, Chardonnay
Sage	Fruity, oaky, slightly sweetish, light red	New World Merlot, Alentejo
Tarragon	Smooth, slightly sweet, oaky white	Chardonnay, Chenin Blanc
Thyme	Spicy, earthy red or acidic white	Sauvignon Blanc
Vanilla	Sweet, spicy white	Pacherenc du Vic-Bilh, Tokaji

Herbs add to the savoury dimension of a dish and make the dish a little more interesting for the wine. Many wines even have spicy or herbal notes to them and thus are natural accompaniments. Obviously the amount of the herb used will determine the extent of its flavouring. The way in which it is used is also important. If the herbs are used in a bouquet garni and infused in a big pot of stock, then the flavours will gently permeate whatever you are cooking. But if you take the same bouquet garni and grill or roast it alongside your meat, then their influence becomes much heavier and you will need a more assertive and up-front wine, less complex and subtle than the one you would use for the former dish.

Herbs and spices can also alter the taste and texture of wine, and that's where the matching comes in. Some clash with tannins or oaks, while others – such as chilli, mustard or horseradish – simply blitz the palate and numb the tastebuds, let alone what they might do to the wine. Another factor to consider is that a lot of the spices and herbs used in international cuisine are from countries where wine is not produced, so it is no wonder that finding a match might be difficult. Although this book is about food and wine, do not be shy if you prefer beer with your Thai, tequila with your Mexican, or vodka with your Russian.

A Brief History of English Cooking

It seems as though the French and the English have always been fighting over something. One of the favourite topics of debate is cuisine, and for once we can safely say that England is enjoying a worthy respite from its traditional role as the home of boring, indigestible, colourless, unimaginative and equally unidentifiable substances. London is being touted as the world's gastronomic capital. In fact, every aspect of its culture is being celebrated. Why the change or heart – or should I say, stomach? Or is it really true to say that there been one? For the stereotype of dreadful English cooking is totally inaccurate. In fact, the best English cooking has always been exceptional. Why do you think we gave the French such a run for their money?

Fresh, home-grown produce was always the rule in England, not the exception, and these quality foods were enhanced by the exotic spices and herbs which were brought back from far regions explored or conquered. So culinarily aware were the English that even rice was first served in 1390, a full thirty years before the French. In the seventeenth century, the English became increasingly impressed by French cuisine simply because of the culinary advances being made there. François la Varenne, for example – a chef whose book's impact reached far into the eighteenth century – reformed French *haute cuisine* to such an extent that the English began to suffer from a serious inferiority complex.

As a result, the English began a backlash against French cooking. The eighteenth-century English despised French cooking and could not understand its rising popularity. It was thought to be 'sneaky', in that everything was covered in elaborate sauces to the extent that you could not tell what was underneath. Elisabeth Ayrton recounts in her book *The Cookery of England*, that in one particular English household they were preparing a meal for some French guests. The cooks realized they had run out of pheasants so one of them decided 'they would be French'. They add a chicken to the pheasants and covered all the poultry in a thick French sauce – assuming that their pretentious guests would not know the difference! Even then, the British had a taste and preference for simple, unadorned food, as evidenced by the publication of Mrs Glasse's *The Art of Cookery Made Plain and Easy* in 1747, in which she states, 'But if Gentlemen will have French Chefs, they must pay for French Tricks'.

In the nineteenth and twentieth centuries, wealth began to spread to more than just the gentry, a prosperous middle class emerged and eating habits changed as a result. The classes were allowed to mix for the first time and food and wine, in the form of entertainment, became more than ever before social-climbing accoutrements. The reason dinner parties took place in so many rooms of a house (dining room, (with)drawing room, billiard room, smoking room, and so on) was to provide as many opportunities as possible to show off one's best possessions. Food and wine were the focal point of this parade.

So what happened that relegated modern English cooking to the shadows? Again, I refer to Elisabeth Ayrton, who explains that it was 'when the mistress of a house which cannot support steward or housekeeper leaves the kitchen that the food loses its savour'. She blamed rapid

BORDEAUX AND BRITISH CLASSICS

Dish	Wine to serve
Welsh rarebit Pâté on toast Cocktail sausages with mustard Raw vegetables with anchovy or herb dip	Light red, white or rosé, slightly chilled
Devilled crab	White Graves
Chilled cucumber soup Fish and chips	Young, light red Bordeaux Supérieur
Lamb with mint sauce	St-Emilion, Pomerol or Pauillac
Cold lamb, pork and chicken	Slightly chilled Bordeaux rosé or Clairet
Tossed green salad with Stilton	Young, red Graves, Bordeaux Supérieur or Sauternes
Crumbles of dark brown sugar and black cherries	Pomerol
Apricot and almond crumble	Sauternes
Rhubarb and strawberry crumble	Barsac

Source: *Conseil Interprofessionnel du Vin de Bordeaux*

urbanization and the vast 'increase of prosperity for the great landowners and the ruling classes in general, which sent the gentry to Europe in search of education'. In other words, the housewives of the middle classes could not afford a proper live-in foreign chef (especially later, after World War 1), but as they had great pretensions of grandeur, had a housekeeper do the cooking as they sat in the parlour and entertained. *Voilà*, the 'debasement' of urban cook:ng. Everything became a 'frantic, inept imitation of the fashionable and upper-class world which could afford to import its chefs'.

Today, there are numerous factors that account for England's great culinary success: a more relaxed social structure; the increase of restaurant dining; the influx of foreign cuisines; the broader holiday horizons; the availability and choice of foodstuffs; a greater awareness of food and wine via the media; the arrival of New World wine; a greater amount of leisure time and the acceptance of food and drink as a leisure activity – it has become 'cool' to cook and eat. To say that England is simply enjoying a flash of culinary trendiness would be unjust. Rather, England is basking in a full-blown gustatory Renaissance.

The Diversity of International Cuisines

We know to look to regional wines to match our food in countries like France, Italy and Germany. The exercise is also viable when extended to the New World but the rules change a bit, for not only is the wine 'new' in these countries, so is the culinary scene, in so far as they are cultural melting pots. Immigration, emigration, foreign travel and other factors

have all made for original and fresh cuisines, and they have produced a whole new genre of cuisine with a myriad of exotic spices, textures and flavours called 'Mediterrasian', 'Modern British', 'fusion' or 'Pacific Rim'. Still, we have no problem figuring out that red Burgundy would suit a coq au vin; a Californian red Zinfandel would beautifully complement a venison steak with juniper and sweet potatoes; and a Chilean Merlot makes a great companion for empanadas.

But what about those countries that either do not produce their own wines or produce too little to be relevant outside the specific regions? (You won't find a bottle of Chinese Rkatsiteli on the shelf at Oddbins!) Sadly, their cuisine is sometimes relegated to the category of takeaways, but these cuisines are as multidimensional, complex and diverse as those with which we are most familiar. China, for example, is a vast country with indigenous cooking styles in its many different regions. It, too, has its Alsace, Burgundy and Bordeaux, even though the average consumer only knows of the stereotyped, generic favourites. Authentic Chinese dishes are a riot of texture, colour and contrasting flavours and we can often find a whole range of taste sensations in a single dish. What follows is a brief overview of the dominant flavours in the dishes of these countries. For specific dishes and their wine matches, see Part 3.

In general, oriental dishes are hot (using chillies and peppers); salty (from the soy and oyster sauces); sweet (with sugar and honey); and bitter (from the use of vinegar). Pick out the dominant flavour in the dish and match that to the dominant characteristics in the wine. You will find, however, that often even spicy or bitter dishes have a sweetish backbone and need wines with low tannins; this is why whites work so well. Also try dry rosés and sparkling wines.

Chinese Food

Chinese food is a lot more than chicken chow mein and crispy noodles. The dominant flavours are ginger, garlic, spring onions, soy sauce, salt, sugar, pepper, chillies, sesame oil, oyster sauce and coriander. The resulting sauces are sweet and sour, peanut, ginger and oyster; all of which fall into either the sweet or salty taste groups.

This means that your best matches are going to be sweetish, spicy or fruity white wines with a bit of residual sugar. If reds are matched, choose low-tannin, unoaked reds (especially with duck dishes) because salty foods make a wine's tannins taste more bitter. Acidic wines are also a bad idea unless you have a fatty duck dish which can take it. And oaked wines are not a good idea unless the dish contains smoked meats. A slightly oaked

Chardonnay would, however, work with sesame seed-based sauces or a peanut sauce. Or try an Alsatian Gewürztraminer with the ginger and peanut sauces, and a slightly sweet Vouvray, New World Chardonnay or Sémillon with most others. Light, crisp rosés and sparkling wines also are a very good match as their texture can either cut through any heaviness in a dish, or underline the delicacy of the more fragile ones, such as wontons and other steamed dumplings.

China has about 90 wineries and the recent focus, after decades of sweet white wines made from unpronounceable hybrids, is medium-dry whites for domestic and foreign consumption.

Japanese Food

The overall flavours of Japanese cuisine are bitter and vinegary: think of wasabi (green horseradish), vinegar, soy sauces and onions.

When serving wine with Japanese food, avoid acidic wines and go for

---

SERVING WINE DURING A MEAL

Here are some guidelines on how to serve wines from different regions at the same meal.

☙ Chilled wines come before room-temperature wines.

☙ Younger wines are served before older ones.

☙ Lighter wines come before heavier, coarser ones.

☙ White wine before red.

☙ Red wine before sweet white wines (unless the sweet white wine has been served as an apéritif or with a first course like foie gras).

☙ Wines served from the same wine region should be served in order of vintage, the younger before the old, even if the younger is a better growth – although there may of course be a few exceptions to this. The idea is to save the heaviest, more complex wines for last so as not to spoil the palate for lighter wine.

chilled, off-dry, fruity white wines and any sparkling wines with most dishes like sashimi or sushi. For the slightly heavier dishes, such as tempura or *yakitorri* (grilled chicken and chicken livers with spring onions), choose fuller, fruitier styles: red Chinon, Saumur or Sancerre would work. Again, good brut Champagne will always save the day.

White wine grapes (Koshu) have been grown near Mount Fuji since 1186! But the rest of Japan's annual 7,220,000 cases are an odd mix of European-styled wines from European varieties which sadly tend to be characterless and diluted due to the heavy rainfall in the region. Worth trying, however, is Suntory's Château Lion, a sweet white of botrytized Sémillon; but it is very expensive.

Thai Food

Thai food uses more aromatic, spicy flavours and its playful contrasting tastes make it very difficult to match indeed. Thai food indulges in generous heaps of fresh chillies, lime leaves, lemon grass, citrus juices, coriander, ginger and basil, just to name a few. The antidote here is crisp, dry whites, not spicy, slightly sweet ones. Try New World Sauvignon Blanc, Marsanne or Chardonnay for creamy curries, biranis and even meat satays. A fruity, robust Shiraz will do very nicely with chilli and beef dishes. My favourite – as you may have already guessed – is a brut Champagne.

Mexican Food

Another very difficult cuisine to match with wine, Mexican food is chilli dominated – and everyone will tell you that chilli does not affect the wine, only your palate – burning it until you cannot tell water from molasses.

Very hot and spicy foods need equally spicy wines with a touch of residual sugar to counteract the spice. Try chilled, fruity whites and acidic rosés to temper all that heat. Low-tannin reds that are fruity and spicy like New World Merlot or Pinot Noir, or a good Beaujolais Cru, will also work. Apart from the chillies, the Mexican diet seems to contain a lot of cornflour and beef – tamales, chilli con carne, chile con queso, carnitas. Mexicans usually accompany their meals with beer, tequila or chocolate drinks.

The irony of Mexico is that it has been producing wine since the end of the nineteenth century but because it was considered too hot for wine, 80 per cent of the harvest goes directly into brandy and vermouth production. You might be surprised to know that international companies such as Domecq, Freixenet, Hennessy, Martell, Suntory, Seagram and Cinzano have all heavily invested in Mexico for their brandy trade. Despite this, the wines have become more serious since 1980 and are increasingly being relocated to cooler plateaux or coastal regions.

Indian Food

Think Indian, and you think curry, curry and more curry. The basic staple of Indian cuisine is the rice and wheat for the doshai, chapatis and paratha breads. There is also a great variety of vegetables and fruit and the coconut both for its milk and its flesh. And while, yes, curry seems to be a common denominator, let's not forget chilli, turmeric, coriander, mustard seeds, ginger, cloves, cinnamon, pepper, cumin, lime, tamarind, cardamom and fennel.

All these spices, which are usually incorporated in a creamy, yoghurt or milk-based sauce, need wines of low alcohol and tannin content that are fruity and sweet – and with definitely no oak. Straightforward Merlots, Zinfandels and Syrahs can work. Try a full-bodied rosé from Bordeaux with samosas and pakoras, or Gewürztraminer with tandoori. Try full-bodied sparkling wines, rosé Champagne for example. If you can find it, try Indian sparkling wine.

Until the Portuguese came along in the fifteenth century, the Indians had 2,000 years of haphazard winemaking under their belt. Now the 167,000 annual cases produced are rather decent modern imitations of European models.

Middle Eastern Food

The exotic perfumes of figs, raisins, cinnamon, nuts and turmeric are warm and sweet. Soft, fruity reds and whites complement Middle Eastern flavours best, and although our rule of matching sweet food with sweet wine still applies, it needs to be done carefully. The texture and weight of Middle Eastern food can render some sweet wines too heavy and the entire meal loses its nuances and becomes sickeningly sweet. Try Beaujolais and New World Pinot Noir and Château Mûsar, Lebanon's masterpiece of Cabernet Sauvignon/Cinsault.

Mediterrasian, Pacific Rim, Modern British Food

This most trendy of cuisines is rather easier to match with wine than you might think. Certainly there are no safe local or regional wines to refer to, and every single spice and condiment imaginable can be used in a same dish, sometimes in a very confrontational manner. The goal is to surprise, wake up and startle.

Not much room for a wine in all of that, you might say. But the best complements to all of these outspoken dishes are the equally outspoken and up-front New World varietals. The new style is to take the Old World classic staples and 'sunkiss' them to the extreme: we want everything to taste, look, and smell as though it has just been picked under a high noon sun. My husband calls it 'zapping the tastebuds'.

I like to think that the popularity of this new cuisine, along with the revival of ethnic cuisine, is in response to our modern culture and the fact that our attention spans have seriously lessened. We are, and you've surely heard this before, the generation of 'instant gratification'. After four bites (one = inquiry, two = confirmation, three = satisfaction, four = indulgence), we want to move on to something else. Ethnic foods, with their varied spices and numerous small dishes, fit the bill perfectly. Ask someone to dig their way through a bowl of game casserole and they lose interest half-way through. The idea is to take the basics of a traditional cuisine and simplify yet magnify the dominant flavours. The Americans have perfected the technique with Italian food and call it 'Cal-Ital'. We seem to have embraced the entire Mediterranean basin, so the obvious vinous mate will be the big, obvious, exaggerated, hot-climate varietals: 'a' Syrah, 'a' Merlot, 'a' Cabernet Sauvignon, 'a' Chardonnay or 'a' Sauvignon Blanc, and so on.

Matching Food and Wine

If I may, I wish to quote Matt Kramer (*Making Sense of Wine*) quoting Richard Olney (1986 Interview in the *Wine Spectator*): 'The general mode of thinking always leans on the cliché and on the abstract. People do not return to their palates. People are afraid that they do not know how to taste. They prefer to lean on rules. With rules you don't have to think; you don't have to taste. You just have to follow the rules – and they'll destroy you every time.'

Was he talking only of food and wine?!

What an appropriate way in which to begin the section on food and wine pairing guidelines! Can we really say that there are no rules? I don't think so. Perhaps what might best be said is that

---

As UK editor of the Paris wine magazine *Vintage*, I was able to participate in food and wine 'experiments' as research for our cuisine articles, usually by Elizabeth de Meurville, the French food writer. She would call a chef and explain what she wanted to experiment with: oysters and wines at Cap Vernet, Côtes du Rhônes chez Guy Savoy, or Loires chez Jean Bardet in Tours. It was strenuous, believe it or not, keeping up with her and the magical combinations placed before us, but we were up to the challenge. She has taught me a great deal about food. There were also the weekly, if not daily lunches and dinners hosted by château owners: another comprehensive exercise in food and wine pairings.

With hundreds of wines a week as homework, my palate was, and still is, continually being worked-out. I couldn't begin to list my favourite discoveries – they would fill a book themselves! – but here a few worth mentioning:

Coquilles Saint Jacques des Côtes d'Armor aux senteurs pérogourdines (layers of scallops, foie gras and truffles in filo pastry)
with Chablis Premier Cru Côte de l'échet 1990
Tirel-Guérin Restaurant, Saint-Meloir des Ondes (near St Malo), February 1994

Risotto aux morilles (wild mushroom risotto)
with Bandol Rouge Château Pibarnon 1985
Prepared by and enjoyed with Alain Ducasse Louis IV, Monte Carlo, the day he became the only chef in the world to have two Michelin three-star restaurants, spring 1996.

Saumon mi-fumé, poêlé sur barbe de capucin, vinaigrette au jus de betteraves (partially smoked salmon pan-fried on a bed of nasturtium and a beetroot juice vinaigrette)
with Château de France Bordeaux Blanc 1993
Hôtel Ritz, April 1996

Gâteau de pommes de terre au foie gras (potato pancakes with foie gras)
with Château Lascombes 1985 and 1992
Carré des Feuillants, chez Alain Dutournier, April 1996

Blanquette de sole coquilles Saint Jacques au jus de cerfeuil, concombre et gingembre (blanquette of sole and scallops with a chervil, cucumber and ginger sauce)
with Champagne Gosset Celebris
Hotel de Brissac, September 1995

taste is subjective, so that a combination that a certain individual might put together because he or she likes it, is then, by definition, an acceptable pairing. Because putting personal, subjective taste aside, there are rules. Nobody sat down and wrote them up, they are simply laws of nature, of chemistry. Acid and bitter tastes reinforce each other. Sweet tastes change acidic and bitter tastes, as well as salty tastes. (Sweet wines with salty foods work – whereas tannic or alcohol reds with salty foods taste bitter.) The bitterness and acidity of a tannic red wine will make fish or creamy cheese taste metallic. Now, if you happen to enjoy the taste of a copper penny on your tongue – go to it. Because Mr Olney is quite right in that you should taste something for yourself rather than let someone decide for you.

If in a match, both personalities are distinct yet compatible, success has been achieved, and if in a match, both personalities are not only distinct and compatible but also draw out the hidden tastes or qualities of the other, then nirvana has been reached. In fact, matching food and wine is very much analogous to finding one's soul mate. Not an easy task, but certainly an enjoyable exercise.

Food as an Enemy

When we say that a particular food item or dish is an enemy to wine, we mean that it alters detrimentally the taste of wine. From one of my oldest copies of the *Larousse Gastronomique* in its original French: *'Nous n'indiquons de vins ni pour les potages ni pour les oeufs; seuls conviennent de petits vins de carafe. Avec les crudités et les salades, il est préférable de boire un verre d'eau fraîche'.* In other words, soups and eggs only merit carafe wines, and a glass of fresh water is the only solution for raw vegetables and salads. Not true, not true! Where is their imagination? There is always a solution to these culinary quandaries, and at the risk of repeating myself, there is always Champagne!

What follows are some guidelines to some classic friends and foes of wine. For specific recipe and wine matches, refer to Part 3.

Grilled and Poached Seafood or Shellfish

Dry whites are the perfect match in texture, weight and flavour to poached seafood or shellfish, while dry rosés are perfect for the grilled dishes. Try whites such as Entre-deux-mers, Graves, Chablis, Pouilly-Fuissé for poached fish, and slightly more flavourful whites such a Condrieu (Viognier), New Zealand Sauvignon Blanc or Californian Chardonnay for those that are grilled. Tasty rosés such as Tavel, Cassis, Bandol or Lirac are also good, slightly heavier or more full-bodied matches.

Fish in Sauce

For fish in sauces, the same matches as above still apply. But if the sauce has a bit of personality and spice in it, you will need whites which also have a bit more character, such as Meursault, white Hermitage, Riesling and again, most of the New World Chardonnays and Sauvignon Blancs. If the accompanying sauce is slightly sweet, a Vouvray, Coteaux du Layon or Monbazillac can be a spectacular companion. Fish in a red wine sauce works if the fish is meaty, like monkfish, tuna or swordfish, and if the red wine is light or medium-bodied, like a Merlot or an Italian Barbera.

Oysters

If ever there was an unlikely, fraught relationship, this is it. With their high levels of salt and acid, and pronounced flavour of the sea, oysters have a reputation for killing wines. Oysters, like wines, have 'producers' and 'growths' (think of Bordeaux). Furthermore, their taste can vary enormously depending on their size (and therefore age) and, more especially, on the *terroir* and the method used to raise them. Oysters can vary very much in texture and taste: they can be salty and wiry, sweet and fleshy, or meat-like and complex. Good oysters, like good wine, are not even commercialized until they are three years old. And unlike other food and wine matches, it is the oyster that might dominate a wine.

The predictable conclusion in this match is to not serve oysters with a very expensive *grand vin* but rather with a well made and sufficiently powerful wine, such as a Sancerre. Expensive wines are too refined and subtle to emerge unscathed from such an encounter with the flavour of the ocean. The Sauvignon Blanc stands up to the opponent beautifully. Other perfect matches are Muscadet or Riesling (a crisp, fresh one), or a white Bordeaux, such as a Graves. What should you not drink? White Côtes du Rhône, Sylvaner and Chardonnays seem to go flat and bitter.

Grilled White Meats

Grilled white meats like chicken breast, turkey or pork, need smooth reds that are not coarse or rustic. Try a Saumur-Champigny or Chinon (Loire), a Volnay or Beaune (Burgundy), a Médoc or Chinon. This is because although a white meat may take a white wine, the cooking method means that the dish can move up to a red, but only if it is soft, smoothly textured and of low tannin content. Rustic, big, tannic reds would dominate the white meat, even if grilled.

White Meats in White Wine Sauce

Ideally, make your sauce using the same wine you serve with the meal. White wines that lend themselves to creamy, mushroom sauces for meat are Champagne, Meursault, Graves, Sauternes or Riesling. A trick might be to use a reasonably priced, good-quality Chardonnay for the cooking, but a better Burgundy, like the Meursault, for the drinking. Most of us cannot really afford to throw a bottle of Meursault into the saucepan!

White Meats in Red Wine Sauce

Fruity, moderately tannic and moderately alcoholic reds work best with white meats: Chambertin, Beaujolais, Chinon, Bourgueil, St-Emilion all work well. As you can see, the common denominator is not the grape variety, as the above wines represent Pinot Noir, Gamay, Cabernet Sauvignon, Cabernet Franc and others. It has more to do with the fruitiness and slightly acidic background that keeps the texture and flavours light enough for the meat.

Grilled or Roasted Red Meats

Grilled or roasted red meats are not difficult to match. Think Sunday roast and July barbecues; think full, ripe and mature; think Pomerol, New World Cabernet Sauvignons and Syrahs, Cornas, Hermitage, Châteauneuf-du-Pape, St-Emilion and Zinfandel. Both the red meat and the methods of grilling and roasting can take heavier textures and weights, so bring on the tannins, acids and ripe fruit. No fresh, young things allowed here!

Stews and Casseroles

Stews and casseroles can handle the same sort of reds as grilled red meat, only there is a slight nuance to respect. Long, slow cooking really seals in the flavour of the meat and whatever flavourings are used, changing the texture of the meat. Stews have more complex flavouring and texture and therefore your red wine should be a bit more coarse or rustic. Try a Bordeaux Supérieur, Fronsac or Cahors instead of a St-Emilion or Pomerol; go for a Santenay or Mercurey instead of a Beaune; and try a Côtes du Rhône instead of a Hermitage or Châteauneuf-du-Pape. New World reds might be too fruity and one-dimensional for a stew, which would render them thin and weak – stick to inexpensive classics from south-west France.

Salad with Vinegar-based Dressing

The solution here is to use lemon juice instead of vinegar in the dressing and add protein ingredients such as cheese and nuts to balance the wine. But if you have made the salad and are staring at a plate of vinegar, remember to match a fruity, aromatic but lightly dry white wine with equal acidity as the dressing. Sauvignon Blanc, either as a New World varietal or in the guise of a Loire Valley wine, will do nicely.

When making your own salad, remember to choose the young leaves for the salad, as the older leaves will dominate the wine. The type of lettuce you choose will also have an effect. Bitter salad leaves, such as rocket or lollo rosso, need more acidic wines than, say, iceberg lettuce. Again, the ingredients, as well as the dressing will have a lot to do with the wine you choose, as you will see in the listings in Part 3.

Eggs

While we may not wish to drink a glass of wine at 9 a.m. with our boiled egg and bread soldiers, but by 12 p.m., our eggs Benedict, quiche, soufflés and egg-based béarnaise or hollandaise are all crying out for some vinous sustenance. This is not such an enemy as you might think. Sparkling wine is perfect for the soft texture of most egg dishes, and it won't overpower their subtle, delicate flavours.

Smoked Foods

When foods are correctly smoked, their personalities are not extinguished (excuse the pun!) and the smoke simply adds another texture and flavour dimension. Even the type of wood should be considered, and oak seems to be preferred because it best lends itself to the subtleties of most foods and wines. The two methods, cold smoking or hot smoking, give entirely different tastes. Cold smoking, or curing, is when the smoke simply coats the food and the food is not allowed to cook. Hot smoking, on the other hand, cooks the food and gives it a smoky flavour by raising the temperature. The thinly sliced smoked salmon that we are all most familiar with should be cold smoked and does very well with an unoaked Chardonnay, such as steely Chablis. Actually, most smoked food is ideal with very lightly oaked or unoaked wines. Smoked shellfish is still rather unusual. You really have to acquire a taste for it – and wouldn't we rather eat fresh, anyway? That said, if you find that a Scottish smoked oyster has found its way on to your plate, wash it down with a grassy New World Sauvignon Blanc.

Meat and poultry are often marinated before being smoked, so it is a good idea to find out what was used for the marinade. If that is not possible, try a Pinotage, Zinfandel or Shiraz, as the more subtle flavours of a more complex blend would be completely dominated. Smoked cream cheese is one of my favourites, and although I might put a rich white wine with a cream cheese, I wouldn't when it is smoked. The rich blackcurrant and gentle tannins of mature and classic Bordeaux would be perfect.

Mushrooms

A classic, in my book. What we have to assume here is that we are eating the mushrooms on their own as a separate side dish, otherwise, if the mushrooms are in a wine sauce, the wine in the sauce would give us our lead. If we knew our mushrooms a bit better, we would have an easier time marrying them to dishes and wines for our sauces. There are so many different sorts of mushroom and you just know that I am going to mention the words *terroir* and climate again. I am, and I am going to add another: season. Are we eating morels in the spring, girolles (a highly prized form of the chanterelle mushroom) and meadow

MUSHROOMS AND WINE

Ceps	Pauillac	Bordeaux	Dry red
	St-Emilion	Bordeaux	Dry red
Chanterelles	Bergerac	South-west France	Dry red
	Saumur-Champigny	Loire	Dry red
Girolles	Bergerac	South-west France	Dry red
	Fronsac	Bordeaux	Dry red
	Mercurey	Burgundy	Dry red
Greek mushrooms	Anjou	Loire	Dry red
	Côtes de Provence rosé	Provence	Dry rosé
Morels	Cahors	South-west France	Dry red
	Champagne	Champagne	Sparkling
	Meursault	Burgundy	Dry white
Mushrooms (general)	Echezeaux	Burgundy	Dry red
	Pinot Noir	New World	Dry red
	Pinotage	South Africa	Dry red
	Volnay	Burgundy	Dry red
Pleurottes	Arbois rosé	Jura	Dry rosé
	Mercurey	Burgundy	Dry red
Porcini (see also **Ceps** and **Wild mushrooms**)	Gattinara	Italy	Dry red
Wild mushrooms	Syrah	Rhône or New World	Dry red
	Valdepeñas	Spain	Dry red
	Vosne-Romanée	Burgundy	Dry red

agaric in summer, or ceps, field mush-rooms (agaric), craterelles, pieds-de-mouton, lactarius, royal agaric (Caesar's mushroom) and other wild treasures, in the autumn? Not to mention the various cousins that are at their peak year round!

With mushrooms, cooking method becomes important as it can greatly alter their taste and texture. There are as many different ways of preparing them as there are varieties. Fricasséed, with garlic or shallots, gilded in butter, draped in cream, in soup, in pastry, in quiches, as a garnish for meat or fish, as part of the sauce for chicken, liver or kidneys, or in an omelette or scrambled eggs. The varied textures of plumpness and tenderness, the intensity of one variety or the deli-cacy of another, the sharpness of some types, the earthiness of very lightly cooked young mushrooms, the fleshy aromas of riper mushrooms. The flavours are infinite and the choice of wine depends very much on the particular dish. Another factor to be considered is the style of the meal. Is it a rustic family dinner or a sophisticated soirée?

Use the cooking method (mushrooms fried up in a quick cream sauce vs mush-rooms cooked overnight in a stew) as your first guide, spices as your second. Generally, mushrooms require an elegant wine, despite the dish or preparation method. A robust red wine whose tannins are silky is the best idea. There are a few whites that might work: ones of character, strength and a certain distinctiveness such as a Jura, an Arbois Vin Jaune, a white Côtes du Rhône, or a mature, full-bodied Meursault or other white Burgundy.

Cheese

There are so many different flavoured and textured cheeses that it is impossible to make a blanket wine suggestion. Fruity red wines kill the flavourful hard cheeses, while tannic red wines kill the creamier cheeses. Your best bet is usually whites, both dry and sweet. Try dry whites with goats' cheese and sweet whites with blue cheese. If I had to offer any rule of thumb, I would suggest matching cheese to its local wines, as cheese is very faith-ful to its home *terroir* and climate. On the next few pages, I offer some specific cheese and wine combinations.

SOME CLASSIC FOOD AND WINE COMBINATIONS

Barbecued ribs with Zinfandel

Beef stew or game casseroles with Barolo

Brie with Meursault

Caviar with Champagne

Charcuterie with Beaujolais Crus

Crottin de Chavignol with Sancerre

Farmhouse Cheddar with sweet Jurançon

Foie gras with Sauternes

Seafood with Muscadet sur Lie

Ratatouille with Côtes de Provence rosé

Roast spring lamb with Pauillac

Roquefort with Sauternes

Sole with white Burgundy

St-Maure with Vouvray

Stilton with vintage Port

CHEESE AND WINE

Cheese	Region of origin	Wine style
Appenzell	Switzerland	Full-bodied Syrah or Shiraz
Asiago d'Allevo	Italy	Oaky New World Chardonnay
Baby Bel	France	Light Beaujolais-style red
Bavarian Blue (Cambozola)	Bavaria, Germany	Dry Riesling
Beaufort	Haute Savoie, France	Lightly oaked Chardonnay, Meursault, Chasselas
Beenleigh Blue	Devon, England	Port
Bel Paese	Italy	Light Chardonnay or Barbera
Bleu d'Auverne	Auverne, France	Sauternes, Touraine Sauvignon
Bleu de Bresse	Burgundy, France	Light to medium reds, Fleurie, Mâcon
Bleu de Gex Haut Jura	Jura, France	White Burgundy, Arbois, Ponsard
Bonchester	Scotland	Merlot, Bordeaux
Boursault	Normandy, France	Rioja
Boursin	France	Sancerre, Sauvignon Blanc
Brebis	France	Cahors, Buzet, Pacherence du Vic-Bilh
Brie	France	Full Chardonnay, German dessert wines, Pomerol
Brillat Savarin	Normandy, France	Champagne
Bridamour	Corsica, France	Provence red
Cabrales	Spain	Oloroso Sherry, red or white Rioja
Caerphilly	Wales	Sweet white Rioja
Camembert	Normandy, France	Normandy cider, Médoc, Cotes du Rhône, Corbières, Bandol
Cantal	Auvergne, France	Rioja, Côtes de Provence rosé, St-Pourçain
Cashel Blue	Ireland	Light fruity red
Cave Cheese	Denmark	White mature Burgundy
Chabichou du Poitou	Loire, France	New World Sauvignon Blanc, spicy Cabernet Franc
Chaource	Champagne, France	Champagne or Cadillac
Cheddar	England	Periquita, Zinfandel, Gewürztraminer vendanges tardives

Cheshire	England	Meursault, sweet white
Chèvre	France	Sancerre, Riesling, Crémant d'Alsace
Colby/ Longhorn	Wisconsin, USA	Zinfandel
Comté	Haute-Savoie, France	Chianti Classico Reserva, spicy white
Cornish Yarg	Cornwall, England	Mature red Bordeaux or Burgundy
Coulommiers	France	Côtes du Rhône, unoaked Chardonnay
Cream cheese	Everywhere	New World Pinot Noir
Crottin de Chavignol	Central France	Sancerre, Entre-deux-mers, Graves
Danish blue	Denmark	Schnapps, Sauternes
Edam	Netherlands	Syrah, Zinfandel, Pauillac
Emmental	Switzerland	Côtes du Rhône, Shiraz
Epoisses	Burgundy	Mature red or white Burgundy
Esrom	Denmark	Valpolicella
Feta	Greece	Ouzo, Chardonnay
Fontina	North-west Italy	Barbaresco
Fourme d'Ambert	Central France	Côtes du Rhône, Port, l'Etoile
Gaperon	Auvergne, France	Tokaji, vodka
Gjetost	Norway	Madeira, sweet white
Gloucester	England	Zinfandel
Gorgonzola	Northern Italy	Barolo, sweet white, Gigondas
Gouda	Netherlands	Chardonnay, white Burgundy, Chinon
Grana Padano	Northern Italy	Vino Nobile di Montepulciano
Gruyère	Switzerland	Bordeaux, Chasselas, Alsace Pinot Gris
Gubbeen	Southern Ireland	Oaky, mature white Burgundy
Havarti	Denmark	Light young red
Idiazabal	Northern Spain	White oaked Rioja
Kefalotiri	Greece	Bordeaux
Lanark Blue	Scotland	Sauternes
Lancashire	England	Burgundy, fresh Pinot Noir
Langres	France	Mature red Burgundy, Champagne
Leicester	England	Red Provence, full, rustic red

Limburg	Germany	Garrafeira red, Tokay Pinot Gris
Livarot	Normandy, France	Ste-Croix-du-Mont, Bonnezeaux
Mahon	Spain	Rioja
Manchego	Spain	Amontillado
Maroilles	France	Pacherence du Vic-Bilh
Morbier	Juras, France	Arbois white, Gevrey-Chambertin
Monterey Jack	California, USA	New World Chardonnay
Mozzarella	Italy	Chablis, Orvieto, Soave, Pinot Grigio
Munster	Alsace, France	Gewürztraminer, Loupiac, Coteaux du Layon
Parmigiano-Reggiano	Northern Italy	Barolo, Barbaresco, Taurasi
Pont l'Evêque	Normandy, France	Mature red and white Burgundy, Bourgueil
Port Salut	Brittany, France	Bergerac, red Burgundy
Provolone	Italy	Young Chianti, Bardolino, Dolcetto d'Alba
Raclette	Switzerland	Chasselas, Chablis, Côtes de Duras
Reblochon	Savoie, France	Chardonnay, Crépy, Lirac, Sancerre
Robiola	Italy	Prosecco
Roquefort	France	Sauternes, Port, Châteauneuf-du-Pape, Vin de Paille
St-Nectaire	Auvergne, France	Côtes du Rhône, Sancerre, Fronsac, Mâcon
Ste-Maure	Loire, France	Chinon, Sancerre, Coteaux du Layon, Alsace Pinot Gris
Selles-sur-Cher	Central France	Sancerre, Romorantin, Reuilly
Shropshire Blue	England	Bordeaux, Cadillac
Stilton	England	Port, Sauternes, Ste-Croix-du-Mont
Taleggio	Italy	Soave, Chianti
Tête de Moine	Switzerland	Côtes du Rhône, mature white Burgundy
Tetilla	Spain	Cava
Tilsit	Germany	Gewürztraminer
Tomme de Savoie	France	Beaujolais, Varois
Vacherin Mont d'Or	Savoie, France	Tokay Pinot Gris, Chablis, Corton, Barsac

Fresh Fruit

Fruits that are high in acid can make wines taste metallic and thin. In general, drink sweet whites, especially botrytized, late harvest, or sparkling wines. These are the best solutions for fruit, whether it be in a salad or as part of a dessert. Actually, sweet white wines and sparkling wines can take a most meals from appetizers to dessert and coffee. Try it sometime.

Chocolate

Faced with such an aromatic prospect as chocolate, the task of finding a suitable wine seems daunting. A general rule, however, is that a good Port or Banyuls with most chocolate desserts, or chocolate alone, does well. With a very dark and strong chocolate, try a Mas Amiel (Maury). To accompany milk chocolate desserts or fruit and chocolate deserts, try a Gewürztraminer vendanges tardives, or a Muscat de Beaumes-de-Venise. Dry red wines such as a Bordeaux like St-Julien, or a Rasteau or Côtes du Rhône can also work very well.

ALSACE: Portrait of a Region

Alsace is a perfect French region in which to study food and wine matches, as it makes wine varietals and not blends. There is also a strong regional cuisine.

Sylvaner

Fresh, fruity and light, Sylvaner is ideal to accompany oysters and other shellfish, snails, fish, quiche lorraine and delicatessen platters. It is heavenly with a *salade Vosgienne* (mushrooms, red potatoes, Munster cheese, cumin, smoked lardons, croûtons and poached eggs), with their famous onion and béchamel sauce tart, or with *flammenküeche* (a thin, flat bread dough rectangle filled with lightly fried onions, cream and smoked bacon).

Riesling

The pride of Alsace, with its delicate fruit and subtle bouquet, Riesling is perfect with fish, shellfish (especially lobster and crab), white meats and, of course, *choucroute* (a dish of sauerkraut, boiled meats and potatoes). Its perfect mate, however, is a *kougelhopf* (or savoury brioche) of salmon and pike. *Kougelhopf* can, in fact, be either savoury or sweet, but are always made in the shape of a large brioche.

Gewürztraminer

This noble, full-bodied and structured nectar is ideal with exotic, spicy dishes and strong cheeses, as well as with desserts such as crème brûlée, or alone as an aperitif. Try it with a *brioche de foie gras* (duck pâté en croûte) instead of the usual Sauternes. It works beautifully with pork tenderloin in a sweet and sour sauce. And, of course, the local *grumbeerekiechle* (potato pancakes) with salmon and horseradish and their *tarte aux pommes à l'alsacienne* (an apple tart with a ground almond filling).

Pinot Blanc

Fresh and supple, Pinot Blanc marries well with almost everything, but does better with fish, especially trout or sole with dill seed, and shellfish, especially oysters.

Tokay Pinot Gris

A grape variety that fits in somewhere between the steely crispness of a Riesling and the sweeter opulence of a Gewürztraminer. It complements foie gras and most fowl (turkey, goose, *magret de canard*, sweetbreads in cream and morel mushrooms) and game (venison or wild boar). Also try it with mussels and lobster tails in a saffron and cream sauce. My favourite match is with *baeckaoffa* (a slow-cooked marinated meat stew with onions, potatoes and seasoning).

Pinot Noir

Not to be confused with the Burgundian style of Pinot Noir, here it is lighter (it is often a rosé) and fruitier. It goes very well with lamb and other red meats, delicatessen platters and cheeses such as goats' cheese and Cheddar. Try it with gamier poultry with tarragon sauce or turkey stuffed with ceps and minced veal and pork.

Crémant d'Alsace

Like Champagne, this goes with everything, although a heavy game dish might overpower it. Otherwise try it with foie gras or a sweet *kougelhopf*. This is often a better accompaniment than the heavy, classic Sauternes or Gewürztraminer. Then drink it throughout the rest of the meal with the seafood, cheese, dessert and then, of course, continue long into the night!

A special treat, Clos de Zahnacker is the deliciously unique concoction of Riesling, Tokay Pinot Gris and Gewürztraminer (produced by my good friends at the Caves de Ribeauvillé in Ribeauvillé) with a *presskopf* (a sort of terrine) of fresh wild salmon, lobster and oysters in a creamy sauce of caviar, parsley, tarragon and chives.

PROVENCE: Portrait of a Region

Garlic, basil, olive oil, ripe plum tomatoes – delicious. Just mention the word 'Provence' and my mouth waters. I think if I had to say that I learned to taste wines while living in Paris, it was living in Nice for a couple of years that taught me how to cook and eat, and seriously shop for fresh, quality ingredients.

There are eight AOC appellations in Provence: Côtes de Provence, Coteaux d'Aix-en-Provence, Coteaux d'Aix-en-Provence les Baux, Palette, Bandol, Cassis, Bellet and the Coteaux Varois.

The reds and rosés are mostly composed of Mourvèdre (robust and aromatic), Grenache (full-bodied and vital), Cinsault (fresh and fruity), Syrah (rich and spicy), Tibouren (fine and elegant) and Cabernet Sauvignon, apart from Bellet, which is principally of Braquet, Folle Noir and Cinsault. The whites are herby brews of Bourboulenc, Clairette, Ugni Blanc, Sauvignon Blanc, Marsanne, Rolle and Sémillon. Their aromas vary from pears and lemons to roses and lavender with hints of exotic spices.

Légumes farcies (meat-filled vegetables) with a rosé from Bandol or Bellet.

Tapenade (anchovy, garlic and olive spread) with a fruity rosé.

Anchoîade (purée of anchovies, olive oil and seasonal vegtables) with a light, fruity Côtes de Provence rosé.

Pan bagna (bread coated in olive oil, garlic and tomatoes) with a red Côtes de Provence or Cassis.

La tourte de blette (a savoury tart of chard leaves and courgettes) with a herby, substantial white Bandol.

La bouillabaisse (a medley of fish and seafood cooked in a sauce of white wine, olive oil, tomatoes, garlic, saffron, parsley and herbs) with a Côtes de Provence rosé.

Ravioli niçoise (ravioli filled with the juice of daube de boeuf) with a red Bandol.

La daube de boeuf (beef braised in red wine and herb sauce) with a red Côtes de Provence or Coteaux d'Aix-en-Provence.

Ratatouille niçoise (onions, courgettes, aubergines, peppers and tomatoes in olive oil and herbs) with Côtes de Provence rosé or white.

Salade niçoise (tomatoes, cucumber, broad beans, peppers, onion, eggs, anchovies, olives, olive oil, garlic and basil) with rosés from Bellet, Palette, Cassis, or Bandol.

Fromage Mont-Vento (a local cheese) with whites from Côtes de Provence or Palette.

Le socca (a chick pea cake) with sweet and fruity rosés.

Crystallized fruits and *fougasse* (a fruit-cake-like bread) with Muscat de Beaumes-de-Venise.

PIEDMONT: Portrait of a Region

Barbaresco, Barolo, Barbera d'Alba, Barbera d'Asti, Boca, Bramaterra, Brachetto d'Acqui – bbbeautiful! Why is it that the names of most of my favourite Italian wines begin with the letter 'b' and are from Piedmont? Bordering France and Switzerland, nestled at the foot of the Alps and the Apennines (hence its name: 'Piemonte', or foot of the mountain), this region is only seventh among Italy's regions in terms of total production, but it has the most DOC and DOCG quality designation zones and the most vine-yards dedicated to classified production.

Almost all of these classified wines are issued from indigenous grape varieties such as Nebbiolo, Barbara, Freisa, Grignolino and Brachetto. They are elaborate, sensual, complex, stunning, sometimes fresh (Freisa), sometimes slightly acidic (Barbara) but on the whole, thoroughly succulent wines. And they are perfect mates for the region's equally ample cuisine: game, buttery sauces, polenta, white truffle, risotto. Where else would you find a fondue dish served with two kinds of pasta, wheat-based and potato-based (gnocchi) in the same meal? My kind of country. For the more timid, Piedmont also has the fruity, gentle Dolcetto, and an entire gamut of whites.

Salada di coconi (mushroom salad with anchovy and hard-boiled eggs) with Asti Spumante or Barbera.

Brasato al Barolo (braised beef) with a Barolo, naturally.

La bagna caoda (anchovy dip with hot oil for vegetables) with a Freisa or a Barbera.

Bollito (boiled meats with spicy hot sauces) with Barolo or Barbaresco.

Fonduta (melted Fondina cheese, butter and eggs over polenta or pasta) with a Dolcetto, Barbera or Barolo.

Carbonata (rich beef stew with polenta) with a Barolo.

Vitello tonnato (veal in a tuna and anchovy sauce) with Grignolino d'Asti or Dolcetto.

Lepre in salmi Val d'Aosta (hare casserole in Barbera) with a mature Barbera.

Bunet Piemontese (amaretto biscuit and egg custard pudding) with Asti Spumante.

PART THREE
WINES AND
FOODS

Wines and foods

THE following food and wine cross-reference is not meant to be finite and all-encompassing. Indeed such a feat would be beside the point, as the idea is not to create a gustatory dictate or dictionary, but rather a guide to pleasurable frolicking for your tastebuds.

The foods and wines listed are an odd mix from the very general to the very specific, hoping to capture larger flavour groups as well as more specific and illustrative examples. These matches are a smattering of ideas meant to get your own tastebuds activated and to encourage you to invent your own taste pairings. Do not consider the suggestions to be exhaustive or inflexible – just because Chilean Chardonnay is matched to carrot soup does not mean that this is the only Chardonnay that will do. I have used it as an example either because I personally find a certain *je ne sais quoi* in the combination, or because I am trying to represent equally the geographical distribution of the world's Chardonnay production.

I have included some wines which may be more expensive or more difficult to find, if I felt that they were the very best example I could give, but all the wines listed are available in the UK. If you do find the wine listed is too expensive or hard to come by, you can buy the New World version for every day and save the real thing for special occasions.

'Why so much detail on specific wines?' I hear you ask. Well, if when cooking your Sunday roast, you choose your spices, gravy and vegetables with care, then the natural evolution is to include the wine in the equation in the same way. Consider the wine as something on your plate, and not in the glass next to the plate – it is part of the meal, not an adjunct.

There are enough wines listed to be able to extrapolate a taste theme. When the European wines are cited, you can use the Which Grapes Make Which Wines? table on page 32 to find New World grape variety substitutes. For example, the Rhône Valley's Condrieu is issued from the white grape variety Viognier – so you can eat your ceviche just as pleasurably with a Viognier grown elsewhere – variations on its theme, assumed and permitted.

Old World appellation and vineyard subtleties are slightly bowed to, yet it would be a bit too restrictive to insist that only a Gevrey-Chambertin could do the trick and that a Chambertin just couldn't possibly. There are also references to a wine's classification, such as Villages, Premier Cru, or Grand Cru. As we move up to the next quality classification, we are looking for a more serious version bearing greater weight and concentration, which is a result of the more attentive viticultural and viniculture practices (such as lower yields, less oak, and so on, as discussed in Part 2).

When discussing varietals such as Chardonnay and Cabernet Sauvignon, the term 'New World' is used to signify that most exported versions of a particular European variety will do very nicely in that particular case. To be honest, I find the nuances amongst the New World exports becoming less significant as 'clean' winemaking techniques are still in international vogue. Just note that most New World versions tend to taste oakier, sweeter and monolithic, whereas their Old World counterparts are more subtle, dry and complex, becoming more opulent with age. Hence the New World wines match the bold, spicy, New World cuisine and the Old World wines are best with their corresponding regional cuisines. Although this is not to say that European wine and food lacks boldness and spice – don't confuse subtle with boring!

Finally, these culinary couplings are a mixture of the 'tried-and-true' as well as those from years of my tasting notes gleaned from the back of lipstick-stained dinner napkins. I know that it is hard to please all of the people all of the time, and I would be quite happy to please somebody just once. In that light, I supplied, if applicable, wines for each food entry that were New World and Old World, sweet and dry, red, white and rosé. I did not always list and match all of a wine's types. For example, I mention red Dão but not white. However, if you refer to the Which Grapes Make Which Wines? index on page 32, you will find a complete listing of wine styles.

The second half of this cross reference, the wines to foods section, was tricky, as there are many more dishes to a wine than there are wines to a dish – so again, for space and clarity, the wine guide is not exhaustive. The point of the exercise is not to tell you what and how to eat and drink, but to provide a quick and easy guide as well as to present a springboard of ideas for your own taste adventures.

Bon appetit!

Foods and Wines Index

Food	Wine name	Region/Country	Wine style

A **Accra** *see* **Appetizers**

Aioli *see* **Sauces**

Almonds *see* **Nuts**

Anchovies and anchovy paste *see* **Fish**

Andouillette *see* **Charcuterie, cured and cold meats**

Antipasti *see* **Appetizers**

APPETIZERS

Food	Wine name	Region/Country	Wine style
Accra	Champagne	Champagne	Sparkling
	Riesling VT	Alsace	Dry to medium-dry white
	Vouvray	Loire	Medium-dry white
Antipasti	Bardolino	Italy	Dry red
	Dolcetto d'Alba	Italy	Dry white
	Falerno del Massico	Italy	Dry white
	Verdicchio	Italy	Dry white
Avocado	Chablis	Burgundy	Dry white
	Champagne (brut)	Champagne	Sparkling
	Sancerre	Loire/Centre	Dry white
	Sauvignon Blanc	New Zealand	Dry white

Blinis *see* **Pancakes and crêpes**

Food	Wine name	Region/Country	Wine style
Bruschetta	Chardonnay	Chile	Dry white
	Soave	Italy	Dry white
	Vernaccia di San Gimignano	Italy	Dry white
Buffalo wings	Buzet	South-west France	Dry red
	Côtes du Roussillon	Roussillon	Dry red
	Zinfandel	California	Dry red

Escargots à la	Aligoté	Burgundy	Dry white
Bourguignonne	Bourgueil	Loire	Dry red
	Chablis	Burgundy	Dry white
	Champagne	Champagne	Sparkling
	(Blanc de Blancs)		
	Côtes du Roussillon	Roussillon	Dry red
	Vacqueyras	Rhône	Dry red
Guacamole	Champagne	Champagne	Sparkling
	Chardonnay	California	Dry white
	Meursault	Burgundy	Dry white
	Pinot Grigio	Italy	Dry white
Melon with	Bardolino	Italy	Dry red
Parma ham	Bergerac	South-west France	Dry red
	Bianco di Scandiano	Italy	Dry white
	Chinon	Loire	Dry red
	St-Joseph	Rhône	Dry red
Melon with Port	Monbazillac	South-west France	Sweet white
	Pineau des Charentes	Cognac	Vin de liqueur
Olives	Amontillado	Spain	Fortified red
	Côtes de Provence	Provence	Dry white
	Manzanilla	Spain	Fortified white
	Riesling	Alsace	Dry white
	Sherry	Spain	Fortified red
Tapas	Amontillado	Spain	Fortified red
	Bandol rosé	Provence	Dry rosé
	Fino Sherry	Spain	Fortified white
	Sancerre	Loire/Centre	Dry white
Tapenade	Lirac rosé	Rhône	Dry rosé
	Palette	Provence	Dry red
	Patrimonio	Corsica	Dry red
Taramasalata	Chablis	Burgundy	Dry white
	Muscadet	Loire	Dry white
	Patrimonio	Corsica	Dry white
	Sancerre rosé	Loire/Centre	Dry rosé

Apples and apple-based desserts *see* **Desserts and cakes**

Apricots and apricot-based desserts *see* **Desserts and cakes**

Artichokes *see* **Vegetables**

Asparagus *see* **Vegetables**

Aubergines *see* **Vegetables**

Avocado *see* **Appetizers**

B

Baclava see **Desserts and cakes**

BACON AND HAM

Bacon	Beaujolais	Burgundy	Dry red
	Chardonnay	Burgundy or NW	Dry white
	Pinot Noir	New World	Dry red
Ham, baked	Beaujolais	Burgundy	Dry red
	Chinon	Loire	Dry red
	Pinot Noir	New World	Dry red
Ham, baked with	Bourgueil	Loire	Dry red
pineapple	Côtes de Montravel	South-west France	Dry white
	Saumur	Loire	Medium-dry white
Ham, smoked	Chardonnay (oaked)	New World	Dry white
	Pacherenc du Vic-Bilh	South-west France	Sweet white
	Riesling Spätlese	Germany	Sweet white
	Riesling VT	Alsace	Sweet white
Jambon persillé	Chablis	Burgundy	Dry white
	Chardonnay	Chile	Dry white
	Pouilly-Fumé	Loire	Dry white
	Rully	Burgundy	Dry white
	Sauvignon Blanc	Chile	Dry white

Baeckaoffa see **Meat dishes**

Baked beans see **Pulses and grains**

Bananas and banana-based desserts see **Desserts and cakes**

Barbecued meats see **Meat dishes**

Basque chicken see **Chicken dishes**

Bass see **Fish**

Bean and pasta soup see **Soups**

Béarnaise sauce see **Sauces**

BEEF DISHES
see also **Meat dishes**, **Pasta dishes**

Beef bourguignon	Barolo	Italy	Dry red
	Brouilly	Beaujolais	Dry red
	Clos de Vougeot	Burgundy	Dry red
	Gigondas	Rhône	Dry red
	Kékfrankos	Hungary	Dry red
	Saumur	Loire	Dry red
Beef dishes	Barolo	Italy	Dry red
(general)	Cabernet Sauvignon/ Cinsault	Lebanon	Dry red
	Corbières	Languedoc	Dry red

Beef dishes	Gigondas	Rhône	Dry red
(continued)	Juliénas	Beaujolais	Dry red
	Pomerol	Bordeaux	Dry red
Beef potpie	Rioja	Spain	Dry red
	St-Emilion	Bordeaux	Dry red
	Zinfandel	California	Dry red
Beef Stroganoff	Bordeaux rosé	Bordeaux	Dry rosé
	Kékfrankos	Hungary	Dry red
	Mavrud	Bulgaria	Dry red
	Merlot	New World	Dry red
	Meursault	Burgundy	Dry white
	Vacqueyras	Rhône	Dry red
Beef tacos	Riesling	Alsace or New World	Dry white
	Zinfandel	California	Dry red
Beef Wellington	Champagne (brut)	Champagne	Sparkling
	Malbec	Argentina	Dry red
	Merlot	New World	Dry red
	St-Emilion	Bordeaux	Dry red
Boeuf en daube	Bandol	Provence	Dry red
	Barolo	Italy	Dry red
	Hermitage	Rhône	Dry red
	Shiraz	Australia	Dry red
	Vin de Corse	Corsica	Dry red
Chateaubriand	Barolo	Italy	Dry red
	Echezeaux	Burgundy	Dry red
	Margaux	Bordeaux	Dry red
Chilli con carne	Cabernet Sauvignon	Argentina or Chile	Dry red
	Côtes du Rhône	Rhône	Dry red
	Pinotage	South Africa	Dry red
	Shiraz	Australia	Dry red
	Zinfandel	California	Dry red
Goulash	Gigondas	Rhône	Dry red
	Mavrud	Bulgaria	Dry red
	Penedès	Spain	Dry red
	Zinfandel	California	Dry red
Hamburgers	Beaujolais	Burgundy	Dry red
	Cabernet Sauvignon	California	Dry red
	Chianti	Italy	Dry red
	Shiraz	Australia	Dry red
	Zinfandel	California	Dry red
Oxtail	Brunello di Montalcino	Italy	Dry red
	Châteauneuf-du-Pape	Rhône	Dry red
	Periquita	Portugal	Dry red

Pot-au-feu	Anjou	Loire	Dry red
	Bergerac	South-west France	Dry red
	St-Emilion	Bordeaux	Dry red
Sirloin steak	Barolo	Italy	Dry red
	Cabernet Sauvignon	California	Dry red
	Chianti Classico	Italy	Dry red
	Merlot	New World	Dry red
	Pomerol	Bordeaux	Dry red
	Shiraz	Australia	Dry red
Sirloin steak with	Cabernet Sauvignon	California	Dry red
wild mushrooms	Chinon	Loire	Dry red
	Mercurey	Burgundy	Dry red
	Merlot	New World	Dry red
	Pomerol	Bordeaux	Dry red
Steak and	Buzet	South-west France	Dry red
kidney pie	Cahors	South-west France	Dry red
Steak tartare	Cahors	South-west France	Dry red
	Cornas	Rhône	Dry red
	Crozes-Hermitage	Rhône	Dry red
	St-Amour	Beaujolais	Dry red
	St-Véran	Burgundy	Dry red
Stews and	Amarone della	Italy	Dry red
casseroles, red	Valpolicella		
meat	Brunello di Montalcino	Italy	Dry red
	Cahors	South-west France	Dry red
	Copertino	Italy	Dry red
	Cornas	Rhône	Dry red
	Pauillac	Bordeaux	Dry red
	Periquita	Italy	Dry red
	Shiraz	Australia	Dry red
	Vino Nobile di	Italy	Dry red
	Montepulciano		

Black forest gateau see **Desserts and cakes**

Black pudding see **Charcuterie, cured and cold meats**

Blackcurrants and blackcurrant-based desserts see **Desserts and cakes**

Blanquette de veau see **Veal**

Blinis see **Pancakes and crêpes**

Boar see **Game**

Boeuf en daube see **Beef dishes**

Bolognese sauce see **Sauces**

Borscht see **Soups**

Brandy-based desserts *see* **Desserts and cakes**

Bread and butter pudding *see* **Desserts and cakes**

Bresaola *see* **Charcuterie, cured and cold meats**

Brown sugar *see* **Desserts and cakes**

Brownies *see* **Desserts and cakes**

Bruschetta *see* **Appetizers**

Buffalo wings *see* **Appetizers**

Butter-based sauces *see* **Sauces**

Buttermilk pancakes *see* **Pancakes and crêpes**

Cabbage *see* **Vegetables**

Cabbage, red with apples *see* **Vegetables**

Caesar salad *see* **Salads**

Cajun-style meats *see* **Meat dishes**

Calamari *see* **Seafood dishes**

Caramel-based desserts *see* **Desserts and cakes**

Caramelized oranges *see* **Desserts and cakes**

Carbonara sauce *see* **Pasta dishes**

Carp *see* **Fish**

Carpaccio *see* **Charcuterie, cured and cold meats**

Carrot cake *see* **Desserts and cakes**

Carrot soup *see* **Soups**

Cassis-based desserts *see* **Desserts and cakes**

Cassoulet *see* **Pulses and grains**

Caviar *see* **Seafood dishes**

Ceviche *see* **Fish**

C

CHARCUTERIE, CURED AND COLD MEATS
see also **Bacon and ham, Pâtés and terrines, Pork**

Andouillette, grilled with mustard	Arbois	Jura	Dry white
	Grenache	France or New World	Dry red
	Minervois	Languedoc-Roussillon	Dry red
	Palette	Provence	Dry red
Black pudding	Côtes de Provence	Provence	Dry white
	Côtes du Rhône	Rhône	Dry red
	Dolcetto d'Alba	Italy	Dry red
	Fronsac	Bordeaux	Dry red

101

Bresaola	Chianti	Italy	Dry red
	Sangiovese	California	Dry red
	Valpolicella	Italy	Dry red
Carpaccio (raw	Champagne (rosé)	Champagne	Sparkling rosé
beef in vinaigrette	Chianti	Italy	Dry red
sauce)	Reguengos	Portugal	Dry red
	Sangiovese	California	Dry red
Charcuterie	Bardolino	Italy	Dry red
	Beaujolais	Burgundy	Dry red
	Cabernet Sauvignon	Chile	Dry red
	Chinon	Loire	Dry red
	Côtes du Rhône	Rhône	Dry red
	Rully	Burgundy	Dry red
Chorizo (spicy	Chacoli de Guetaria	Spain	Dry white
Spanish sausage)	Corbières	Languedoc	Dry red
	Irouléguy	South-west France	Dry red
	Navarra	Spain	Dry red
	Pinotage	South Africa	Dry red
	Zinfandel	California	Dry red
Merguez sausages	Grenache	New World	Dry red
(spicy North African	Rioja	Spain	Dry red
sausages)	Shiraz	Australia	Dry red
Prosciutto	Barbera d'Asti	Italy	Dry red
	Pinot Grigio	Italy	Dry white
	Valpolicella Classico	Italy	Dry red
Salami	Barbera d'Asti	Italy	Dry red
	Bardolino	Italy	Dry red
	Montepulciano d'Abruzzo	Italy	Dry red
	Rosso Cònero	Italy	Dry red
	Tavel	Rhône	Dry rosé
	Zinfandel	California	Dry red
Terrines	Barsac	Bordeaux	Sweet white
Tongue	Bergerac	South-west France	Dry red
	Cahors	South-west France	Dry red
	Chardonnay	Chile	Dry white

Chateaubriand *see* **Beef Dishes**

CHEESE DISHES
see also **Wine and Cheese** *on pages 87-9 for individual cheese and wine pairings.*

Blue cheese dip	Aligoté	Burgundy	Dry white
	Cadillac	Bordeaux	Sweet white
	Champagne	Champagne	Sparkling

Cheese fondue	Chardonnay	California	Dry white
	Chasselas	Alsace or Switzerland	Dry white
	Côtes du Rhône	Rhône	Dry red
	Mâcon	Burgundy	Dry white
	Patrimonio	Corsica	Dry white
Croque monsieur	Anjou Gamay	Loire	Dry red
or madame	Bordeaux	Bordeaux	Dry red
	Chardonnay	Australia	Dry white
	Sylvaner	Alsace	Dry white
Gougère	Chablis	Burgundy	Dry white
	Côtes du Rhône	Rhône	Dry red
	Pinot Gris	Alsace	Dry white
	Pouilly-Fuissé	Burgundy	Dry white

Macaroni cheese see **Pasta dishes**

Raclette	Chasselas	Alsace or Switzerland	Dry white
	Côtes du Rhône	Rhône	Dry red
	Pinot Gris	Alsace	Dry white
	Valpolicella Classico	Italy	Dry red

Cheesecake see **Desserts and cakes**

Chef's salad see **Salads**

Cherries and cherry-based desserts see **Desserts and cakes**

Chestnut-based desserts see **Desserts and cakes**

CHICKEN DISHES
see also **Offal, Poultry**

Basque chicken	Châteauneuf-du-Pape	Rhône	Dry red
	Corbières	Languedoc	Dry red
	Fronsac	Bordeaux	Dry red
	Madiran	South-west France	Dry red
Chicken chasseur	Bourgueil	Loire	Dry red
	Entre-deux-mers	Bordeaux	Dry white
	Médoc	Bordeaux	Dry red
	Savigny-lès-Beaune	Burgundy	Dry red
	Sémillon	California	Dry white
Chicken in cream	Chablis Premier Cru	Burgundy	Dry white
and morels sauce	Chardonnay	New World	Dry white
	Corbières	Languedoc	Dry white
	Pinot Noir	Oregon, USA	Dry red
	Riesling	Alsace	Dry white

Chicken curry see **Indian food**

Chicken korma see **Indian food**

Chicken paprika

Kékfrankos	Hungary	Dry red
Shiraz	Australia	Dry red
Zinfandel	California	Dry red

Chicken piri-piri
(a Portuguese dish
with chillis)

Periquita	Portugal	Dry red
Renguengos	Portugal	Dry red
Sauvignon Blanc	France or New World	Dry white
Vinho Verde	Portugal	Dry white

Chicken salad see **Salads**

Chicken in sweet
and sour sauce

Gewürztraminer VT	Alsace	Medium-dry white
Muscat de Rivesaltes	Roussillon	Vin doux naturel
Pomerol	Bordeaux	Dry red
Sylvaner	Alsace	Dry white

Chicken tahine see **Pulses and grains**

Chicken teriyaki

Sancerre	Loire/Centre	Dry white
Sauvignon Blanc	New Zealand	Dry white
Soave	Italy	Dry white

Chicken tikka masala see **Indian food**

Coq au vin

Châteauneuf-du-Pape	Rhône	Dry red
Corbières	Languedoc	Dry red
Côtes du Rhône	Rhône	Dry red
Gevrey-Chambertin	Burgundy	Dry red
Pinot Noir	California	Dry red

Creole chicken

Gewürztraminer	Alsace	Dry white
Sancerre	Loire/Centre	Dry white
Sauvignon Blanc	New Zealand	Dry white
Savennières	Loire	Dry white

Jambalaya

Poulsard	Jura	Dry white
Sancerre	Loire	Dry white
Sauvignon Blanc	New Zealand	Dry white

Lemon chicken

Champagne (rosé)	Champagne	Sparkling rosé
Chenin Blanc	Loire	Dry white
Saumur-Champigny	Loire	Dry red
Vouvray	Loire	Dry white

Roast chicken

Beaujolais	Burgundy	Dry red
Bergerac	South-west France	Dry red
Bordeaux Supérieur	Bordeaux	Dry red
Chardonnay (oaked)	Chile or New World	Dry white
Pinot Noir	New World	Dry red

Southern fried
chicken

Bordeaux Supérieur	Bordeaux	Dry red
Buzet	South-west France	Dry red
Shiraz	Australia	Dry red

Tarragon chicken	Cahors	South-west France	Dry red
	Crozes-Hermitage	Rhône	Dry red
	Mourvèdre	New World	Dry red
	Savigny-lès-Beaune	Burgundy	Dry red

Chinese food see **Oriental food**

Chilli con carne see **Beef dishes**

Chilli sauce see **Sauces**

Chocolate-based desserts see **Desserts and cakes**

Chorizo sausage see **Charcuterie, cured and cold meats**

Choucroute garni see **Pork**

Christmas pudding see **Desserts and cakes**

Chutney see **Indian food**

Cinnamon-based desserts see **Desserts and cakes**

Clam chowder see **Soups**

Clam sauce see **Pasta dishes**

Coconut-based desserts see **Desserts and cakes**

Coffee-based desserts see **Desserts and cakes**

Cognac-based desserts see **Desserts and cakes, Brandy-based**

Cointreau-based dessers see **Desserts and cakes**

Confit de canard see **Poultry**

Coq au vin see **Chicken dishes**

Coquilles St Jacques see **Seafood dishes**

Corn bread see **Vegetables**

Corn chowder see **Soups**

Corn on the cob see **Vegetables**

Cornish pasties see **Meat dishes**

Couscous see **Pulses and grains**

Crab see **Seafood dishes**

Cranberry sauce see **Sauces**

Cream-based sauces see **Sauces**

Crème caramel or brûlée see **Desserts and cakes**

Creole chicken see **Chicken dishes**

Crêpes see **Pancakes and crêpes**

Croque monsieur or madame *see* **Cheese dishes**

Crudités *see* **Vegetables**

Curried tomato soup *see* **Soups**

Curry *see* **Indian food**

 DESSERTS AND CAKES
see also **Fruits, Pancakes and crêpes**

Apple-based desserts	Pineau des Charentes	Cognac	Vin de liqueur
	Vin de Paille	Jura	Vin doux naturel
	Vouvray	Loire	Sweet white or sparkling

Apple crumble *see* **Apple-based desserts**

Apple pie *see* **Apple-based desserts**

Apricot-based desserts	Blanquette de Limoux	Languedoc	Sparkling
	Côteaux du Layon	Loire	Sweet white
	Muscat de Rivesaltes	Roussillon	Vin doux naturel
	Vin de Paille	Jura	Vin doux naturel
Baclava	Samos	Greece	Sweet white
	Moscatel du Setúbal	Portugal	Sweet white
	Muscat de Beaumes-de-Venise	Rhône	Vin doux naturel
Banana-based desserts	Crémant de Bourgogne	Burgundy	Sparkling
	Monbazillac	South-west France	Sweet white
	Muscat de Beaumes-de-Venise	Rhône	Vin doux naturel

Black forest gateau *see* **Chocolate-based desserts**

Blackcurrant-based desserts *see* **Cassis-based desserts**

Brandy-based desserts	Arbois	Jura	Dry white
	Pineau des Charentes	Cognac	Vin de liqueur
Bread and butter pudding	Côtes de Provence	Provence	Dry white
	Loupiac	Bordeaux	Sweet white
	Monbazillac	South-west France	Sweet white
	Pacherenc du Vic-Bilh	South-west France	Sweet white
	Sauternes	Bordeaux	Sweet white
Brown sugar (as a principal ingredient or dominant flavour)	Gewürztraminer	Alsace	Sweet white
	Riesling Auslese	Germany	Sweet white
	Sauternes	Bordeax	Sweet white
	Vosne-Romanée	Burgundy	Dry red

Brownies *see* **Chocolate-based desserts**

Caramel-based desserts	Barsac	Bordeaux	Sweet white
	Champagne (demi-sec)	Champagne	Sparkling
	Moscatel de Setúbal	Portugal	Sweet white
Caramelized oranges	Black Muscat	California	Sweet white
Carrot cake	Crémant du Bourgogne	Burgundy	Sparkling
	Meursault	Burgundy	Dry white
	Tokaji	Hungary	Dry white
Cassis-based desserts	Bergerac	South-west France	Dry white
	Champagne (rosé)	Champagne	Sparkling rosé
	Muscat de Rivesaltes	Roussillon	Vin doux naturel
Cheesecake	Cadillac	Bordeaux	Sweet white
	Champagne	Champagne	Sparkling
	Coteaux du Layon	Loire	Sweet white
	Monbazillac	South-west France	Sweet white
	Pacherenc du Vic-Bilh	South-west France	Sweet white
Cherry-based desserts	Black Muscat	California	Sweet white
	Blanquette de Limoux	Languedoc	Sparkling
	Côteaux du Layon	Loire	Sweet white
	Riesling Beerenauslese	Germany	Sweet white

Cherry tart *see* **Cherry-based desserts**

Chestnut-based desserts	Asti Spumante	Italy	Sparkling
	Chenin Blanc	Loire	Dry white
	Loupiac	Bordeaux	Sweet white
Chocolate-based desserts	Banyuls	Roussillon	Vin doux naturel
	Champagne (Noir de Noirs)	Champagne	Sparkling
	Muscatel du Setúbal	Portugal	Sweet white
	Pineau des Charentes	Cognac	Vin de liqueur
	Port	Portugal	Fortified red
	Sauternes	Bordeaux	Sweet white

Chocolate chip cookies *see* **Chocolate-based desserts**

Chocolate cream pie *see* **Chocolate-based desserts**

Christmas pudding	Asti Spumante	Italy	Sparkling
	Banyuls	Roussillon	Vin doux natural
	Champagne	Champagne	Sparkling
	Sauternes	Bordeaux	Sweet white
	Tokaji Aszú, 5 puttonyos	Hungary	Sweet white
Cinnamon-based desserts	Gevrey-Chambertin	Burgundy	Dry red
	Ste-Croix-du-Mont	South-west France	Sweet white
	Sauternes	Bordeaux	Sweet white
	Volnay	Burgundy	Dry red

Cinnamon cake see **Cinnamon-based desserts**

Coconut-based desserts	Champagne	Champagne	Sparkling
	Chardonnay	New World	Dry white
	Gewürztraminer VT	Alsace	Medium-dry white
	Marsanne	France	Dry white
	Sémillon	France or New World	Dry white
Coffee-based desserts	Banyuls	Roussillon	Vin doux naturel
	Champagne (brut)	Champagne	Sparkling
	Richebourg	Burgundy	Dry red
	Vosne-Romanée	Burgundy	Dry red

Coffee cake see **Coffee-based desserts**

Cognac-based desserts see **Brandy-based desserts**

Cointreau-based desserts	Champagne	Champagne	Sparkling
	Sauternes	Bordeaux	Sweet white
Crème caramel or brûlée	Champagne (demi-sec)	Champagne	Sparkling
	Gaillac	South-west France	Dry white
	Sauternes	Bordeaux	Sweet white
Fruit-based desserts (general)	Asti Spumante	Italy	Sparkling
	Barsac/Sauternes	Bordeaux	Sweet white
	Champagne (Blanc de Blancs)	Champagne	Sparkling
	Coteaux du Layon	Loire	Sweet white
	Loupiac	Bordeaux	Sweet white
	Monbazillac	South-west France	Sweet white
	Muscat de Beaumes-de-Venise	Rhône	Vin doux naturel
	Quarts de Chaume	Loire	Sweet white
	Vouvray	Loire	Sweet white or sparkling
Fruit compote or salad	Muscat de Rivesaltes	Roussillon	Vin doux naturel
	Moscato Spumante	Italy	Sparkling
	Loupiac	Bordeaux	Sweet white
	Champagne (rosé)	Champagne	Sparkling rosé
	Ste-Croix-du-Mont	South-west France	Sweet white
Ginger-based desserts	Muscat	France	Sweet white
	Muscat de Beaumes-de-Venise	Rhône	Vin doux naturel
	Sauvignon Blanc	France or New World	Dry white

Gingerbread cake see **Ginger-based desserts**

Honey-based desserts	Black Muscat	California	Sweet white
	Montrachet	Burgundy	Dry white
	Muscat de Beaumes-de-Venise	Rhône	Vin doux naturel

Ice cream	Champagne	Champagne	Sparkling
	Muscat	France	Sweet white
	Muscat de Beaumes-de-Venise	Rhône	Vin doux naturel
	Passito	Italy	Sweet white
Iles flottantes	L'Etoile	Jura	Dry white
	Loupiac	Bordeaux	Sweet white
	Muscat de Rivesaltes	Roussillon	Vin doux naturel
Kougelhopf	Riesling SGN	Alsace	Sweet white
	Pinot Gris VT	Alsace	Semi-sweet white
	Quarts de Chaume	Loire	Sweet white
Lemon-based desserts	Hermitage	Rhône	Dry white
	Sauternes	Bordeaux	Sweet white
	Vouvray	Loire	Sweet white or sparkling

Lemon meringue pie *see* **Lemon-based desserts**

Meringues	Asti Spumante	Italy	Sparkling
	Champagne	Champagne	Sparkling
	Muscat de Rivesaltes	Roussillon	Vin doux naturel
Mille feuilles	Champagne	Champagne	Sparkling
	Pacherenc du Vic-Bilh	South-west France	Sweet white
Mince pies	Pacherenc du Vic-Bilh	South-west France	Sweet white
	Port	Portugal	Fortified red
	Vouvray	Loire	Sweet white or sparkling
Mint-based desserts	Asti Spumante	Italy	Sparkling
	Muscat de Beaumes-de-Venise	Rhône	Vin doux naturel
Orange-based desserts	Muscat de Rivesaltes	Roussillon	Vin doux naturel
	Ste-Croix-du-Mont	South-west France	Sweet white
Pecan pie	Champagne	Champagne	Sparkling
	Moscatel de Valencia	Spain	Sweet white
	Sauternes	Bordeaux	Sweet white
Pineapple-based desserts	Cadillac	Bordeaux	Sweet white
	Champagne (demi-sec)	Champagne	Sparkling
	Muscat de Rivesaltes	Roussillon	Vin doux naturel
	Orvieto	Italy	Dry white
	Pacherenc du Vic-Bilh	South-west France	Dry to sweet white
Raspberry-based desserts	Beaujolais-Villages	Beaujolais	Dry red
	Champagne (demi-sec)	Champagne	Sparkling
	Coteaux du Layon	Loire	Sweet white

Raspberry-based desserts *(continued)*	Loupiac	Bordeaux	Sweet white
	Monbazillac	South-west France	Sweet white
	Riesling	Alsace	Dry white
	Saumur-Champigny	Loire	Dry red
Sachertorte *see also* **Chocolate-based desserts**	Champagne	Champagne	Sparkling
	Muscat de Beaumes-de-Venise	Rhône	Vin doux naturel
	Riesling Trocken-beerenauslese	Germany	Sweet white
Sorbets *see also* **Desserts with the appropriate fruit base**	Champagne	Champagne	Sparkling
	Pineau des Charentes	Cognac	Vin de liqueur
Strawberry-based desserts	Banyuls	Roussillon	Vin doux naturel
	Champagne	Champagne	Sparkling
	Monbazillac	South-west France	Sweet white
	Saumur-Champigny	Loire	Dry red

Tarte tatin *see* **Apple-based desserts**

Tiramisu *see also* **Coffee-based desserts**	Muscat de Rivesaltes	Roussillon	Vin doux naturel
	Passito	Italy	Sweet white
	Sauternes	Bordeaux	Sweet white
Treacle tart	Champagne	Champagne	Sparkling
	Monbazillac	South-west France	Sweet white
	Moscatel de Valencia	Spain	Sweet white
Trifle	Cadillac	Bordeaux	Sweet white
	Crémant de Bourgogne	Burgundy	Sparkling
	Sémillon	New World	Sweet white
Vanilla-based desserts	Arbois	Jura	Dry rosé
	Bergerac	South-west France	Dry white
	Muscat de Rivesaltes	Roussillon	Vin doux natural

Duck *see* **Poultry**

E **Eels** *see* **Fish**

EGG DISHES

Eggs (general)	Brouilly	Burgundy	Dry red
	Muscadet	Loire	Dry white
	Sauvignon Blanc	France or New World	Dry white
Eggs Benedict	Champagne	Champagne	Sparkling
	Chardonnay (unoaked)	New World	Dry white
	Pinot Blanc	Alsace	Dry white
Omelette	Brouilly	Beaujolais	Dry red
	Champagne	Champagne	Sparkling

Omelette *(continued)*	Pinot Blanc Sancerre	Alsace Loire/Centre	Dry white Dry white
Omelette with **bacon**	Chardonnay Pinot Gris	New world Alsace	Dry white Dry white
Omelette with **cheese**	Chardonnay Pinot Blanc Vosne-Romanée	New World Alsace Burgundy	Dry white Dry white Dry red
Omelette with **mushrooms**	Côtes du Rhône Petit Chablis Saumur-Champigny	Rhône Burgundy Loire	Dry red Dry white Dry red
Omelette with **tomato**	Beaujolais Chianti	Burgundy Italy	Dry red Dry red
Omelette with **truffles**	Chambolle-Musigny Champagne (Blanc de Blancs)	Burgundy Champagne	Dry white Sparkling
Piperade	Bandol rosé Chacoli de Guetaria Champagne (rosé) Pacherenc du Vic-Bilh	Provence Spain Champagne South-west France	Dry rosé Dry white Sparkling rosé Dry white
Quails' eggs	Champagne Crémant de Bourgogne	Champagne Burgundy	Sparkling Sparkling
Quiche lorraine	Bergerac Bianco di Custoza Chinon Pinot Gris Riesling	South-west France Italy Loire Alsace Alsace	Dry white Dry white Dry red Dry white Dry white
Scrambled eggs **with smoked** **salmon**	Cava Champagne (rosé) Chardonnay (oaked) Petit Chablis	Spain Champagne Chile Burgundy	Sparkling Sparkling rosé Dry white Dry white
Soufflé with **broccoli and cheese**	Champagne Muscadet sur Lie Rully Sauvignon Blanc	Champagne Loire Burgundy New Zealand	Sparkling Dry white Dry white Dry white
Soufflé with **spinach**	Champagne (Blanc de Blancs) Chardonnay Frascati Superiore Mâcon St-Véran Vin du Jura	Champagne New World Italy Burgundy Burgundy Jura	Sparkling Dry white Dry white Dry white Dry white Dry white

Soufflé with seafood *see* **Seafood dishes**

Empanadas *see* **Meat dishes**

Escargots *see* **Appetizers**

ETHNIC FOOD

Cajun-style meats *see* **Meat dishes**

Chinese food *see* **Oriental food**

Greek food	Naoussa	Greece	Dry red
see also **Moussaka**	Rioja	Spain	Dry red
	Shiraz	Australia	Dry red
	Zinfandel	California	Dry red

Indian food Indian food

Japanese food *see* **Oriental food**

Mexican food	Cahors	South-west France	Dry red
	Côtes du Rhône	Rhône	Dry red
	Fitou	Languedoc	Dry red
	Valpolicella	Italy	Dry red
Moussaka	Côtes du Rhône	Rhône	Dry red
	Dão	Portugal	Dry red
	Kékfrankos	Hungary	Dry red
	Naoussa	Greece	Dry red
	Nemea	Greece	Dry red
	Pinotage	South Africa	Dry red
	Rioja	Spain	Dry red

F **Fettucine Alfredo** *see* **Pasta dishes**

FISH
see also **Seafood dishes**

Anchovies or	Bandol rosé	Provence	Dry rosé
anchovy paste	Fino Sherry	Spain	Fortified white
(anchoiade)	Greco di Tufo	Italy	Dry white
	Saumur	Loire	Dry white
	Sylvaner	Alsace	Dry white
	Tavel	Rhône	Dry rosé
Barbecued fish	Bordeaux Sec	Bordeaux	Dry white
	Entre-deux-mers	Bordeaux	Dry white
	Sémillon	Australia	Dry white
Bass, grilled	Chardonnay	France or New World	Dry white
	Pouilly-Fuissé	Burgundy	Dry white
	Tocai Friulano Collio	Italy	Dry white
Blackened fish	Chardonnay	Chile	Dry white
	Entre-deux-mers	Bordeaux	Dry white
	Sémillon	Australia	Dry white

Carp, grilled	Pouilly-Fumé	Loire	Dry white
	Sauvignon Blanc	France or New World	Dry white
	Trebbiano	Italy	Dry white
	Ugni Blanc	New World	Dry white
Ceviche (raw fish marinated in lemon juice)	Condrieu	Rhône	Dry white
	Sauvignon Blanc	Chile	Dry white
	Vinho Verde	Portugal	Dry white
Eels with a creamy herb sauce	Pouilly-Fumé	Loire	Dry white
	Riesling	Alsace	Dry white
	Sancerre	Loire/Centre	Dry white
Eels, smoked	Bourgeuil	Loire	Dry red
	Sancerre	Loire	Dry white
	Sauvignon Blanc	New Zealand	Dry white
Fish cakes	Chardonnay	Chile	Dry white
	Muscadet	Loire	Dry white
	Sancerre	Loire/Centre	Dry white
	Sauvignon Blanc	New Zealand	Dry white
	Vouvray	Loire	Dry white
Fish and chips	Bandol rosé	Provence	Dry rosé
	Bergerac	South-west France	Dry white
	Mâcon	Burgundy	Dry white
	Pinot Grigio	Italy	Dry white
	Rully	Burgundy	Dry white
	Sauvignon Blanc	Chile	Dry white
	Verdicchio	Italy	Dry white
Fish in red wine	Barbaresco	Italy	Dry red
	Bardolino	Italy	Dry red
	Graves	Bordeaux	Dry red
Fried fish	Bergerac	South-west France	Dry red
	Pinot Grigio	Italy	Dry white
	Verdicchio	Italy	Dry white
Gravad lax	Champagne (Blanc de Blancs)	Champagne	Sparkling
	Chardonnay	Australia	Dry white
	Riesling Kabinett	Germany	Dry white
Haddock	Arbois	Jura	Dry red
	Graves	Bordeaux	Dry white
	Riesling	Alsace	Dry white
	Sauvignon Blanc	France or New World	Dry white
Herring	Corbières	Languedoc	Dry white
	Entre-deux-mers	Bordeaux	Dry white
	St-Véran	Burgundy	Dry white

Kedgeree	Champagne	Champagne	Sparkling
	Chardonnay	New World	Dry white
	Pinot Blanc	Alsace	Dry white
Kippers	Champagne	Champagne	Sparkling
	Corbières	Languedoc	Dry white
	Entre-deux-mers	Bordeaux	Dry white
Mackerel with	Chablis (oaked)	Burgundy	Dry white
butter and spring	Gaillac	Rhône	Dry white
onions	Graves	Bordeaux	Dry white
	Sémillon	New World	Dry white
Mackerel with	Gros Plant	Loire/Centre	Dry white
green gooseberry	Muscadet	Loire	Dry white
sauce	Sancerre	Loire/Centre	Dry red
	Vinho Verde	Portugal	Dry white
Monkfish	Chardonnay	Chile	Dry white
	Puligny-Montrachet	Burgundy	Dry white
	Sémillon	Australia	Dry white
Pike with garlic	Riesling	Austria	Dry white
	Sauvignon Blanc	Australia	Dry white
	Sylvaner	Alsace	Dry white
Plaice	Chablis	Burgundy	Dry white
	Orvieto	Italy	Dry white
	Riesling	Alsace	Dry white
Red mullet	Bordeaux rosé	Bordeaux	Dry rosé
	Mercurey	Burgundy	Dry red
	Sancerre	Loire/Centre	Dry white
Salmon,	Chardonnay	Long Island, USA	Dry white
cold cooked	Coteaux d'Aix en Provence rosé	Provence	Dry rosé
	Pinot Noir	Alsace	Dry red
Salmon and cream	Chablis	Burgundy	Dry white
cheese bagels	Champagne (brut)	Champagne	Sparkling
	Pinot Noir	Romania	Dry red
Salmon, poached,	Chablis	Burgundy	Dry white
steamed or lightly	Chinon	Loire	Dry red
grilled	Condrieu	Rhône	Dry white
	Sancerre	Loire/Centre	Dry white
Salmon, smoked	Chablis (oaked)	Burgundy	Dry white
	Champagne (brut)	Champagne	Sparkling
	Chardonnay (oaked)	Long Island, USA	Dry white
	Riesling	Alsace	Dry white
	Rully	Burgundy	Dry white

Salt cod balls, deep-fried	Chinon	Loire	Dry red
	Rioja	Spain	Dry white
	Tempranillo	Spain	Dry red
Salt cod with garlic, oil and cream	Côtes de Provence rosé	Provence	Dry rosé
	Mâcon	Burgundy	Dry white
	Sylvaner	Alsace	Dry white
Sardines, grilled	Gaillac	South-west France	Dry white
	Orvieto	Italy	Dry white
	Vinho Verde	Portugal	Dry white
Smoked fish	Chardonnay (oaked)	California	Dry white
	Gewürztraminer VT	Alsace	Medium-dry white
	Riesling Auslese	Germany	Sweet white
Sole meunière	Bellet	Provence	Dry white
	Chablis	Burgundy	Dry white
	Condrieu	Rhône	Dry white
	Riesling	Alsace	Dry white
Swordfish	Chardonnay	New World	Dry white
	Côte-Rôtie	Rhône	Dry white
	Marsanne	New World	Dry white
	Meursault	Chablis	Dry white
Trout	Entre-deux-Mers	Bordeaux	Dry white
	Riesling	Alsace	Dry white
	Rully	Burgundy	Dry white
Tuna	Côtes du Jura	Jura	Dry white
	Côtes de Provence rosé	Provence	Dry rosé
	Merlot	New World	Dry red
	Saumur	Loire	Dry red
Tuna salad see **Salads**			
Turbot	Chablis	Burgundy	Dry white
	Graves	Burgundy	Dry white
	Minervois	Languedoc-Roussillon	Dry red
	Pinot Gris	Alsace	Dry white
	Sauvignon Blanc	New World	Dry white
White fish	Chardonnay (oaked)	California	Dry white
	Chassagne-Montrachet	Burgundy	Dry white
	Muscadet sur Lie	Loire	Dry white
	Sauvignon Blanc	France or New World	Dry white
	Vouvray	Loire	Dry white
White fish, grilled	Chenin Blanc	New World	Dry white
	Orvieto	Italy	Dry or semi-sweet white
	Riesling	Alsace	Dry white
	Trebbiano	Italy or New World	Dry white

White fish, grilled *(continued)*	Viognier	Rhône, Italy or New World	Dry white

Foie gras *see* **Pâtés and terrines**

Fondue, cheese *see* **Cheese dishes**

Fondue, meat *see* **Meat dishes**

Fruit compote or salad *see* **Desserts and cakes**

 GAME

Boar *see* **Wild boar**

Game	Barolo	Italy	Dry red
	Bonnes-Mares	Burgundy	Dry red
	Clos de Vougeot	Burgundy	Dry red
	Corton	Burgundy	Dry red
	Echezeaux	Burgundy	Dry red
	Shiraz	Australia	Dry red
	Syrah	New World	Dry red
	Vosne-Romanée	Burgundy	Dry red
Grouse	Barolo	Italy	Dry red
	Chambertin	Burgundy	Dry red
	Hermitage	Rhône	Dry red
	Richebourg	Burgundy	Dry red
Guinea fowl	Chambertin	Burgundy	Dry red
	Fronsac	Bordeaux	Dry red
	Pauillac	Bordeaux	Dry red
Hare	Bonnes-Mares	Burgundy	Dry red
	Canon-Fronsac	Bordeaux	Dry red
	Cornas	Rhône	Dry red
	Minervois	Languedoc-Roussillon	Dry red
Hare, potted or jugged	Bergerac	South-west France	Dry red
	Buzet	South-west France	Dry red
	Corbières	Languedoc	Dry red
Partridge	Châteauneuf-du-Pape	Rhône	Dry red
	Pomerol	Bordeaux	Dry red
Pheasant	Barolo	Italy	Dry red
	Chambolle-Musigny	Burgundy	Dry red
	Crozes-Hermitage	Rhône	Dry red
	Pomerol	Bordeaux	Dry red
	St-Emilion	Bordeaux	Dry red
Rabbit	Côtes de Duras	South-west France	Dry red
	Pinot Noir	New World	Dry red
	St-Estèphe	Bordeaux	Dry red
	Volnay	Burgundy	Dry red

Venison with	Bandol	Provence	Dry red
cranberries or	Cabernet Sauvignon/	Lebanon	Dry red
juniper berries	Cinsault		
	Chambertin	Burgundy	Dry red
	Mourvèdre	New World	Dry red
	Shiraz	Australia	Dry red
	Zinfandel	California	Dry red
Wild boar	Bandol	Provence	Dry red
	Cabernet Sauvignon/	Lebanon	Dry red
	Cinsault		
	Gigondas	Rhône	Dry red
	Pomerol	Bordeaux	Dry red
	Pommard	Burgundy	Dry red
	Shiraz	Australia	Dry red
	Vino Nobile di	Italy	Dry red
	Montepulciano		

Gammon see **Bacon and ham**

Gazpacho see **Soups**

Ginger-based desserts see **Desserts and cakes**

Goose see **Poultry**

Goulash see **Beef dishes**

Gratin dauphinois see **Vegetables**

Gravad lax see **Fish**

Green salad with oil and vinegar dressing see **Salads**

Grouse see **Game**

Guacamole see **Appetizers**

Guinea fowl see **Game**

Haddock see **Fish**

H

Haggis see **Offal**

Ham see **Bacon and ham**

Hamburgers see **Bacon and ham**

Hare see **Game**

Hazelnuts see **Nuts**

Herbs and Spices see **Part 2** page 74

Herring see **Fish**

Hollandaise sauce see **Sauces**

Honey-based desserts see **Desserts and cakes**

Horseradish sauce *see* **Sauces**

Houmus *see* **Pulses and grains**

Ice cream *see* **Desserts and cakes**

Iles flottantes *see* **Desserts and cakes**

INDIAN FOOD

Chicken curry	Arbois	Jura	Dry white
	Chardonnay	New World	Dry white
	Côtes du Rhône	Rhône	Dry red
	Morgon	Beaujolais	Dry red
	Pinot Gris	Alsace	Dry white
	St-Emilion	Bordeaux	Dry red
Chicken korma	Chardonnay	California	Dry white
	Chenin Blanc	California	Dry white
	Sémillon	New World	Dry white
Chutney	Bellet rosé	Provence	Dry rosé
	Champagne	Champagne	Sparkling
	Gewürztraminer	Alsace	Dry white
	Zinfandel	California	Dry red
Curry sauces	Condrieu	Rhône	Dry white
	Marsanne	New World	Dry white
	Viognier	Rhône	Dry white
Indian food with spicy yoghurt sauces	Bordeaux rosé	Bordeaux	Dry rosé
	Champagne (non-vintage)	Champagne	Sparkling
	Chardonnay	California	Dry white
	Chenin Blanc	Loire or New World	Dry white
	Gewürztraminer VT	Alsace	Medium-dry white
	Orvieto Abboccato	Italy	Medium-dry white
	Sémillon	New World	Dry white
	Viognier	New World	Dry white
Lamb curry	Gewürztraminer	Alsace	Dry white
	Pinot Noir	California	Dry red
	Savigny-lès-Beaune	Burgundy	Dry red
	Shiraz	Australia	Dry red
Tandoori	Cabernet Sauvignon	California	Dry red
	Gewürztraminer	Alsace	Dry white
	Shiraz	Australia	Dry red

Jambalaya *see* **Chicken dishes**

Jambon persillé *see* **Bacon and Ham**

Japanese food *see* **Oriental food**

Kangaroo *see* **Meat dishes**

Kebabs *see* **Meat dishes**

Kedgeree *see* **Fish**

Kidneys *see* **Offal**

Kippers *see* **Fish**

Kleftiko *see* **Lamb**

Kougelhopf *see* **Desserts and cakes**

LAMB
see also **Meat dishes**

Kleftiko (kebabs)	Bairrada	Portugal	Dry red
	Cabernet Franc	New World	Dry red
	Nemea	Greece	Dry red
	Periquita	Portugal	Dry red
	Poulsard	Arbois	Dry red
Lamb (general)	Cabernet Sauvignon	Australia	Dry red
	Médoc	Bordeaux	Dry red
	Navarra	Spain	Dry red
	Pauillac	Bordeaux	Dry red
	Rioja	Spain	Dry red
Lamb chops, grilled	Côtes de Provence rosé	Provence	Dry rosé
	Lirac rosé	Rhône	Dry rosé
	Pomerol	Bordeaux	Dry red
	Saumur-Champigny	Loire	Dry red
Lamb crown roast	Ajaccio	Corsica	Dry red
	Pauillac	Bordeaux	Dry red
	St-Julien	Bordeaux	Dry red

Lamb curry *see* **Indian food**

Lamb with herbes de provence	Cinsault or Mourvèdre	New World	Dry red
	Colli Orientali del Friuli	Italy	Dry red
	Côtes de Provence rosé	Provence	Dry rosé
	Dão	Portugal	Dry red
	St-Emilion	Bordeaux	Dry red
Lamb shoulder	Bordeaux Supérieur	Bordeaux	Dry red
	Côtes de Bourg	Bordeaux	Dry red
	Hermitage	Rhône	Dry red
	St-Emilion	Bordeaux	Dry red

Lamb stew *see* **Meat dishes**

Lancashire hotpot	Bergerac	South-west France	Dry red
	Cabernet Sauvignon	New World	Dry red
	Fitou	Languedoc	Dry red
	Montepulciano d'Abruzzo	Italy	Dry red
Roast lamb with mint sauce	Champagne (rosé)	Champagne	Sparkling rosé
	Margaux	Bordeaux	Dry red
	Mavrud	Bulgaria	Dry red
	Pommard	Burgundy	Dry red
	Vino Nobile di Montepulciano	Italy	Dry red
Shepherd's pie	Bourgueil	Loire	Dry red
	Buzet	South-west France	Dry red
	Pomerol	Bordeaux	Dry red

Lancashire hotpot see **Lamb**

Lasagne see **Pasta dishes**

Lemons and lemon-based desserts see **Desserts and cakes**

Lemon chicken see **Chicken dishes**

Liver see **Offal**

Lobster see **Seafood dishes**

Lobster bisque see **Soups**

M **Macaroni cheese** see **Pasta dishes**

Mackerel see **Fish**

Mayonnaise see **Sauces**

Meatloaf see **Meat dishes**

Melon with Parma ham or Port see **Appetizers**

Merguez sausages see **Charcuterie, cured and cold meats**

Meringues see **Desserts and cakes**

MEAT DISHES
see also **Beef, Game, Lamb, Pork, Veal**

Baeckaoffe	Gewürztraminer	Alsace	Dry white
	St-Veran	Burgundy	Dry white
Barbecued meats	Cabernet Sauvignon/ Cinsault	Lebanon	Dry red
	Gewürztraminer	Alsace	Dry white
	Lirac	Rhône	Dry red
	Mourvèdre	France	Dry red
	Shiraz	Australia	Dry red
	Zinfandel	California	Dry red

Cajun-style meats	Pommard	Burgundy	Dry red
	Syrah	New World	Dry red
	Zinfandel	California	Dry red
Cornish pasties	Côtes du Rhône	Rhône	Dry white
	Sangiovese	California	Dry red
	Viognier	California	Dry white
Empanadas	Malbec	Argentina	Dry red
	Merlot	Chile	Dry red
	Zinfandel	California	Dry red
Fondue, meat	Bordeaux	Bordeaux	Dry red
(à la Bourguignonne)	Côte de Beaune	Burgundy	Dry red
	Côtes du Rhône	Rhône	Dry red
	Saumur	Loire	Dry white
	Shiraz	Australia	Dry red
Kangaroo	Cabernet Sauvignon	Australia	Dry red
	Chardonnay	Australia	Dry white
	Shiraz	Australia	Dry white
Kebabs	Arbois	Jura	Dry red
	Côtes de Provence rosé	Provence	Dry rosé
	Patrimonio	Corsica	Dry red
	St-Joseph	Rhône	Dry red
Meatloaf	Bordeaux Supérieur	Bordeaux	Dry red
	Cabernet Sauvignon	California	Dry red
	Pinot Noir	New World	Dry red
	Zinfandel	California	Dry red
Pot roast	Riesling	Alsace	Dry white
	Gewürztraminer	Alsace	Dry white
	St-Emilion	Bordeaux	Dry red

N NUTS
see also **Chestnut-based desserts**

Almonds, grilled and salted	Chablis Grand Cru	Burgundy	Dry white
	Fino Sherry	Spain	Fortified white
	Moscatel de Setúbal	Portugal	Sweet white
Almonds, walnuts, hazelnuts, peanuts	Amontillado	Spain	Fortified red
	Madiera	Spain	Fortified red
	Manzanilla	Spain	Fortified white
	Port	Portugal	Fortified white
	Samos	Greece	Sweet white

O Octopus see **Seafood dishes**

OFFAL

Foie gras see Pâtés and terrines

Haggis	Baden Spätburgunder	Germany	Dry red
	Bordeaux Supérieur	Bordeaux	Dry red
	Cabernet Sauvignon	New World	Dry red
	Bairrada	Portugal	Dry red
Kidneys	Beaujolais	Beaujolais	Dry red
	Cabernet Sauvignon	New World	Dry red
	Pommard	Burgundy	Dry red
Liver	Champagne (Blanc de Blancs)	Champagne	Sparkling
	Côtes de Provence rosé	Provence	Dry rosé
	Médoc	Bordeaux	Dry red
	Rioja	Spain	Dry red
Sweetbreads	Côte de Beaune	Burgundy	Dry red
	Côtes de Provence rosé	Provence	Dry rosé
	Sylvaner	Alsace	Dry white
Tripe	Meursault	Burgundy	Dry white
	Pacherenc du Vic-Bilh	South-west France	Dry white
	Pouilly-Fumé	Loire	Dry white

Olives see Appetizers

Omelettes see Egg dishes

Onions, creamed see Vegetables

Onion tart see Vegetables

Oranges and orange-based desserts see Desserts and cakes

ORIENTAL FOOD
see also **Ethnic food, Indian food**

Chinese food	Champagne (non-vintage)	Champagne	Sparkling

Chinese food	Chasselas	Switzerland	Dry white
(continued)	Gewürztraminer VT	Alsace	Medium-dry white
	Riesling VT	Alsace	Dry to medium-dry white
	Riesling Spätlese	Germany	Sweet white
	Grüner Veltliner Beerenauslese	Austria	Sweet white
Indian food *see* **Indian food**			
Japanese food	Champagne (non-vintage, Blanc de Noirs)	Champagne	Sparkling
	Pomerol	Bordeaux	Dry red
	Pouilly-Fuissé	Burgundy	Dry white
	Riesling	Austria	Dry white
Peking duck	Gewürztraminer VT	Alsace	Medium-dry white
	Pinot Noir	Australia	Dry red
	Rioja (oaked)	Spain	Dry white
	St-Emilion	Bordeaux	Dry red
Sashimi	Riesling Kabinett	Germany	Dry white
	Sancerre	Loire/Centre	Dry white
	Sauvignon Blanc	New Zealand	Dry white
Satay	Pinot Gris	Alsace	Dry white
	Rully	Burgundy	Dry white
Stir-fries	Pinot Grigio	Italy	Dry white
	Riesling	Alsace	Dry white
	Sauvignon Blanc	New World	Dry white
Sushi	Arbois	Jura	Dry white
	Riesling Kabinett	Germany	Dry white
	Sancerre	Loire/Centre	Dry white
Tempura	Sancerre	Loire/Centre	Dry white
	Chablis	Burgundy	Dry white
	Orvieto	Italy	Dry white
Thai food	Chablis	Burgundy	Dry white
	Colombard	New World	Dry white
	Gewürztraminer VT	Alsace	Medium-dry white
	Sauvignon Blanc	France or New World	Dry white
	Tokaji	Hungary	Dry white
	Vin de Paille	Jura	Vin doux naturel

Osso bucco *see* **Veal**

Oxtail *see* **Bacon and ham**

P Paella *see* **Seafood dishes**

PANCAKES AND CRÊPES

Blinis	Champagne	Champagne	Sparkling
	Crémant de Bourgogne	Burgundy	Sparkling
Buttermilk pancakes	Champagne	Champagne	Sparkling
	Crémant du Loire	Loire	Sparkling
	Sauternes	Bordeaux	Sweet white
Crêpes, savoury	Alto Adige Chardonnay	Italy	Dry white
	Bordeaux Supérieur	Bordeaux	Dry red
	Pinot Blanc	Alsace	Dry white
	Rully	Burgundy	Dry white
	St-Amour	Beaujolais	Dry red
Crêpes, sweet	Champagne (demi-sec)	Champagne	Sparkling
	Muscat de Rivesaltes	Roussillon	Vin doux naturel
	Vin de Paille	Jura	Vin doux naturel
	Vouvray	Loire	Sparkling (mousseux)
Pancakes with maple syrup	Champagne	Champagne	Sparkling
	Riesling beerenauslese	Germany	Sweet white
	Vouvray	Loire	Sparkling (mousseux)

Partridge *see* **Game**

PASTA AND PIZZA DISHES

Fettucine Alfredo	Bardolino	Italy	Dry red
	Alto Adige Chardonnay	Italy	Dry white
	Frascati Superiore	Italy	Dry white
	Rully	Burgundy	Dry white
Lasagne	Barbera d'Asti	Italy	Dry red
	Chianti	Italy	Dry red
	St-Amour	Beaujolais	Dry red
Macaroni cheese	Beaujolais	Burgundy	Dry red
	Chardonnay	California	Dry white
	Soave	Italy	Dry white
	Zinfandel	California	Dry red
Pasta with carbonara sauce	Barbera d'Asti	Italy	Dry red
	Bardolino	Italy	Dry red
	Alto Adige Chardonnay	Italy	Dry white
	Mâcon	Burgundy	Dry white
Pasta with clam sauce	Chardonnay (unoaked)	New World	Dry white
	Chasselas	Alsace	Dry white
	Pinot Grigio	Italy	Dry white

Pasta with pesto sauce	Barbera d'Asti	Italy	Dry red
	Chardonnay (unoaked)	New World	Dry white
	St-Emilion	Bordeaux	Dry red
	Soave	Italy	Dry white
Pasta with meat or béchamel sauce	Barbera d'Asti	Italy	Dry red
	Bardolino	Italy	Dry red
	Montepulciano d'Abruzzo	Italy	Dry red
	Sangiovese	California	Dry red
Pasta with spinach and Ricotta	Bianco di Custoza	Italy	Dry white
	Chianti	Italy	Dry white
	Grave del Friuli	Italy	Sparkling
Pasta with spring vegetables	Colli Berici Pinot Bianco	Italy	Dry white
	Pinot Grigio	Italy	Dry white
	Sauvignon Blanc	New Zealand	Dry white
Pizza bolognese	Barbera d'Asti	Italy	Dry red
	Cabernet Sauvignon/ Cinsault	Lebanon	Dry red
	Chianti	Italy	Dry red
	Côte de Beaune	Burgundy	Dry red
	Sangiovese	California	Dry red
	Zinfandel	California	Dry red
Pizza with seafood	Bianco di Custoza	Italy	Dry white
	Côtes de Provence rosé	Provence	Dry rosé
	Pouilly-Fumé	Loire	Dry white
	Sauvignon Blanc	France or New World	Dry white

PÂTÉS AND TERRINES

Foie gras	Champagne (Blanc de Blancs)	Champagne	Sparkling
	Corton-Charlemagne	Burgundy	Dry red
	Monbazillac	South-west France	Sweet white
	Pineau des Charentes	Cognac	Vin de liqueur
	Pinot Gris VT	Alsace	Dry to medium-dry white
	Riesling Auslese	Germany	Sweet white
	Ste-Croix-du-Mont	South-west France	Sweet white
	Sauternes/Barsac	Bordeaux	Sweet white
	Vin de Paille	Jura	Vin doux naturel
Pâtés *see also* **Foie gras**	Barsac	Bordeaux	Sweet white
	Ste-Croix-du-Mont	South-west France	Sweet white

Pea and ham soup *see* **Soups**

Peanuts *see* **Nuts**

Peanut sauce *see* **Sauces**

Pecan pie see **Desserts and cakes**

Peking duck see **Oriental food**

Pepper sauce see **Sauces**

Peppers see **Vegetables**

Pheasant see **Game**

Pigeon see **Poultry**

Pike see **Fish**

Pineapples and pineapple-based desserts see **Desserts and cakes**

Piperade see **Egg dishes**

Pissaladière (onion tart) see **Vegetables**

Pizzas see **Pasta and pizza dishes**

Plaice see **Fish**

Polenta see **Pulses and grains**

Potato salad see **Salads**

PORK
see also **Bacon and ham, Charcuterie, cured and cold meats, Meat dishes**

Choucroute garni	Chablis (unoaked)	Burgundy	Dry white
	Crozes-Hermitage	Rhône	Dry white
	Pinot Blanc	Alsace	Dry white
	Riesling	Austria	Dry white
Pork chops, grilled	Corbières	Languedoc	Dry red
	Côtes de Duras	South-west France	Dry red
	Pinot Gris	Alsace	Dry white
	Pinot Noir	New World	Dry red
Roast pork	Bairrada	Portugal	Dry red
	Chardonnay	New World	Dry white
	Chianti	Italy	Dry red
	Tempranillo	Spain	Dry red
	Pinot Gris	Alsace	Dry white
Roast pork with apple sauce	Gewürztraminer VT	Alsace	Medium-dry white
	Riesling Spätlese	Germany	Sweet white
Sausage and mash	Corbières	Languedoc	Dry red
	Fitou	Languedoc	Dry red
	Gigondas	Rhône	Dry red
	Kékfrankos	Hungary	Dry red
	Zinfandel	California	Dry red

Toad-in-the-hole	Periquita	Portugal	Dry red
	Navarra	Spain	Dry red
	Shiraz	Australia	Dry red

Pot-au-feu *see* **Beef dishes**

Pot roast *see* **Meat dishes**

POULTRY
see also **Chicken**

Confit du canard	Cahors	South-west France	Dry red
	Merlot	New World	Dry red
	Pommard	Burgundy	Dry red
	St-Emilion	Bordeaux	Dry red
	Saumur-Champigny	Loire	Dry red
Duck à l'orange	Cahors	South-west France	Dry red
	Côtes de Provence	Provence	Dry red
	Gewürztraminer	Alsace	Dry white
	Graves	Bordeaux	Dry red
	Riesling Auslese	Germany	Sweet white
	Rosso Cònero	Italy	Dry red
	Shiraz	Australia	Dry red

Duck liver *see* **Pâtés and terrines**

Duck, Peking *see* **Oriental foods**

Duck, roast	Bonnes-Mares	Burgundy	Dry red
	Châteauneuf-du-Pape	Rhône	Dry red
	Madiran	South-west France	Dry red
	Pomerol	Bordeaux	Dry red
	Pommard	Burgundy	Dry red
	Zinfandel	California	Dry red
Goose stuffed with prunes or other fruit	Champagne	Champagne	Dry sparkling
	Châteauneuf-du-Pape	Rhône	Dry red
	Chianti Classico	Italy	Dry red
	Gigondas	Rhône	Dry red
	Margaux	Bordeaux	Dry red
	Pacherenc du Vic-Bilh	South-west France	Dry or sweet white
	Pomerol	Bordeaux	Dry red
	Shiraz	Australia	Dry red
	Vouvray	Loire	Medium-dry white
Pigeon	Buzet	South-west France	Dry red
	Crozes-Hermitage	Rhône	Dry red
	Pinotage	South Africa	Dry red
	St-Emilion	Bordeaux	Dry red
	Vacqueyras	Rhône	Dry red

Quail	Champagne	Champagne	Sparkling
	Pinot Noir	Italy	Dry red
	St-Emilion	Bordeaux	Dry red
	Saumur-Champigny	Loire	Dry red
	Volnay	Burgundy	Dry red
Turkey, roast with	Chardonnay	California	Dry white
all the trimmings	Châteauneuf-du-Pape	Rhône	Dry red
	Vosne-Romanée	Burgundy	Dry red
	Zinfandel	California	Dry red

Prawns see **Seafood**

Prosciutto see **Charcuterie, cured and cold meats**

PULSES AND GRAINS

Baked beans	Bourgueil	Loire	Dry red
	Cabernet Franc	New World	Dry red
	Zinfandel	California	Dry red
Cassoulet	Barbaresco	Italy	Dry red
	Cahors	South-west France	Dry red
	Corbières	Languedoc	Dry red
	Mourvèdre	France or New World	Dry red
	Shiraz	Australia	Dry red
	Zinfandel	California	Dry red
Couscous	Cabernet Sauvignon/Cinsault	Lebanon	Dry red
	Navarra	Spain	Dry red
	Pinotage	South Africa	Dry red
	Shiraz	Australia	Dry red
Houmus	Furmint	Hungary	Dry white
	Pinot Grigio	Italy	Dry white
	Zitsa	Greece	Dry white
Polenta	Ajaccio rosé	Corsica	Dry rosé
	Côtes de Provence rosé	Provence	Dry rosé
	Vin de Corse	Corsica	Dry red
Risotto alla	Côtes du Rhône	Rhône	Dry red
Milanese	Pinot Grigio	Italy	Dry white
	Soave	Italy	Dry white
	Trebbiano d'Abruzzo	Italy	Dry red
Risotto alla	Bardolino	Italy	Dry red
Parmigiana	Bianco di Custoza	Italy	Dry white
see also **Wine and**	Dolcetto d'Alba	Italy	Dry red
Cheese (page 87–9)			

Tabbouleh	Bandol rosé	Provence	Dry rosé
	Bellet rosé	Provence	Dry rosé
	Côtes du Jura	Jura	Dry red

Pumpkin pie see **Vegetables**

Quail see **Poultry**

Quails' eggs see **Egg dishes**

Rabbit see **Game**

Raclette see **Cheese dishes**

Raspberries and raspberry-based desserts see **Desserts and cakes**

Ratatouille see **Vegetables**

Red cabbage with apples see **Vegetables**

Red mullet see **Fish**

Red wine sauce see **Sauces**

Risottos see **Pulses and grains**

Sachertorte see **Desserts and cakes**

Salade niçoise see **Salads**

SALADS

Caesar salad	Champagne	Champagne	Sparkling
	Chardonnay	Chile	Dry white
	Rully	Burgundy	Dry white
Chef's salad	Chardonnay	California	Dry white
(with eggs,	Soave	Italy	Dry white
tomatoes and	Viognier	California	Dry white
cheese)			
Chicken salad	Beaujolais	Burgundy	Dry red
	Bordeaux rosé	Bordeaux	Dry rosé
	Chardonnay	California	Dry white
	Sauvignon Blanc	New Zealand	Dry white
Green salad with	Aligoté	Burgundy	Dry white
oil and vinegar	Cheverny	Loire	Dry white
dressing	Muscadet	Loire	Dry white
	Sancerre	Loire/Centre	Dry white
	Vinho Verde	Portugal	Dry white
Potato salad	Côtes de Provence rosé	Provence	Dry rosé
	Pinot Noir	Alsace	Dry red
	Riesling	Alsace	Dry white

Salade niçoise	Cheverny	Loire	Dry white
	Coteaux d'Aix en Provence rosé	Provence	Dry rosé
	Côtes du Rhône	Rhône	Dry red
Seafood salad	Soave	Italy	Dry white
	Verdicchio	Italy	Dry white
Tomato salad	Barbera d'Asti	Italy	Dry red
	Riesling Spätlese	Germany	Sweet white
	Sauvignon Blanc	New Zealand	Dry white
Tuna salad	Côtes de Provence rosé	Provence	Dry rosé
	Valpolicella	Italy	Dry red
	Vin de Corse	Corsica	Dry white
Waldorf salad	Muscat de Beaumes-de-Venise	Rhône	Vin doux naturel
	Riesling VT	Alsace	Sweet white
	Sauternes	Bordeaux	Sweet white

Sandwiches *see principal ingredient*

Salami *see* **Charcuterie, cured and cold meats**

Salmon *see* **Fish**

Salt cod *see* **Fish**

Salsa *see* **Sauces**

Saltimbocca alla Romana *see* **Veal**

Sardines *see* **Fish**

Sashimi *see* **Oriental food**

Satay *see* **Oriental food**

SAUCES

Aioli	Bordeaux rosé	Bordeaux	Dry rosé
	Palette rosé	Provence	Dry rosé
	Soave	Italy	Dry white
Béarnaise sauce	Frascati Superiore	Italy	Medium-dry white
	Riesling Kabinett	Germany	Dry white
	Sancerre	Loire/Centre	Dry white
	Vouvray	Loire	Medium-dry white
Bolognese sauce	Cabernet Sauvignon	Australia	Dry red
	Merlot	Chile	Dry red
	Montepulciano d'Abruzzo	Italy	Dry red
	Rosso Cònero	Italy	Dry red
Butter-based sauces	Bâtard-Montrachet	Burgundy	Dry white

Carbonara sauce *see* **Pasta dishes**

Chilli sauce	Côtes de Provence rosé	Provence	Dry rosé
	Côtes du Rhône	Rhône	Dry red
	Fitou	Languedoc	Dry red
	Shiraz	Australia	Dry red

Clam sauce *see* **Pasta dishes**

Cranberry sauce	Mourvèdre	France or New World	Dry red
	Riesling Kabinett	Germany	Dry white
	Shiraz	Australia	Dry red

| **Cream-based sauces** | Bâtard-Montrachet | Burgundy | Dry white |

Cream and morels sauce *see* **Chicken**

Creamy herb sauce *see* **Fish, eels**

Green gooseberry sauce *see* **Fish, mackerel**

Hollandaise sauce	Bâtard-Montrachet	Burgundy	Dry white
	Sancerre	Loire/Centre	Dry white
	Vouvray	Loire	Dry white

Horseradish sauce	Riesling	Alsace	Dry white
	Sancerre	Loire/Centre	Dry white
	Shiraz	Australia	Dry white

| **Mayonnaise** | Chablis (unoaked) | Burgundy | Dry white |
| | Chardonnay (unoaked) | New World | Dry white |

Mint sauce	Cabernet Sauvignon	Australia	Dry red
	Gevrey-Chambertin	Burgundy	Dry red
	Pomerol	Bordeaux	Dry red

Mustard sauce	Chardonnay	Chile	Dry white
	Riesling	Alsace	Dry white
	Sancerre	Loire/Centre	Dry white

Peanut sauce	Gewürztraminer	Alsace	Dry white
	Muscat	Alsace	Dry white
	Pinot Gris	Alsace	Dry white

Pepper sauce	Mourvèdre	France or New World	Dry red
	Pomerol	Bordeaux	Dry red
	Pommard	Burgundy	Dry red
	Shiraz	Australia	Dry red
	Zinfandel	California	Dry red

Pesto sauce *see* **Pasta dishes**

Red wine sauce *use the same wine that is used in the sauce or one of these alternatives.*

| | Barbaresco | Italy | Dry red |
| | Brunello di Montalcino | Italy | Dry red |

Red wine sauce *(continued)*	Cabernet Sauvignon	New World	Dry red
	Côtes du Rhône	Rhône	Dry red
Salsa, red and green	Bandol rosé	Provence	Dry rosé
	Sauvignon Blanc	France or New World	Dry white
	Vinho Verde	Portugal	Dry white

Sauce chasseur *see* **Chicken**

Sweet and sour sauce	Gewürztraminer	Alsace	Dry white
	Pinot Gris VT	Alsace	Semi-sweet white
	Sauvignon Blanc	Australia	Dry white
	Vouvray	Alsace	Sweet white
Tomato sauce	Aligoté	Burgundy	Dry white
	Sancerre	Loire/Centre	Dry white
	Sauvignon Blanc	France or New World	Dry white
Vinaigrette sauce	Cheverny	Loire	Dry white
	Pouilly-Fumé	Loire	Dry white
	Vinho Verde	Portugal	Dry white
White sauce	Chardonnay	New World	Dry white
	Chassagne-Montrachet	Burgundy	Dry white
	Meursault	Burgundy	Dry white
White wine sauce	Chablis	Burgundy	Dry white
	Graves	Bordeaux	Dry white
	Muscadet	Loire	Dry white
	Pinot Gris VT	Alsace	Semi-sweet white
	Sauvignon Blanc	France or New World	Dry white

Satay *see* **Oriental food**

Sauerbraten *see* **Vegetables**

Sausages *see* **Charcuterie, cured and cold meats, Pork**

Sausage and mash *see* **Pork**

Scallops *see* **Seafood dishes**

Scrambled eggs *see* **Egg dishes**

SEAFOOD DISHES
see also **Fish**

Calamari *see* **Squid**

Caviar	Champagne (non-vintage)	Champagne	Sparkling
	Châteauneuf-du-Pape	Rhône	Dry white
	Puligny-Montrachet	Burgundy	Dry white
	Pinot Gris	Alsace	Dry white

Coquilles St Jacques *see* **Scallops**

Crab	Chablis	Burgundy	Dry white
	Crépy	Savoie	Dry white
	Crozes-Hermitage	Rhône	Dry white
	Entre-deux-mers	Bordeaux	Dry white
	Muscadet	Loire	Dry white
Lobster	Bordeaux Sec	Bordeaux	Dry white
	Champagne (Blancs de Blancs)	Champagne	Sparkling
	Chardonnay	California	Dry white
	Condrieu	Rhône	Dry white
	Meursault	Burgundy	Dry white

Lobster bisque *see* **Clam chowder**

Moules et frîtes	Muscadet	Loire	Dry white
	Sancerre	Loire/Centre	Dry white
	Verdicchio	Italy	Dry white
Moules marinière	Chablis	Burgundy	Dry white
	Entre-deux-mers	Bordeaux	Dry white
	Pouilly-Fumé	Loire	Dry white
	Riesling	Alsace	Dry white

Mussels *see* **Moules**

Octopus	Bellet	Provence	Dry white
	Gigondas rosé	Rhône	Dry rosé
	Rioja	Spain	Dry white
	Zinfandel	California	Dry white
Oysters	Aligoté	Burgundy	Dry white
	Entre-deux-mers	Bordeaux	Dry white
	Gavi	Italy	Dry white
	Muscadet	Loire	Dry white
	Sancerre	Loire/Centre	Dry white
Paella	Côtes de Provence rosé	Provence	Dry rosé
	Penedès	Spain	Dry white
	Pouilly-Fumé	Loire	Dry white
	Rioja rosé	Spain	Dry rosé
Prawn cocktail	Bergerac	South-west France	Dry white
	Muscadet	Loire	Dry white
	Sauvignon Blanc	France or New World	Dry white
Prawns	Champagne	Champagne	Sparkling
	Chassagne-Montrachet	Burgundy	Dry white
	Sauvignon Blanc	New Zealand	Dry white
	Sauvignon Colli Orientali del Friuli	Italy	Dry white
	Soave	Italy	Dry white

Scallops in cream and tarragon sauce	Bâtard-Montrachet	Burgundy	Dry white
	Champagne	Champagne	Sparkling
	Meursault	Burgundy	Dry white
	Sauvignon Blanc	New Zealand	Dry white
Scallops, grilled	Graves	Bordeaux	Dry white
	Muscadet	Loire	Dry white
	Savennières	Loire	Dry white
Seafood dishes	Bianco di Custoza	Italy	Dry white
	Sancerre	Loire/Centre	Dry white
	Sauvignon Blanc	France or New World	Dry white
	Verdicchio	Italy	Dry white

Seafood salad see **Salads**

Squid cooked in their own juices	Ajaccio	Corsica	Dry red
	Côtes de Bordeaux	Bordeaux	Dry white
	Gaillac	France	Dry white
	Mâcon	Burgundy	Dry white
	Valdepeñas	Spain	Dry red

Shepherd's pie see **Lamb**

Sole see **Fish**

Sorbets see **Desserts and cakes**

Soufflés see **Egg dishes**

SOUPS

Bean and pasta soup	Bergerac	South-west France	Dry red
	Buzet	South-west France	Dry red
	Côte-Rôtie	Rhône	Dry red
	Shiraz	Australia	Dry red
Borscht	Chianti	Italy	Dry red
	Copertino	Italy	Dry red
	Kékfrankos	Hungary	Dry red
Bouillabaisse	Riesling	Alsace	Dry white
	Tavel	Provence	Dry rosé
	Vin de Corse	Corsica	Dry white
Carrot soup	Chablis Grand Cru	Burgundy	Dry white
	Chardonnay	California	Dry white
	Viognier	Italy	Dry white
Clam chowder	Chablis Grand Cru	Burgundy	Dry white
	Chardonnay	Long Island, USA	Dry white
	L'Etoile	Jura	Dry white
	Riesling	Alsace	Dry white
	Pinot Gris	Alsace	Dry white

Corn chowder	Chardonnay	California	Dry white
	Meursault	Burgundy	Dry white
	Rully	Burgundy	Dry white
Curried tomato soup	Crozes-Hermitage	Rhône	Dry white
	Gewürztraminer	Alsace	Dry white
	Marsanne	New World	Dry white
	Rioja Reserva	Spain	Dry red
Gazpacho	Buzet	South-west France	Dry red
	St-Georges-St-Emilion	Bordeaux	Dry red
	Sauvignon Blanc	New Zealand	Dry white
	Soave	Italy	Dry white
	Viognier	New World	Dry white
Minestrone	Alenquer	Portugal	Dry white
	Chianti	Italy	Dry white
	Corbières	Languedoc	Dry white
Pea and ham soup	Chardonnay	Chile	Dry white
	Madiran	South-west France	Dry red
	Pinotage	South Africa	Dry red
Vichyssoise	Bergerac	South-west France	Dry white
	Sancerre	Loire/Centre	Dry white
	Vacqueyras	Rhône	Dry white

Southern fried chicken *see* **Chicken dishes**

Squid *see* **Seafood dishes**

Steak *see* **Beef dishes**

Steak and kidney pie *see* **Beef dishes**

Steak tartare *see* **Beef dishes**

Stir-fries *see* **Oriental food**

Strawberries and strawberry-based desserts *see* **Desserts and cakes**

Sushi *see* **Oriental food**

Sweet potatoes, candied *see* **Vegetables**

Sweetbreads *see* **Offal**

Swordfish *see* **Fish**

Tabbouleh *see* **Pulses and grains**

Tandoori *see* **Indian food**

Tapas *see* **Appetizers**

Tapenade *see* **Appetizers**

Taramasalata *see* **Appetizers**

T

Tarragon chicken *see* **Chicken dishes**

Tarte tatin *see* **Desserts and cakes**

Tempura *see* **Oriental food**

Terrines *see* **Pâtés and terrines**

Thai food *see* **Oriental food**

Tiramisu *see* **Desserts and cakes**

Toad-in-the-hole *see* **Pork**

Tomato salad *see* **Salads**

Tomatoes *see* **Sauces**

Tongue *see* **Charcuterie, cured and cold meats**

Treacle tart *see* **Desserts and cakes**

Trifle *see* **Desserts and cakes**

Tripe *see* **Offal**

Trout *see* **Fish**

Truffles *see* **Vegetables**

Tuna salad *see* **Salads**

Turkey *see* **Poultry**

 Vanilla-based desserts *see* **Desserts and cakes**

VEAL
see also **Meat dishes**

Blanquette de veau	Côtes de Provence rosé	Provence	Dry rosé
	Minervois rosé	Languedoc-Roussillon	Dry rosé
	Muscadet	Loire	Dry white
	Riesling Grand Cru	Alsace	Dry white
Osso bucco	Barbera d'Asti	Italy	Dry red
	Crozes-Hermitage	Rhône	Dry white
	Dolcetto d'Alba	Italy	Dry red
	Gigondas	Rhône	Dry red
	Patrimonio	Corsica	Dry red
	Valpolicella	Italy	Dry red
Saltimbocca alla Romana	Barbera d'Asti	Italy	Dry red
	Rosso Cònero	Italy	Dry red
	Sangiovese	California	Dry red
Roast veal or veal cutlets	Côte de Beaune	Burgundy	Dry red
	Graves	Bordeaux	Dry white

Roast veal or veal cutlets *(continued)*	Margaux	Bordeaux	Dry red
	Pinot Gris	Alsace	Dry white
	Riesling	Alsace	Dry white
Wiener schnitzel	Chinon	Loire	Dry red
	Grüner Veltliner	Austria	Dry white
	Sancerre	Loire/Centre	Dry white
	Weissburgunder	Germany	Dry red

VEGETABLES

Artichokes	Chardonnay (unoaked)	Burgundy or New World	Dry white
	Rully	Burgundy	Dry white
	Sauvignon Blanc	New Zealand	Dry white
	Viognier	Rhône or New World	Dry white
Asparagus	Bourgueil	Loire	Dry red
	Chinon	Loire	Dry red
	Gewürztraminer	Alsace	Dry white
	Muscat (dry)	Alsace	Dry white
	Sauvignon Blanc	New Zealand	Dry white
Asparagus in cream sauce	L'Etoile	Jura	Dry white
	Meursault	Burgundy	Dry white
	Muscat	Alsace	Dry white
	Petit Chablis	Burgundy	Dry white
Asparagus in vinaigrette sauce	St-Véran	Burgundy	Dry white
	Tavel	Rhône	Dry rosé
Aubergine	Corbières	Languedoc	Dry red
	Dão	Portugal	Dry red
	Vin de Corse	Corsica	Dry red
	Zinfandel	California	Dry red
Aubergine with Parmesan	Barbaresco	Italy	Dry red
	Barolo	Italy	Dry red
	Brunello di Montalcino	Italy	Dry red
Brussels sprouts	Arbois	Jura	Dry white
	Côtes de Provence	Provence	Dry red
	Pinot Noir	New World	Dry red
Cabbage, stuffed	Bourgueil	Loire	Dry red
	Crozes-Hermitage	Rhône	Dry red
	Shiraz	Australia	Dry red

Carrot cake *see* **Desserts and cakes**

Corn bread	Chardonnay	California	Dry white
	Côtes du Jura	Jura	Dry red
	Merlot	New World	Dry red
	Vin de Corse	Corsica	Dry red

Corn on the cob   Chardonnay   California   Dry white
                      Pinot Gris   Alsace   Dry white

Crudités *see* **Vegetables, raw**

Gratin dauphinois Châteauneuf-du-Pape Rhône   Dry white
                      L'Etoile   Jura   Dry white
                      Riesling   Alsace   Dry white

Mushrooms *see page 85*

Onions, creamed   Gewürztraminer   Alsace   Dry white
                      Palette   Provence   Dry white
                      Riesling   Alsace   Dry white

Onion tart   Arbois rosé   Jura   Dry rosé
(pissaladière)   Bellet rosé   Provence   Dry rosé
                      Corbières   Languedoc   Dry white
                      Côtes de Provence   Provence   Dry white
                      Pinot Blanc   Alsace   Dry white
                      Pinot Gris   Alsace   Dry white
                      Tavel   Rhône   Dry rosé

Peppers, roasted or Bandol rosé   Provence   Dry rosé
stuffed   Bellet rosé   Provence   Dry rosé
                      Mâcon   Burgundy   Dry white
                      Regaleali Rosato   Italy   Dry rosé
                      Pinot Gris   Alsace   Dry white

Pumpkin pie   Monbazillac   South-west France   Sweet white
                      Savennières   Loire   Dry white
                      Sémillon   New World   Sweet white

Ratatouille   Corbières   Languedoc   Dry red
                      Côtes de Provence rosé Provence   Dry rosé
                      Minervois   Languedoc-Roussillon Dry red
                      Zinfandel   California   Dry red

Red cabbage with Champagne   Champagne   Sparkling
apples   Gewürztraminer   Alsace   Dry white
                      Riesling Auslese   Germany   Sweet white
                      Shiraz   Australia   Dry red

Sauerbraten   Baden Spätburgunder Germany   Dry red
                      Barbaresco   Italy   Dry red
                      Gewürztraminer VT   Alsace   Medium-dry white
                      Morgon   Beaujolais   Dry red
                      Pinot Noir   Alsace   Dry red

Sweet potatoes,   Crozes-Hermitage   Rhône   Dry white
candied   Monbazillac   South-west France   Sweet white
                      Viognier   California   Dry white

Tomatoes *see* **Sauces, tomato**

Truffles, black and white	Barbaresco	Italy	Dry red
	Cahors	South-west France	Dry red
	Champagne (Blanc de Blancs)	Champagne	Sparkling
	Chassagne-Montrachet	Burgundy	Dry white
	Echezeaux	Burgundy	Dry red
	Pomerol	Bordeaux	Dry red
	Vosne-Romanée	Burgundy	Dry red
Vegetables, grilled or roasted	Beaujolais-Villages	Burgundy	Dry red
	Cassis	Provence	Dry white
	Corbières	Languedoc	Dry white
	Palette	Provence	Dry white
	Rueda	Spain	Dry white
	St-Joseph	Rhône	Dry white
Vegetables, raw	Bardolino	Italy	Dry red
	Beaujolais	Burgundy	Dry red
	Pinot Blanc	Alsace	Dry white
	Pinot Grigio	Italy	Dry white
	Sauvignon Blanc	France or New World	Dry white

Venison see **Game**

Vichyssoise see **Soups**

Vinaigrette sauce see **Sauces**

Waldorf salad see **Salads**

W

Walnuts see **Nuts**

Weiner schnitzel see **Veal**

White sauce see **Sauces**

Wild boar see **Game**

Wines and Foods Index

Wine	Region	Colour/Style	Food
A **Ajaccio**	Corsica	Dry red	Lamb crown roast Roast pork Spicy sausages Squid cooked in their own juices
		Dry rosé	Polenta Bouillabaisse Ratatouille
Alenquer	Portugal	Dry white	Grilled sardines Minestrone Salt cod balls Tapas
Aligoté	Burgundy	Dry white	Cod Blue cheese dip Escargots à la Bourguignonne, oysters and mussels Green salad with oil and vinegar dressing Tomato sauce-based dishes Trout
Alto Adige Chardonnay	Italy	Dry white	Chicken salad Fettucine Alfredo, pasta with carbonara sauce Savoury crêpes Tuna salad
Amarone della Valpolicella	Italy	Dry red	Rissotto alla Parmigiana Red meat stews and casseroles
Amontillado Sherry	Spain	Fortified red	Almonds, walnuts, hazelnuts and peanuts Chorizo Manchego cheese and ewe's milk cheeses Olives and tapas Wild boar

Anjou	Loire	Dry red	Bacon, gammon and ham dishes Charcuterie Pot-au-feu White meats
Arbois	Jura	Dry red	Game Spicy meat dishes
		Dry rosé	Chutney Lamb dishes Onion tart
		Dry white	Andouillette, grilled with mustard Brandy-based desserts Brussels sprouts Cauliflower cheese Chicken curry Haddock and white fish dishes Kebabs Sushi
Asti Spumante	Italy	Sparkling	Chestnut, mint or fruit-based desserts Christmas pudding Meringues
Baden Spätburgunder	Germany	Dry red	Goulash, beef stews and casseroles Sauerbraten
Bairrada	Portugal	Dry red	Garlic-based sauces Haggis Roast pork Roast vegetables in oil and herbs
Bandol	Provence	Dry red	Barbecued meats Boeuf en daube Ravioli niçoise Roasted vegetables Venison with cranberries or juniper berry sauce Wild boar
		Dry rosé	Anchovies or anchovy paste Fish and chips Roasted or stuffed peppers Piperade Salade niçoise Tabbouleh Tapas
Banyuls	Roussillon	Vin doux naturel	Chocolate, coffee or strawberry-based desserts Christmas pudding

B

141

Barbaresco	Italy	Dry red	Aubergine with Parmesan Cassoulet Fish in red wine and red wine sauce dishes Sauerbraten Truffles, black and white
Barbera d'Asti	Italy	Dry red	Anchovy paste and dips Bolognese sauce, lasagne and pizza or pasta with meat and béchamel sauce Osso bucco Pasta with carbonara or pesto sauce Prociutto Risottos, especially mushroom Salami-based dishes Saltimbocca alla Romana Tomato salad

Bardolino	Italy	Dry red	Antipasti and charcuterie
			Melon with Parma ham
			Pasta with carbonara sauce
			Pasta dishes with meat and béchamel
			  sauce
			Raw vegetables
			Risotto alla Parmigiana and other
			  risottos
			Salami-based dishes

Barolo	Italy	Dry red	Aubergine with Parmesan Beef bourguignon, boeuf en daube, brasato al Barolo Game, grouse and pheasant Sirloin steak
Barsac	Bordeaux	Sweet white	Caramel and fruit-based desserts Pâtés and terrines Spicy ethnic foods
Bâtard- Montrachet	Burgundy	Dry white	Hollandaise sauce Most butter or cream-based sauces Scallops in cream and tarragon sauce White fish dishes
Beaujolais	Burgundy	Dry red	Bacon and ham Charcuterie and boudin blanc (white pudding) Chicken salad Grilled, roast and raw vegetables Hamburgers Kidneys

Beaujolais *(continued)*			Macaroni cheese Raspberry-based desserts Refried beans, Mexican and chilli dishes
Bellet	Provence	Dry rosé	Pissaladière Roasted or stuffed peppers Tabbouleh
		Dry white	Octopus Salade niçoise Sole meunière
Bergerac	South-west France	Dry red	Bean and pasta soup Fried fish Potted or jugged hare Lancashire hotpot Melon with Parma ham Pot-au-feu Roasted meats, both white and red Tongue
		Dry white	Cassis-based desserts Fish and chips Quiche lorraine Prawn cocktail Vichyssoise
Bianco di Custoza	Italy	Dry white	Pasta with spinach and ricotta Pizza with seafood and other seafood dishes Quiche lorraine Risotto alla Parmigiana
Bianco di Scandiano	Italy	Dry white	Melon with Parma ham Pasta with cream and cheese sauces Poached oysters in vegetable broth Seafood dishes
Black Muscat	California	Sweet white	Cherry-based desserts Chocolate Caramelized oranges
Blanquette de Limoux	Languedoc	Sparkling	Apricot and cherry-based desserts Lemon chicken Sweet and savoury soufflés
Bonnes-Mares	Burgundy	Dry red	Beef and chicken potpies Dry sausages Hare, game, grouse and partridge Mushroom and red wine sauces Roast duck or goose Savoury cheese dishes

Bordeaux and Bordeaux Supérieur	Bordeaux	Dry red	Barbecued red meats Cold lamb or beef Croque monsieur or madame Meat fondue Southern fried chicken
		Dry rosé	Aioli Beef Strognanoff Chicken salad Indian food with spicy yogurt sauces
		Dry white	Barbecued fish Haggis Light, white meat dishes Lobster Meatloaf Roast chicken Savoury crêpes
Bourgeuil	Loire	Dry red	Asparagus Baked beans Baked ham with pineapple Chicken chasseur Smoked eels Escargots à la Bourguignonne Shepherd's pie Stuffed cabbage
Brouilly	Burgundy	Dry red	Beef bourguignon Cold meats Grilled and roasted vegetables Omelette with tomato, quiches and pizzas
Brunello di Montalcino	Italy	Dry red	Aubergine with Parmesan Oxtail Red meat stews and casseroles Red wine sauce-based dishes
Buzet	South-west France	Dry red	Bean and pasta soup Buffalo wings Gazpacho Pigeon Potted or jugged hare Shepherd's pie Southern fried chicken Steak and kidney pie
C **Cabernet Sauvignon**		Dry red	All beef dishes Herbs: thyme, rosemary and mint

Cabernet Sauvignon (continued)	Argentina		Chilli con carne, spiced pork and sausages
	Australia		Bolognese sauce Kangaroo Roast lamb with mint sauce
	California		Hamburgers Meatloaf Sirloin steak
	Chile		Charcuterie
	New World		Haggis and kidneys Red wine sauce-based dishes
Cabernet Sauvignon/ Cinsault	Lebanon	Dry red	Barbecued meats Couscous Lamb with herbes de provence Pizza bolognese Venison with cranberry or juniper berry sauce Wild boar
Cadillac	Bordeaux	Sweet white	Blue cheese dip Cheesecake Pineapple-based desserts Trifle
Cahors	South-west France	Dry red	Cassoulet Confit du canard Duck à l'orange Red meat stews and casseroles Refried beans and other Mexican dishes Steak and kidney pie Steak tartare Tarragon chicken Tongue Truffles, black and white
Cassis	Provence	Dry white	Grilled and roasted vegetables Light lamb dishes
Cava	Spain	Sparkling	Custard dessesrts Quiches, scrambled eggs with smoked salmon Tapas
Chablis	Burgundy	Dry white	Avocado Bagels with salmon and cream cheese Crab, escargots à la Bourguignonne, moules marinières

Chablis *(continued)*			Gougère Jambon persillé Salmon, sole meunière, plaice and other white fish dishes Taramasalata Tempura Thai food White wine sauce-based dishes
		Grand Cru	Almonds Carrot soup Clam chowder
		Premier Cru	Chicken in cream and morels sauce
		Oaked	Smoked salmon
		Unoaked	Mayonnaise Choucroute garni
Chacoli de Guetaria	Spain	Dry white	Chorizo and other dried spicy sausages Piperade Spicy casseroles
Chambertain	Burgundy	Dry red	Grouse and guinea fowl Venison with cranberry or juniper berry sauce
Chambolle-Musigny	Burgundy	Dry red	Meat and mushroom dishes Pheasant Omelette with truffles

Champagne	Champagne	Sparkling	Everything!
			Accra
			Bagels with salmon and cream cheese
			Blinis and buttermilk pancakes
			Caesar salad
			Cheesecake
			Cheeses, especially blue and goats'
			Chocolate, coffee, brandy and fruit-
			  based desserts
			Christmas pudding
			Guacamole
			Ice cream and sorbets
			Indian food
			Japanese food
			Kedgeree
			Kippers
			Lobster, prawns and scallops in cream
			  and tarragon
			Omelettes, eggs Benedict and quail's
			  eggs

Champagne *(continued)*			Quail Red cabbage with apples Soufflés with broccoli and cheese, spinach and chocolate Truffles, black and white
		Blanc de Blancs	Escargots Foie gras Liver
		Brut	Avocado Beef Wellington Smoked salmon
		Demi-sec	Caramel-based desserts Sweet crêpes
		Non-vintage	Caviar Chinese food Indian food
		Rosé	Carpaccio Cassis-based desserts Lamb with mint sauce Lemon chicken Scrambled eggs with smoked salmon
Chardonnay		Dry white oaked	Kippers Roast chicken Smoked salmon White fish dishes
	Burgundy	Unoaked	Artichokes Asparagus Bacon Carrot soup and pea and ham soup Chef's salad and chicken salad Cheese fondue Chicken in cream and morels sauce Cold salmon and smoked salmon Croque monsieur or madame Omelette with cheese and eggs Benedict Pasta with clam sauce Roast pork Tongue Soufflé with spinach White sauce-based dishes
	New World		Blackened fish Bruschetta Caesar salad

Chardonnay *(continued)*			Clam chowder Corn bread, corn chowder and corn on the cob Fish cakes and grilled bass Guacamole Indian food Kangaroo Lancashire hotpot Lobster dishes Mayonnaise Mustard sauce Pesto sauce Scrambled eggs with smoked salmon
Chassagne-Montrachet	Burgundy	Dry white	Mushrooms Prawns and delicate seafood dishes Tarragon Truffles, black and white White sauces
Chasselas	Alsace or Switzerland	Dry white	Cheese fondue Chinese food Crab Mild curry dishes Pasta with clam sauce Raclette
Châteauneuf-du-Pape	Rhône	Dry red	Basque chicken and coq au vin Caviar Goose stuffed with prunes Gratin dauphinois Oxtail Partridge Roast duck Roast turkey with traditional trimmings
Chénas	Burgundy	Dry red	*See* **Beaujolais**
Chenin Blanc	Loire or New World	Dry white	Chestnut-based desserts Grilled fish Indian food Lemon chicken and other poultry dishes Oriental dishes containing soy sauce, garlic, ginger and honey Vegetable and fruit salads
Cheverny	Loire	Dry white	Green salad with oil and vinegar dressing Salade niçoise Vinaigrette sauce

Chianti	Italy	Dry red	Borscht Bresaola and carpaccio Goose stuffed with prunes or other fruit Hamburgers Lasagne Omelette with tomato Pizza bolognese Roast pork Sirloin steak
		Dry white	Chicken dishes Light pasta dishes Minestrone Pasta with spinach and Ricotta
Chinon	Loire	Dry red	Asparagus Baked ham and charcuterie Melon with Parma ham Poached, steamed or lightly grilled salmon Quiche lorraine Salt cod balls Sirloin steak with wild mushrooms Wiener Schnitzel
Chiroubles	Burgundy	Dry red	*See* **Beaujolais**
Clos de Vougeot	Burgundy	Dry red	Beef bourguignon Chateaubriand Game
Colli Berici Pinot Bianco	Italy	Dry white	Pasta with spring vegetables Seafood dishes
Colli Orientali del Friuli	Italy	Dry red	Lamb with herbes de provence Lemon chicken Light pasta dishes
Colombard	New World	Dry white	Melon with Parma ham Poached white fish dishes Most salads Thai food
Condrieu	Rhône	Dry white	Ceviche Curry Indian food Lobster Poached, steamed or lightly grilled salmon Sole meunière
Copertino	Italy	Dry red	Borscht Heavy pasta dishes

Copertino *(continued)*			Red meat stews and casseroles Spicy and dried sausages
Corbières	Languedoc	Dry red	Aubergine Cassoulet Chicken in cream and morels sauce, Basque chicken and coq au vin Chorizo Hare Herring Kippers Minestrone Onion tart Pork chops Ratatouille Roasted meats, especially beef Sausage and mash
Cornas	Rhône	Dry red	Hare Red meat stews and casseroles Steak tartare
Corton	Burgundy	Dry red	Duck Game Red meat dishes Red wine sauce-based dishes
Corton- Charlemagne	Burgundy	Dry red	Foie gras Scallops Veal dishes White oily fish dishes White wine sauces with morels
Côte de Beaune	Burgundy	Dry red	Meat fondue Sweatbreads Pizza bolognese Veal dishes
Côte de Brouilly	Burgundy	Dry red	*See* **Beaujolais**
Côte-Rôtie	Rhône	Dry red	Bean and pasta soup Roasted meats, game and poultry Smoked meats
Coteaux d'Aix en Provence	Provence	Dry rosé or white	Cold salmon Lamb chops Red mullet Salade niçoise
Coteaux du Layon	Loire	Sweet white	Boudin blanc (white pudding) Cheesecake Fruit-based desserts and fruit salad

Côtes de Bourg	Bordeaux	Dry red	Casseroles and stews Heavy bean and rice dishes Lamb shoulder Pasta in tomato and meat sauces
Côtes de Duras	South-west France	Dry red	Casseroles and stews Rabbit and hare Roast pork dishes
Côtes du Jura	Jura	Dry red	Corn bread and cornmeal-based dishes Roasted meats, especially lamb and game Tabbouleh
		Dry white	Soufflé with spinach *See also* **Arbois, Poulsard**
Côtes de Provence	Provence	Dry red	Anchovy and olive pastes Brussels sprouts and baked or roasted vegetable dishes Duck à l'orange Mediterranean dishes
		Dry rosé	Blanquette de veau Kebabs Lamb chops and lamb with herbes de provence Liver and sweetbreads Paella Polenta Potato and tuna salad Ratatouille Salt cod with garlic, oil and cream Seafood pizza
		Dry white	Black pudding Olives
Côtes du Rhône	Rhône	Dry red	Black pudding Charcuterie Cheese fondue and raclette Chicken curry and coq au vin Chilli con carne Cornish pasties Meat fondue Gougère Mexican food Moussaka Omelette with mushrooms Red wine sauce-based dishes Risotto alla Milanese Salade niçoise

Côtes du Roussillon	Roussillon	Dry red	Buffalo wings Escargots à la Bourguignonne
Crémant de Bourgogne	Burgundy	Sparkling	Banana-based desserts Blinis Carrot cake Trifle
Crémant de Loire	Loire	Sparkling	Buttermilk pancakes Creamy fish dishes Custard-based dishes
Crépy	Savoie	Dry white	Cheese fondue and raclette Chinese food Crab Mild curry dishes Pasta with clam sauce
Crozes-Hermitage	Rhône	Dry red	Pigeon and pheasant Steak tartare Stuffed cabbage Tarragon chicken
		Dry white	Candied sweet potatoes Choucroute garni Crab Curried tomato soup Osso bucco
D **Dão**	Portugal	Dry red	Lamb with herbes de provence Moussaka and aubergine dishes Pork dishes
Dolcetto d'Alba	Italy	Dry red	Antipasti Black pudding Fonduta Osso bucco Pasta with meat sauces Risotto alla Parmigiana
E **Echezeaux**	Burgundy	Dry red	Venison, game and roasted meats Mushrooms and mushroom sauces Rich wine sauces Truffles, black and white *See also* **Vosne-Romanée**
Entre-deux-Mers	Bordeaux	Dry white	Barbecued and blackened fish Chicken chasseur Crab Herring Kippers Moules marinières and oysters

L'Etoile	Jura	Dry white	Asparagus in cream sauce Clam chowder Gratin dauphinois Iles flottantes
Falerno del Massico	Italy	Dry white	Antipasti Pasta with Parmesan sauce Veal dishes
Fino Sherry	Spain	Fortified white	Almonds Anchovies or anchovy paste Olives Tapas
Fitou	Languedoc	Dry red	Andouillette Chilli sauce and Mexican dishes Lancashire hotpot Sausage and mash
Fleurie	Burgundy	Dry red	See **Beaujolais**
Frascati Superiore	Italy	Demi-sec white	Béarnaise sauce Fettucine Alfredo Soufflé with spinach
Fronsac	Bordeaux	Dry red	Black pudding Basque chicken Guinea fowl Hare
Furmint	Hungary	Dry white	Curry dishes Goulash Houmus Poultry casseroles
Gaillac	South-west France	Dry white	Crème caramel or brulée Grilled sardines Mackerel with butter and spring onions Squid cooked in their own juices
Gavi	Italy	Dry white	Creamy pasta dishes Mushroom risotto Oysters
Gevrey- Chambertin	Burgundy	Dry red	Coq au vin Mint sauce Mushroom soufflés, tarts and risottos Roast duck and duck à l'orange
Gewürztraminer Vendanges Tardives (VT)	Alsace	Medium-dry white	Baeckaoffa Barbecued meats Brown sugar-based desserts Chinese food, especially chicken or other meats in sweet and sour sauce

F

G

Gewürztraminer **Vendanges** **Tardives** *(continued)*			Creamed onions Curried tomato soup Duck à l'orange Indian food, especially lamb curry Pot roast Red cabbage with apples Roast pork in mustard sauce Sauerbraten Smoked fish Thai food
Gigondas	Rhône	Dry red	Beef bourguignon and goulash Goose stuffed with prunes Octopus Osso bucco Sausage and mash Wild boar
Grave del Fruili	Italy	Sparkling	Light pasta dishes, especially cream or cheese-based Seafood dishes
Graves	Bordeaux	Dry red	Duck à l'orange Fish in red wine Roast beef or steak Steak and kidney pie
		Dry white	Grilled scallops Haddock Mackerel with butter and spring onions Veal White wine sauce-based dishes
Greco di Tufo	Italy	Dry white	Anchovies or anchovy paste Green salad Olives and olive paste Pasta in tomato and cheese sauce Risotto
Grenache	France or New World	Dry red	Andouillette and merguez sausages Beef casseroles Chilli con carne and other spicy meat dishes Steak tartare
Gros Plant	Loire/Nantes	Dry white	Avocados or guacamole Mackerel with green gooseberry sauce and other oily fish dishes Raw vegetables and salads Sashimi

Grüner Veltliner	Austria	Sweet white	Chinese food Roast pork Wiener schnitzel
Hermitage	Rhône	Dry red	Beef Wellington Boeuf en daube and other red meat stews and casseroles Grouse Lamb shoulder	**H**
Irouléguy	South-west France	Dry red	Barbecued meats Basque chicken Chorizo	**I**
Juliénas	Burgundy	Dry red	*See* **Beaujolais**	**J**
Kékfrankos	Hungary	Dry red	Beef bourguignon and beef Stroganoff Moussaka Sausage and mash	**K**
Lirac	Rhône	Dry red	Barbecued meats	**L**
		Dry rosé	Lamb chops Tapenade	
Loupiac	Bordeaux	Sweet white	Bread and butter pudding Chestnut, fruit and raspberry-based desserts and fruit salad or compote Iles flottantes	
Mâcon	Burgundy	Dry white	Cheese fondue Fish and chips Pasta with carbonara sauce Roasted or stuffed peppers Salt cod with garlic, oil and cream Squid cooked their own juices	**M**
Madeira	Spain	Fortified red	Almonds, walnuts, hazelnuts, peanuts Christmas pudding Marzipan desserts	
Madiran	South-west France	Dry red	Basque chicken Pea and ham soup Roast duck	
Malbec	Argentina	Dry red	Beef Wellington Empanadas Roast lamb	
Manzanilla Sherry	Spain	Fortified white	Almonds, walnuts, hazelnuts, peanuts Garlic-based sauces Gazpacho Olives	

Margaux	Bordeaux	Dry red	Chateaubriand Goose stuffed with prunes or other fruit Roast lamb with mint sauce Veal dishes
Marsanne	New World	Dry white	Coconut-based dishes Curry dishes and curried tomato soup White fish in creamy sauces
Mavrud	Bulgaria	Dry red	Beef Stroganoff, goulash, hotpots and casseroles Roast lamb with mint sauce
Médoc	Bordeaux	Dry red	Chicken chasseur Grilled meats Lamb dishes Liver Roast pork and chicken
Mercurey	Burgundy	Dry red	Charcuterie Ham and bacon dishes Macaroni cheese Red mullet Sirloin steak with wild mushrooms Toad-in-the-hole
Merlot	Chile	Dry red	Beef Stroganoff Beef Wellington Bolognese sauce, pizza and hearty pasta dishes Confit de canard Empanadas Sirloin steak
Meursault	Burgundy	Dry white	Asparagus Beef Stroganoff Corn chowder Creamy, buttery dishes Eggs Benedict Guacamole Lobster dishes and scallops in cream and tarragon sauce Tripe White sauce-based dishes
Minervois	Languedoc-Roussillon	Dry red	Andouillette, grilled with mustard Blanquette de veau Grilled meats with garlic and herbs Hare and rabbit Ratatouille

Monbazillac	South-west France	Sweet white	Bread and butter pudding Candied sweet potatoes Cheesecake Foie gras Fruit-based desserts Goats' cheese and blue cheeses Melon with port Pumpkin pie Thai dishes Treacle tart
Montepulciano d'Abruzzo	Italy	Dry red	Bolognese sauce, pizza and pasta dishes with meat and béchamel sauce Lancashire hotpot Salami-based dishes Toad-in-the-hole
Montravel	South-west France	Dry white	Baked ham with pineapple Blue cheeses Chinese food Honey-based sauces and desserts Seafood dishes
Morgon	Burgundy	Dry red	*See* **Beaujolais**
Moscatel de Valencia	Spain	Sweet white	Almond biscuits Fruit-based desserts Treacle tart
Moulin-à-Vent	Burgundy	Dry red	*See* **Beaujolais**
Mourvèdre	France or New World	Dry red	Barbecued meats Cassoulet Cranberry sauce Pepper sauce Tarragon chicken Venison with cranberry or juniper berries
Muscadet and **Muscadet sur Lie**	Loire	Dry white	Blanquette de veau Crab, scallops, oysters, prawn cocktail and moules et frîtes Egg dishes such as soufflés and quiches Fish cakes Green salad with oil and vinegar dressing Mackerel with green gooseberry sauce and other oily fish dishes Taramasalata White fish dishes White wine sauce-based dishes

Muscat de Beaumes-de-Venise	Rhône	Vin doux naturel	Baclava Chocolate-based desserts, especially sachertorte Fruit, ginger and mint-based desserts Ice cream Stewed fruit Waldorf salad
Muscat de Rivesaltes	Roussillon	Vin doux naturel	Apricot, cassis, ginger, orange and pineapple-based desserts Chicken in sweet and sour sauce Dried fruits such as figs and raisins Grapes, fruit compote and salad Iles flottantes and meringues Sweet crêpes Tiramisu
Moscatel de Setúbal	Portugal	Sweet white	Almonds, grilled and salted Baclava Caramel and chocolate-based desserts
Moscato Spumante	Italy	Sparkling	Fruit-based desserts, fruit compote and salad Caramel and chocolate-based desserts
N Naoussa	Greece	Dry red	Aubergine purée Greek food, especially kleftiko and moussaka
Navarra	Spain	Dry red	Chorizo Couscous Toad-in-the-hole
Nemea	Greece	Dry red	Aubergine purée Greek food, especially kleftiko and moussaka
O Oloroso Sherry	Spain	Fortified white	Christmas pudding Nut cakes Praline and chocolate ice cream Treacle and chocolate puddings
Orvieto	Italy	Dry or semi-sweet white	Creamy pasta dishes Grilled sardines Indian food with spicy yoghurt sauces Light fish dishes Tempura
P Pacherenc du Vic-Bilh	South-west France	Dry to sweet white	Bread and butter pudding Cheesecake Chutney

Pacherenc du Vic-Bilh *(continued)*			Goose stuffed with prunes or other fruit Mille feuilles Mince pies Pineapple-based desserts Piperade Smoked ham Tripe
Palette	Provence	Dry red	Aioli Tapenade
		Dry rosé	Andouillette, grilled with mustard
		Dry white	Creamed onions Grilled or roasted vegetables
Passito	Italy	Sweet white	Ice cream Italian biscuits or shortbread Tiramisu
Patrimonio	Corsica	Dry red	Cheese fondue Kebabs Osso bucco Tapenade
		Dry white	Salade niçoise Sardines and anchovies Taramasalata
Pauillac	Bordeaux	Dry red	Guinea fowl, pigeon and quail Lamb Red meat stews and casseroles
Penedès	Spain	Dry red	Empanadas Goulash
		Dry white	Paella Spanish fish stew Spanish omelette with potatoes, garlic and oil
Periquita	Portugal	Dry red	Chicken piri-piri Kleftiko Oxtail Red meat stews and casseroles Roast pork Toad-in-the-hole
Pineau des Charentes	Cognac	Vin de liqueur	Apple, chocolate and brandy-based desserts Foie gras Melon with port Sorbets

Pinot Blanc	Alsace	Dry white	Choucroute garnie Eggs Benedict, cheese omelette and other egg dishes Kedgeree Onion tart Raw vegetables and salads Savoury crêpes

Pinot Grigio	Italy	Dry white	Fish and chips and other fried fish
			  dishes
			Guacamole
			Houmus
			Pasta with clam sauce or spring
			  vegetables
			Prosciutto
			Raw vegetables
			Risotto alla Milanese
			Stir-fries

Pinot Gris	Alsace	Dry white	Caviar Chicken curry Clam chowder Corn on the cob Gougère Omelette with bacon and quiche lorraine Onion tart Pork chops and roast pork Raclette Roasted or stuffed peppers Satay Veal dishes
		Vendanges Tardives	Foie gras Kougelhopf Sweet and sour sauce White wine sauce-based dishes
Pinot Noir	Alsace	Dry red	Cold salmon Potato salad Quail Sauerbraten

	New World		Bacon and baked ham
			Bagels with salmon and cream
			  cheese
			Brussels sprouts and green
			  vegetables
			Coq au vin and chicken in cream and
			  morels sauce

Pinot Noir *(continued)*			Lamb curry Meatloaf Pork chops Rabbit Roast chicken
Pinotage	South Africa	Dry red	Beef Wellington Chilli con carne Chorizo Couscous Moussaka Pea and ham soup Pigeon Roast beef and steak
Pomerol	Bordeaux	Dry red	Beef and steak dishes Chicken in sweet and sour sauce Goose stuffed with prunes or other fruit Grilled lamb chops Mint sauce and pepper sauce Partridge and pheasant Roast duck Shepherd's pie Truffles, black and white Wild boar
Pommard	Burgundy	Dry red	Cajun-style meats Confit de canard Kidneys Pepper sauce Roast duck and roast lamb with mint sauce Wild boar
Port	Portugal	Fortified red	Almonds, walnuts, hazelnuts and peanuts Chocolate-based desserts Melon and Port Mince pies
Pouilly-Fumé	Loire	Dry white	Eels with a creamy herb sauce Goat's cheese Grilled carp Jambon persillé Moules marinières, oysters and seafood pizza Paella Tripe Vinaigrette sauce

Pouilly-Fuissé	Burgundy	Dry white	Cold salmon Grilled bass Fish terrines Quiches and soufflés Japanese food
Poulsard	Arbois	Dry red	Game Jambalaya Kleftiko Spicy meat dishes
Puligny-Montrachet	Burgundy	Dry white	Caviar Creamy and buttery sauces Lobster Monkfish Roast veal
Q **Quarts de Chaume**	Loire	Sweet white	Chocolate-based desserts Exotic fruit-based desserts and fruit salads Kougelhopf
R **Regaleali Rosato**	Italy	Dry rosé	Roasted or stuffed peppers
Regnié	Burgundy	Dry red	*See* **Beaujolais**
Reguengos	Portugal	Dry red	Carpaccio Chicken piri-piri
Retsina	Greece	Dry white	Aubergine dishes Olives and anchovies Spicy sausages
Richebourg	Burgundy	Dry red	Calves' liver Coffee-based desserts Grouse, venison and roast meats
Riesling	Alsace	Dry white	Baeckaoffa and pot roast Blanquette de veau Boudin blanc (white pudding) Bouillabaisse Chicken in cream and morels sauce Creamed onions Horseradish sauce Mustard sauce Olives Potato salad or creamy potato dishes Quiche lorraine Raspberry-based desserts Seafood in creamy sauces and moules marinières Smoked salmon White fish dishes

Riesling *(continued)*		Vendanges Tardives	Accra Chinese food Smoked ham Waldorf salad
Riesling	Germany	Dry to sweet white Kabinett	Béarnaise sauce Cranberry sauce Gravad lax Sashimi and sushi
		Spätlese	Chinese food Roast pork with mustard sauce Smoked ham Tomato salad
		Auslese	Brown sugar-based desserts Duck à l'orange Foie gras Red cabbage with apples Smoked fish
		Beerenauslese	Cherry-based desserts Pancakes with maple syrup Sachertorte and other chocolate-based desserts
Riesling	New World	Dry white	Apple-based desserts Choucroute garnie Curry dishes Japanese food Pike with garlic and poached white fish dishes
Rioja	Spain	Dry red	Beef potpie Curried tomato soup Greek food, especially moussaka Lamb Liver Merguez sausages Roast pork
		Dry rosé	Paella
		Dry white	Octopus Roasted spicy sausages Salt cod balls Stuffed onions Tapas
Rosso Cònero	Italy	Dry red	Bolognese sauce-based dishes Duck à l'orange Salami and spicy meats

Rosso Cònero *(continued)*		Dry rosé	Cured meats Saltimbocca alla Romana and other veal dishes Roast lamb
Rueda	Spain	Dry white	Salads Sausages, dried or smoked Spicy meat casseroles Grilled or roasted vegetables
Rully	Burgundy	Dry red	Charcuterie Coq au vin Roast pork Escargots à la Bourguignonne
		Dry white	Artichokes Caesar salad Jambon persillé Savoury crêpes Smoked salmon Satay Soufflés with broccoli and cheese
S **St-Amour**	Burgundy	Dry red	*See* **Beaujolais**
St-Emilion	Bordeaux	Dry red	Beef potpie Beef Wellington Camembert and English cheeses Chestnut and dried fruit stuffings Chicken curry Confit de canard Game and venison Lamb with herbes de provence Pasta with pesto sauce Pheasant, pigeon and quail Pot roast and pot-au-feu Roasted meats such as chicken, turkey and beef Sausage and mash
St-Estèphe	Bordeaux	Dry red	Lamb with flageolets or light meat casseroles Rabbit Roast lamb
St-Georges- **St-Emilion**	Bordeaux	Dry red	*See* **St-Emilion**
St-Joseph	Rhone	Dry red	Boiled or roast vegetables Grilled meats or kebabs Melon with Parma ham *See also* **Syrah** *or* **Marsanne**

St-Julien	Bordeaux	Dry red	Lamb crown roast Roast turkey with traditional trimmings *See also* **St-Estèphe**
St-Véran	Burgundy	Dry white	Artichokes Asparagus in vinaigrette sauce Herring Soufflés with spinach and cheese Steak tartare
Ste-Croix-du- Mont	South-west France	Sweet white	Cheeses Foie gras and other pâtés Fruit salad and orange-based desserts *See also* **Sauternes**
Samos	Greece	Sweet white	Baclava Nuts, almonds and honey-based desserts Pastries and breads

Sancerre	Loire/Centre	Dry white	Avocado
			Béarnaise sauce
			Creole and teriyaki chicken
			Hollandaise sauce and mustard sauce
			Omelettes
			Red mullet and fish cakes
			Poached, steamed or lightly grilled
			  salmon
			Sashimi and sushi
			Seafood dishes, especially smoked
			  eels
			Taramasalata
			Tomato sauce-based dishes
			Vichyssoise
			Wiener schnitzel

Sangiovese	California	Dry red	Bresaola and carpaccio Pasta dishes with meat and béchamel sauce Cornish pasties Pizza bolognese Saltimbocca alla Romana *See also* **Brunello di Montalcino**
Saumur and **Saumur- Champigny**	Loire	Dry red	Anchovies or anchovy paste Baked ham with pineapple Beef bourguinon Confit de canard Grilled lamb chops Lemon chicken

Saumur and **Saumur-Champigny** (continued)			Meat fondue Quail Raspberry and strawberry-based desserts
Sauternes	Bordeaux	Sweet white	Bread and butter pudding Brown sugar-based desserts Buttermilk pancakes Cheeses, especially blue cheeses Chocolate, Cointreau and lemon- based desserts Christmas pudding Crème caramel or brûlee Foie gras Pecan pie Tiramisu Waldorf salad

Sauvignon Blanc	France	Dry white	Artichokes
			Avocado
			Ceviche
			Egg dishes, soufflés and quiches
			Fish and chips
			Jambon persillé
			Pike with garlic, grilled carp or
			   haddock
			Pizza with seafood, prawn cocktail
			   and other seafood dishes, especially
			   scallops in cream and tarragon sauce
			Smoked eels
			Stir-fries
			Thai food
			White fish dishes
			White wine sauce-based dishes

	New World		Asparagus Chicken creôle Chicken piri-piri and teriyaki chicken Chicken salad Fish cakes and prawns Gazpacho Ginger-based desserts Jambalaya Pasta with spring vegetables Salsa, red and green and other tomato-based sauces Sashimi Stir-fries Tomato salad and raw vegetables

Sauvignon Colli Orientali del Friuli	Italy	Dry white	Mozzarella and Ricotta cheeses Prawns, scampi and seafood pasta dishes *See also* **Sauvignon Blanc**
Savennières	Loire	Dry white	Creole chicken Goats' cheese Grilled scallops Pumpkin pie *See also* **Chenin Blanc**
Savigny-lès-Beaune	Burgundy	Dry red	Chicken chasseur Lamb curry Mushroom and red-wine sauces Tarragon chicken *See also* **Pinot Noir**, New World

Sémillon	New World	Dry white	Barbecued and blackened fish
			Blue cheeses
			Chicken chasseur
			Chinese food
			Coconut-based desserts and savoury
			  dishes
			Ham and pork dishes
			Honey-based dishes
			Indian food with spicy yoghurt sauces
			Mackerel with butter and spring
			  onions and other oily fish dishes
			Monkfish and other seafood
			Pumpkin pie
			Spicy white meat dishes
			Trifle

Sherry	Spain	Fortified red	*See* **Amontillado, Fino, Manzanilla** or **Oloroso**

Shiraz	Australia	Dry red	Barbecued meats
			Bean and pasta soup
			Boeuf en daube, cassoulet and other
			  red meat stews and casseroles
			Chicken paprika and Southern fried
			  chicken
			Chilli con carne and chilli sauce
			Couscous
			Cranberry sauce
			Duck à l'orange
			Game
			Greek food
			Hamburgers
			Horseradish sauce

Shiraz *(continued)*			Lamb curry Meat fondue Merguez sausages Pepper sauce Sirloin steak Stuffed cabbage Toad-in-the-hole Venison and wild boar
Soave	Italy	Dry white	Aioli Bruschetta Chef's salad and other salads Gazpacho Macaroni cheese Pasta with pesto sauce Prawns, seafood salad and light, white fish dishes Risotto alla Milanese Teriyaki chicken
Sylvaner	Alsace	Dry white	Anchovies or anchovy paste Baeckaoffa Chicken in sweet and sour sauce Croque monsieur or madame Onion tarts Pike with garlic Quiche lorraine Salt cod with garlic, oil and cream Sweetbreads
Syrah	New World	Dry red	Cajun-style and barbecued meats Game Mushroom and red-wine sauces *See also* **Hermitage, Cornas, Côte-Rôtie, Crozes-Hermitage, St-Joseph**
T **Tavel**	Rhône	Dry rosé	Anchovies or anchovy paste Asparagus in vinaigrette sauce Bouillabaisse Onion tart Salami-based dishes
Tempranillo	Spain	Dry red	*See* **Rioja**
Tokaji	Hungary	Dry to sweet white	Carrot cake Christmas pudding Thai food *See also* **Muscat de Beaumes-de-Venise, Ste-Croix-du-Mont, Sauternes**

Tokaji Aszú, 5 puttonyos	Hungary	Sweet white	Christmas pudding
Trebbiano d'Abruzzo/Ugni Blanc	Italy or New World	Dry white	Egg dishes with ham or bacon Creamy spinach and pasta dishes Grilled carp Risotto alla Milanese
Vacqueyras	Rhône	Dry red	Beef Stroganoff Escargots à la Bourguinonne Pigeon *See also* **Grenache**
Valdepeñas	Spain	Dry red	Squid cooked in their own juices
Valpolicella Classico	Italy	Dry red	Bresaola Italian garlic and tomato dishes Mexican food Mushroom risotto Osso bucco Proscuitto Raclette Tuna salad
Verdicchio	Italy	Dry white	Antipasti Fish and chips and other fried fish dishes Light, creamy pasta dishes Moules et frîtes Seafood salad and other seafood dishes
Vernaccia di San Gimignano	Italy	Dry white	Bouillabaisse Bruschetta Grilled white fish, especially bass Pesto-based pasta dishes
Vin de Corse	Corsica	Dry red	Aubergine Boeuf en daube Corn bread Merguez sausages Polenta
		Dry white	Bouillabaisse Tabbouleh Tuna salad
Vin de Paille	Jura	Vin doux naturel	Apple and apricot-based desserts Foie gras Sweet crêpes Thai food *See also* **Pacherenc du Vic-Bilh, Tokaji**

V

Vinho Verde	Portugal	Dry white	Ceviche Chicken piri-piri Green salad with oil and vinegar dressing Grilled sardines Mackerel with green gooseberry sauce Salsas, red and green Vinaigrette sauce
Vino Nobile di Montepulciano	Italy	Dry red	Roast lamb with mint sauce Red meat stews and casseroles Wild boar *See also* **Brunello di Montalcino, Sangiovese**

Viognier	Rhône, Italy
	  or New
	  World
		Dry white	Artichokes
			Carrot soup
			Chef's salad
			Cornish pasties
			Curry
			Gazpacho
			Indian food with spicy yoghurt sauces
			See also **Condrieu**

Volnay	Burgundy	Dry red	Mushroom and red-wine dishes Quail Rabbit Roast beef Veal dishes *See also* **Echezeaux**
Vosne-Romanée	Burgundy	Dry red	Brown sugar-based desserts Coffee-based desserts Game Roast turkey with traditional trimmings Truffles, black and white

Vouvray	Loire	Dry to sweet
		  white
			Accra
			Apple, fruit and lemon-based desserts
			Béarnaise and hollandaise sauce
			Goat's cheese
			Goose stuffed with prunes or other
			  fruit
			Quiches and soufflés
			Sweet and sour sauce
			White fish dishes

		Sparkling (mousseux)	Apple, fruit and lemon-based desserts Mince pies Pancakes with maple syrup Sweet crêpes

Weissburgunder	Germany	Dry red	Braised beef, stews and casseroles Roast pork Wiener schnitzel	**W**

Zinfandel	California	Dry red	Aubergine-based dishes
			Baked beans
			Barbecued meats
			Beef potpie
			Beef tacos
			Buffalo wings
			Cajun-style meats
			Cassoulet
			Chicken paprika
			Chilli con carne
			Chorizo sausage
			Empanadas
			Goulash
			Greek food
			Hamburgers
			Meatloaf
			Pepper sauce
			Pizza bolognese
			Ratatouille
			Roast duck
			Roast turkey with traditional
			  trimmings
			Salads
			Sausage and mash
			Venison with cranberries or juniper
			  berries
				Z

		Dry white	Grilled white fish Pasta dishes Octopus Roasted vegetables	
Zitsa	Greece	Dry white	Anchovies Houmus Olives Spicy sausages Tapas	

Conclusion

Here are a few simple rules to help you make the perfect matches with your food and wine.

~♀ Rule Number One: when in doubt, drink Champagne!

~♀ Match food and wine flavours: herbal Sauvignon Blancs match vegetables; peppery Cabernet Sauvignons match steak in pepper sauce; buttery, oaky Chardonnays match fish and pasta in creamy sauces.

~♀ Match food and wine textures: the sweet, unctuousness of Sauternes matches foie gras; crisp, lively Sancerre matches oysters.

~♀ Match food and wine weights: again, Sauternes and foie gras match in richness; heavy Barolos match robust game dishes; light, poached fish match light dry wines.

~♀ Always cook with wine that you would also drink, or drink the same wine that was used in the food's preparation.

~♀ Learn and rely upon regional and local associations: Sancerre and Chavignol, for example.

~♀ The new 'Pacific rim' and 'Mediterrasian' cooking goes well with New World varietals.

~♀ Follow the sauce of the dish and use its dominant flavour as your guide.

~♀ Remember that opposites attract: like sweet and sour sauce, a sweet wine balances an acidic or sour food.

~♀ Strive for balance and respect between wine and food: an older, more complex wine takes centre stage and should be served with very simple foods – not heavy sauces that will drown it.

~♀ Remember that there are wines types that will go with just about everything, just as there are foods, like roast chicken, that will go with almost any wine.

~♀ Hard-to-match foods such as chocolate, strong cheeses, grapefruit, asparagus and pickles should be teamed with the wines from the same region as the dish.

~♀ Keep in mind the cooking method of the dish as well as the winemaking technique.

~♀ Match the wine to the occasion and environment as well as the food: picnic? beach? work dinner?

Wine Vocabulary

Acid, acetic Acid found in all wine, though usually present in tiny quantities. Excess amounts cause the wine to turn to vinegar.

Acid, ascorbic Acid with an anti-oxidising effect, often added to wine just before bottling. It is only effective in the presence of **sulphur dioxide.**

Acid, citric Acid found particularly in citrus fruit but also present in lesser quantities in grapes. White grapes, especially those affected by **noble rot**, contain more than red grapes. As an additive, it is strictly controlled by law.

Acid, lactic Acid which appears during the malolactic fermentation of the wine when malic acid changes into carbon dioxide and lactic acid. Eventually this fades and becomes imperceptible in tasting.

Acid, malic Once the grape ripens, the malic acid present at high levels in the green grapes decreases. Its tart taste of green apples makes it easily recognizable. The hotter the year, the faster it decreases during the ripening process, which is why it is more apparent when the weather has been colder.

Acid, tartaric Regarded as the most 'noble' acid, tartaric acid has more acidifying power than the other acids contained in wine, and is not commonly found in fruits other than grapes. The tartaric acid content goes down as the grape ripens, then varies depending on the weather.

Acidify To add lemon juice or vinegar to a sauce or cooked dish.

Acidity, fixed The total of all the acids contained in the fruit itself, such as tartaric acid, malic acid, lactic acid.

Acidity, real Intensity of acidity, usually expressed in **pH** (potential hydrogen), is expressed on a scale from 0 to 7, with 7 representing total neutrality. The usual pH varies around 3 to 4 on this scale.

Acidity, total Combined total of **volatile acidity** and **fixed acidity**. This naturally varies depending upon whether seasons are cold (when the grapes are too acid) or hot (when the grapes are over-ripe). It is on the basis of these figures and of the legal standards that the decision to acidify or to disacidify a wine is made.

Acidity, volatile In small quantities (from 0.3 to 0.4 grams per litre), excess volatile acids are strictly controlled by law. Only levels below 0.9 grams per litre (production) and 1 gram per litre (retail trade) are tolerated, quantities higher than this making the wine too sour. This acidity, mainly made up of acetic acid, increases as the wine ages.

Acidulation Adding acid to wine made from grapes deficient in natural acid in order to bring the wine into balance. Acidulation is legal in California (where the warmer climates keep acid levels down) but illegal in France. It is interesting to note that adding sugar (**chaptalization**) is legal in France but illegal in California.

Aioli A Mediterranean mayonnaise made with garlic, egg yolks and oil.

Al dente A term used for describing the perfect texture of cooked pasta: tender but still slightly firm to the bite. As each type of pasta (lasagne, fettucini, penne, tagliatelli, rigatoni, fusilli, etc.) demands a different cooking time, it is essential to test pasta regularly during its preparation.

Alcohol An essential element in wine, alcohol is produced during fermentation, when enzymes created by the yeasts change the sugar content of the grape juice into alcohol, carbon dioxide and heat. The level of alcohol varies between under 7 degrees and over 15 degrees in wine. To obtain one degree of alcohol, 18 grams of sugar must be added per litre for white wines and 17 grams per litre for red.

Anthocyanin The red pigments in grapes which give red wine its colour. The purpley-red colour of young wine is almost exclusively caused by fairly unstable anthocyanin molecules which, in the course of ageing, join up with **tannins** to give the wine its ruby-red colour. This polymerization of tannin and anthocyanin is helped by the dissolution of oxygen in the wine, which produces stable polymers.

Appellation The geographic origin of a wine, not synonymous with the term *terroir*.

AOC *Appellation d'origine contrôlée,* a designation created by the French authorities to establish specific areas of production, grape varieties, minimum levels of sugar in the must and of alcohol in the wine, maximum yield per hectare, pruning of the vine, and cultivation and vinification methods.

Aromas These are the scents that a wine gives off, as absorbed by the taster's nose and palate. Three levels of aromas can be distinguished: primary, or varietal aromas; secondary aromas resulting from the fermentation; and tertiary aromas which develop as the wine ages. Together they form the wine's **bouquet**.

Aromatic esters The term used for the compounds formed most often during fermentation by the wine's acids and alcohols.

Au gratin The cooking term used for dishes that are browned in the oven or under a grill. Gratins are often made with béchamel sauce, cheese or eggs.

Auslese German white wines made from late-harvest grapes with a high sugar concentration.

Balance The harmony between the various elements of a wine, such as acidity, sweetness, alcohol and tannin content.

Barrel fermented Wine that is fermented in oak barrels as opposed to stainless steel tanks.

Barrique A French term for a barrel, the capacity of which may vary from one region to another: in the Bordeaux area, where it is most commonly used, it contains 225 litres (four *barriques* make one *tonneau*); in the Muscadet area, it contains 228 litres; while in Touraine-Anjou it holds 232 litres. The traditional English equivalent is the hogshead. In France, other names are used depending on the region and capacity.

Beerenauslese QmP German wines made from grapes affected by *Botrytis cinerea*, or **noble rot**.

Blanc, Blanco, Branco French, Spanish, Portuguese for white.

Blanc de Blancs 'White of whites', meaning a white wine made of white grapes, such as Champagne made from Chardonnay. It is also used as the names of some wineries' special blends of still white wines, ranging from dry to medium-dry.

Blanc de Noirs White wine made from red or black grapes.

Bleeding The bleeding process, or *saignee*, consists in drawing off some of the wine during fermentation. The light-coloured wine drawn off is used to make rosé wines such as Clairet in Bordeaux and Clarete in Rioja.

Blending Blending, or *assemblage*, is the mixing of several vats of wine varieties to make a more balanced wine and is usually performed after each variety has fermented individually. For example, Bordeaux are usually a blend of Cabernet Sauvignon, Cabernet Franc and Merlot.

Bodega An agricultural estate in Spain. However, wines labelled 'bodega' do not necessarily contain grapes which all come from the estate in question.

Body Used to describe a wine with good tannic structure and good ageing potential.

Botrytis A mould which attacks grapes, it manifests itself either as **grey rot**, which may then endanger the harvest; or, in certain atmospheric conditions, as **noble rot**, which is used to make dessert wines such as Sauternes, Barsac, Monbazillac, certain Anjou wines and German wines like Auslese, Beerenauslese or Trockenbeerenauslese, or the famous Hungarian Tokaji.

Botrytis cinerea Literally 'noble rot', *edelfäule* in German, which dehydrates grapes left late on the vine and concentrates their juice.

Bottle sickness Unbalance of wine flavour after bottling or after rough travel, caused by excessive aeration; clears up when wine is allowed to rest.

Bouche The French word for mouth is used to describe the body and impressions of the wine when tasting.

Bouquet Complex emanation from a wine, perceptible in the nose, resulting from maturation and oak ageing. Bouquet is more complex and encompasses **aroma**, which is present only with young wines.

Brettanomyces An undesirable yeast found on grapes, and therefore in wines, which produces very disagreeable odours when in excess and which is a sign of poor hygiene in the winery. In small amounts it escapes unnoticed, or shows itself as an earthy, manure-like smell we sometimes appreciate.

Broker *see* **Courtier**

Brut A French term for sparkling wines, it indicates very low level of sugar (up to 15 grams per litre). There is no sugar present in *Brut intégral* or *Brut zéro* Champagne.

Capers The unopened flower buds of the Mediterranean caper bush, a sort of creeper. They are pickled in vinegar and used as a seasoning.

Carbonic maceration The type of vinification during which red wine grapes are put into vats as they are, without being crushed. This used to be a natural process, with the grapes being left to ferment without interference. Now the vat is closed and filled with carbon dioxide which causes the malic acid to break down and intra-cellular fermentations to take place, changing part of the sugar into alcohol. A few days later the free-run wine is drained off to be blended at a later stage with the **press wine**. The alcoholic fermentation is then allowed to finish. This process has proved particularly effective for Gamay wines, such as the Beaujolais Primeurs, that are sold and consumed when young.

Chaptalization Named after Chaptal, this technique consists of adding sugar (cane or beet or rectified, concentrated must) to the must before fermentation to give the wine a higher alcoholic content. It is strictly forbidden in many countries and is usually controlled by law in those countries that permit it (in France a maximum of three kilos of sugar per hectolitre of grape juice is allowed). The new EU regulations have added to this legislation, defining certain parameters: chaptalization should be authorized only under certain conditions relative to the degree of ripeness, the climatic conditions and the production methods used. Chaptalization is a necessary evil in difficult years; however in France it has become something of a habit, allowing growers to harvest maximum volume in the sure knowledge that they can boost the degree of alcohol by chaptalizing. The EU would like French growers to use only rectified concentrated musts, or RCMs, when chaptalizing. Today, new appliances are used to detect fraudulent chaptalization by nuclear magnetic resonance.

Château To the north-west of Bordeaux, in the Médoc, most country residences have vineyards which have become famous. As a result, the term has come to designate the wine from a particular estate. A real 'château' does not necessarily stand on every property.

Clairet Light red wine obtained by **bleeding** in the course of fermentation of red wine. Not to be confused with **Claret**, the British name for the red wines of Bordeaux.

Claret The British name for the red wines of Bordeaux.

Climat French term originating in Burgundy to indicate a legally defined geographical area. It has nothing to do with weather. However, different climats can have varying weather climates in them or between them.

Clos A French term which originally referred to a vine-growing parcel of land surrounded by a wall, particularly in Burgundy. Many of the original walls even in the oldest properties are still standing.

Cold stabilization A method of clarifying wine by lowering the temperature of the wine to 0°C/32°F for a short period, allowing the suspended particles to drop out.

Complex The term used to describe a wine which has many different levels and layers of flavours and textures.

Concentrated The term used to describe a wine that has a lot of extracted matter, and is intense and rich. The extract comprises the non-volatile solids of a wine: sugars, acids, minerals, phenolics, glycerol, and so on.

Corked The expression used for a wine that has a very strong smell of rotten cork. The wine is usually undrinkable. This rather rare occurrence is caused by the development of moulds on the cork.

Courtier A courtier or broker is an intermediary between the grower and the **négociant**.

Cru Literally, in French, a 'growth' or tract of land such as a vineyard, the term is principally used to mean a vineyard's rank in the 1855 classification or ranking of Bordeaux vineyards and their wines into five classes or Crus. Eighty-three Médoc, Graves and Sauternes châteaux were thus classified in 1855, but since then hundreds more around Bordeaux have classified themselves as first to fifth Crus or as Crus Exceptionnels or as Crus Bourgeois (the lesser-quality categories preceding the Crus).

Crush The physical act of crushing the grapes, as well as the term referring to the harvest season.

Cuvaison, Cuvage The French term for the essential stage in the making of a wine, from when the musts from the harvest are put into the fermentation vats, up to the draining off or *égouttage*.

Cuve A vat designed to hold the fermenting musts, or to store wines. Some vats are closed with an upper lid fitted with a hatch, as in Bordeaux; others are open, as in Burgundy. The vats are made of various materials: wooden vats were once used, but nowadays stainless steel vats are preferred for cleanliness and, principally, temperature control.

Cuvée A French term literally meaning a 'vatful', the word signifies a specific selection of wine that may or may not have been blended. *See* **Blending**.

Daube A method of cooking meat, usually beef, which braises the meat in a red wine sauce, often with garden vegetables and seasonings.

Decanting The process of separating the sediment of a wine from the clear liquid. During the decanting operation a young wine comes into contact with the air, so that the addition of oxygen makes it more palatable. Should the wine be too old, such an operation can be disastrous, as it accelerates the process of deterioration.

Declassification When a wine exceeds certain norms (in terms of yield), or falls short (in degree of alcohol), the wine is declassified and loses its **AOC** classification. The decision may be taken voluntarily by the winemaker. Such wine may be used to make vinegar or pure alcohol.

Dekkera The spore-producing form of the yeast genus Brettanomyces.

Demi-sec EU classification for white wines with a sugar content of less than nine grams per litre. In Champagnes, it is one category below Sec in terms of dryness, and considered the ideal accompaniment to dessert pastries.

Deposit The sediment of solid particles found in wine that separate from the wine during fermentation and ageing. In the case of white wines, these are often fragments of colourless crystalline deposits; in red wines, they are usually a combination of tannins and pigments. *See* **Decanting**.

Dessert wine US legal term for wines over 14 per cent and not over 24 per cent in alcoholic strength by volume; includes appetizer wines such as Sherry.

Distillation The operation during which the alcohol is separated by heating the alcoholic mixture, on the principle that alcohol has a boiling point lower than that of water: the first vapours to be given off are alcoholic ones that are condensed by cooling.

DO *Denominacion de origen*; the Spanish equivalent of the French **AOC**.

DOC *Denominazione di origine controllata*; the Italian equivalent of the French **AOC**. The classification underwrites the origin of the wine, but not necessarily the quality. There are over 220 at present.

Doce, Dolce, Dulce Sweet in Portuguese, Italian, Spanish.

DOCG *Denominazione di origine controllata garantita*. An Italian guarantee that refers to testing by sensory analysis. Existing ones are Barbaresco, Barolo, Brunello, Chianti and Vino Nobile di Montepulciano.

Dry Something of a *faux-ami:* of a Champagne, it in fact means sweet, the driest Champagnes actually being called Brut or Extra dry.

Earthy The positive characteristics of loamy topsoil, mushrooms or truffles sometimes found in red wines.

Elevage Literally 'raising', this French term describes the operations of maturing and blending young wines to attain better balance.

En primeur Rather than being sold when it is ready to drink, wine is most often offered at a much earlier stage. In Bordeaux, the Grands Crus usually sell all or part of a year's harvest (usually in September) the following March or April, in what are known as the sales *en primeur.*

Enology, Oenology The science and study of winemaking.

Espumoso, Espumante Spanish and Portugese for sparkling wine, such as Champagne.

Estate-bottled This originally meant that the wine was produced and bottled entirely at the winery adjoining the proprietor's vineyard, but amendments have broadened it to include any vineyards controlled by the same proprietor or owned by members of a co-operative winery within the same delimited viticultural area as the winery.

Esters Volatile bodies resulting from the combination of an alcohol and an organic acid. They do not have such a marked influence on the wine's bouquet as is commonly thought.

Extra dry The quality of sparkling or still wine containing between 12 and 20 grams of sugar per litre.

Fermentation, alcoholic Transformation of the sugar contained in the must, into alcohol and carbon dioxide, in the presence of yeasts.

Fermentation, malolactic This follows the alcoholic fermentation. Malic acid is affected by specific bacteria and changed into lactic acid and carbon dioxide. Because lactic acid is less harsh than malic acid, the wine becomes softer and more pleasant to drink than when young.

Fining Fining, or collage, is a way of clearing wines before they are bottled. With this method, a 'colloid' is added to the wine to absorb suspended particles and to fall to the bottom of the container. Products used are beaten egg white, fish glue, casein or bentonite, a type of clay. The wine is then drawn off and sometimes filtered before bottling.

Flintstone This evokes the smell of two flints being rubbed together, characteristic of Pouilly-Fumé in the Loire Valley and some other wines, usually made from the Sauvignon grape.

Fortified Said of a wine to which wine spirit (brandy) has been added, such as Port or Sherry.

Foxy In general, this term describes wine with an unpleasant and aggressively gamey smell. Specifically, it refers to the red Concord grape, native of North America and belonging to the *Vitis labrusca* species (grapes from *Vitis vinifera* are the best for winemaking and indeed all those varieties with which we are familiar are *Vitis vinifera*).

Fruity A characteristic of a young wine, or of a wine that has retained its fruity aromas.

Glycerine A trialcohol with a slightly sweet flavour, one of the important constituents of wine. On the palate it is often more pronounced in wines matured in new oak.

Gnocchi Italian potato, egg and flour dumplings.

Grassy or herbaceous Aromas and flavours resembling new-mown grass, a negative characteristic when dominant.

Graves Soils made up of gravels and drift boulders. Graves is also one of the seven major Bordeaux appellations.

Green Used to describe a wine with excessive fruit acidity, especially if it has a malic (apple-like) aroma.

Grey rot *see* **Rot, grey**

Hectolitre 100 litres, the equivalent of 22 imperial or 26.5 US gallons. In the EU, wine production is referred to in hectolitres per hectare (hl/ha).

Herbaceous Aromas and flavours which are reminiscent of herbs or the leafy and branchy parts of the plant. They are not desirable if they are too strong.

Hybrid A cross between two species of vine. As a result of the phylloxera crisis and the subsequent crossings of American and European species, phylloxera-resistant hybrids have been produced. Such hybrids have not been encouraged because the quality of the wine has tended to be mediocre.

Jammy In red wines, this describes the taste of ripe fruitiness combined with natural berry-like flavours.

Kabinett High-quality German dry white wines (**QmP**) that are never **chaptalized**.

Larousse Gastronomique The wine and food lovers' bible by Prosper Montagné – a gastronomic encyclopedia filled with over 8,500 recipes and 1,000 illustrations, providing not only practical recipes, but a history of cooking, anecdotes and explanations with sources from Rabelais, Brillat Savarin, August Escoffier and more. The first French edition was published in 1938; the first English translation in 1961. It is truly a great read and an indispensable tool.

Lees Made up of yeasts in a latent state, tartaric acid and other residual matter from the harvest, the lees form a dark yellowy deposit at the bottom of the cask. They are removed during **racking**.

Madeirized A term meaning oxidized or baked, such as by the heat-treatment method practised in Madeira and some other countries. It can also mean when a white wine oxidizes badly and browns in colour (usually because of poor storage and/or excessive age). The phenomenon takes its name from the taste of Madeira, and is due to the presence of harmful levels of ethyl aldehyde.

Malic Apple-like aroma of malic acid from incompletely ripened grapes.

Marc The solid parts of the grape, obtained after pressing, forming a cake which is sometimes used for distillation in two different processes: the marc can be sprayed with water and drained off before distillation, or it can be placed in special stills into which steam is forced. The resulting spirit is called eau de vie de marc, or just marc for short.

In Champagne, the term is the loading unit for the press, corresponding to 4,000 kilos of grapes.

Marinate Food (usually meats) are marinated in marinades to tenderize them and to impart flavour. The marinade is usually of an oil base with an acidic element such as lemon, vinegar or soy sauce.

Maturation The maturation of a wine is the function of its composition, its origin (***terroir***), and its vintage. No one knows for certain what happens during the ageing process. We know that there is an olfactive evolution, or a change from simple aromas to a complex bouquet. During bottle ageing, red wines deposit little plaques, grains of colouring agents and other molecules which bond and fall to the bottom of the bottle. The heavier clusters settle faster and quicker than the smaller ones, which need years to settle. As these colouring agents settle in the bottles, the intensity of the wine's colour diminishes, becoming more and more reddish-brick, and finally yellowish, as the anthocyanins, or colouring agents, in the tannins soften and diminish as the tannins do. Polymerization progresses continually as the wine ages so that tannic wines for long ageing become gradually harder and more tannic before reaching a peak where they are more tannic than when they were in barrel. Then the slope starts a gradual decline. The extra-large molecules lose their ability to combine with other proteins and their astringency diminishes. At the same time they are combining with other components in the wine, becoming insoluble and precipitating to form the characteristic deposit. At this point the wine is in its mature, mellow phase and is softer, richer and rounder: this is maturity.

Mercaptan From the Latin, meaning 'capturing mercury', a chemical term referring to the skunk-like smelling compounds formed by yeast reacting with the sulphur in the lees after the primary alcoholic fermentation.

Méthode champenoise The originality of this way of making sparkling wines lies in the creation of effervescence in the bottle. The wines used have completed their fermentations (alcoholic and sometimes malolactic) and are what the Champenois call 'clear wines', to which *liqueur de tirage*, made up of sugar solution and yeasts, is added.

This provokes a second alcoholic fermentation in the bottle, which is carefully closed with a metal capsule (or cork). This fermentation produces carbon dioxide which is trapped in the bottle and mixes into the wine; this is how the effervescence is formed. The bottles are then stored in a cellar *sur lattes* (slats of wood) until they are released on to the market (they can be kept for several years in this way without detracting from their freshness).

When the wines are being prepared for shipping, the deposits of dead yeasts that have fallen by force of gravity to the lower side of the bottle are removed. The operation involves raising the bottle progressively on to *pupitres* (racks) and giving it a quarter turn daily (riddling) so that the deposit forms against the cork. Today this traditional way of making Champagne is often replaced by an automatic mechanical operation using *giropallets*, which gives excellent results. The bottles come out neck-down and with the deposit collected against the cork. The neck is immersed in a saline solution which freezes a few centilitres of the wine, forming a plug of ice that includes the deposit. The capsule is then removed in the stage known as *dégorgement* (disgorging). A *liqueur d'expédition* is then added; this is a mixture of old wine, pure spirit (or cognac), citric acid when necessary, anhydride sulphite and, most important, a sugar solution in quantities that will determine the designation: Brut (from 0 to 15 grams), Extra dry (from 12 to 15 grams), Sec (from 17 to 35 grams), Demi-sec (from 33 to 50 grams). The bottle can then be corked, wired and labelled.

Microclimate An area where soil, combined with other environmental factors, produce a distinctive wine. The more American term for the French *climat*.

Mildew A parasitic mould that attacks the green parts of the vine. It used to be treated with copper sulphate but today synthetic substances are used.

Moelleux Describes sweet white wines, the sugar content of which may vary between 12 and 45 grams per litre, according to a 1984 EU directive.

Musky A characteristic of wines made with the Muscatel grape as the base, especially during fermentation, when a smell reminiscent of musk is given off.

Must Unfermented grape juice obtained by crushing or pressing.

NV A contraction for non-vintage, used on Port, Champagne or other wines: non-vintage wines can also be marketed as VSR (very special reserve).

Native yeast A natural yeast attached to the skins of the grapes, sometimes solely used to start fermentation. If fermentation cannot be started by native, or indigenous, yeasts then fabricated or synthetic yeasts are used.

Négociant The person who buys wine from the grower or château to sell to wholesalers or foreign importers.

Négociant éleveur The *négociant* who first buys wines from grower, then stores them in order to mature or blend them, or both. *See* **Elevage**.

Négociant manipulant A term used for traders in Champagne who buy grapes at harvest time for the preparation of their own Champagne. It is abbreviated to NM on the label.

New World The European ex-colonies which began to produce wine in the fifteenth century. See **Old World**.

Noble rot *see* **Rot, noble**

Nouveau Wine of the most recent vintage, which means that, after 31 August of the year following the vintage, wines can no longer claim this designation. Beaujolais Nouveau is the classic example. Now an increasing number of wine-producing regions always declare their vintage on the label; but in the regions of Oporto and Champagne the vintage is still declared by the trade in the best years only.

Oidium A disease of the vine caused by a microscopic mould that attacks the flowers, leaves and grapes. The grapes dry out and a whitish dust covers the vine. The only remedy is sulphur treatment.

Old World The term Old World refers to the countries of Europe and the Mediterranean basin which began to produce wine in the fourth century, as opposed to the term New World, which refers to the European ex-colonies that began producing wine around the fifteenth century. Old World winemakers, in principal, use more traditional winemaking techniques (blending grapes rather than producing single-variety wine, and insisting on smaller yields, for example) rather than modern science. They strive for individual style rather than a homogenous one and consider **terroir** to be real and important. It might be suggested that the differences between the two are slowly fading, as some Old World winemakers are increasingly producing easy, non-committal wines for export and to compete in this New World market; while some New World wines countries are embracing more traditional and less commercial styles. That said, the Old World still has time and experience on its side and, in my opinion, hold the ace card as far as possessing the indigenous grape varieties which are so at home in their climates and soils.

Olive oil Oil extracted from the flesh and stones of the olive. Like wine, the quality of the oil depends greatly on the type of olive, the harvest year, the climate and the soil. Extra virgin is the highest quality as it is unrefined from the first pressing (without the aid of heat or chemicals) of the olives. This method is also known as cold pressed extra virgin olive oil. The second pressing of the olives produces virgin olive oil, of lesser quality. The oil must be purified and filtered but it is not refined. The third type is pure olive oil, and it is a blend of extra virgin and refined olive oil – the least expensive and most common style.

Organoleptic Smell, colour and taste make up what are called the organoleptic qualities perceived by the senses.

Overcropping The practice of allowing vines to produce more fruit than they can ripen.

Oxidation When oxygen in the air comes into direct contact with the wine, oxidation may cause changes in colour and taste.

Oxidized Sherry-like, madeirized or nutty flavour caused by the action of oxygen on wine, due mainly to exposure to air, heat and light.

Passerillage The over-ripening of the grapes at harvest, causing drying out of the grape and higher sugar levels; this is how Vins de Paille, some Muscatels and the sweet wines of the Juras are prepared. Not to be confused with the sweet wines obtained as a result of **noble rot**.

Pasteurization To stabilize low-quality wines and get rid of any micro-organisms, the wine can sometimes be pasteurized or heat-sterilized.

Perlant Said of wines that are very slightly sparkling, but less so than semi-sparkling wines.

Pesto Italian sauce made of basil, Parmesan, garlic, pine nuts and olive oil.

pH Measuring unit expressing potential hydrogen, or the concentration of H+ ions. For wines this means their degree of dryness (between 2.9 and 3.1 for the wines with the best bearing). The lower the pH, the safer the wine is from disease and oxidation, and therefore the greater its ageing potential. *See also* **Acidity, real**.

Phylloxera This plant louse, imported from the United States, attacks the vine at its roots, and was the cause of the destruction of the European vineyards between 1860 and 1880.

Polymerization The process by which smaller molecules form and bind together to create larger ones. When wine ages, the phenolic molecules form and become larger tannin polymers, which become so large that they fall out of the wine and form sediment.

Pourriture noble French for the Botrytis cinerea mould, literally 'noble rot', *edelfäule* in German, which dehydrates grapes left late on the vine and concentrates their sweet juice.

Press wine Press wine, or *vin de presse,* is obtained by pressing the more solid elements which are left over in the vat after the draining off of the free-run wines. Press wines are sometimes blended with the free-run wines at a later stage to obtain the best possible balance for the particular vintage.

Pressing The operation whereby the grape juice is produced.

Primary aromas Those smells in an unaged wine that actually emanate from the grape itself, and are usually straightforward, fresh, fruity smells. These change and become secondary (and tertiary when discussing Burgundies) after the wine has been oak-aged. We then actually call the combination of aromas, the wine's **bouquet**. A young wine cannot therefore have a bouquet.

Primeurs These wines, designed to be drunk very young, enjoy this designation provided they are marketed from 21 November until 31 January of the following year. (Not to be confused with **en primeur.**)

QbA Qualitätswein bestimmter Anbaugebeite; German wines that have been **chaptalized**.

QmP Qualitätswein mit Prädikat, a designation reserved for German wines of quality that have not been **chaptalized**.

Quinta Portuguese equivalent of an estate or property. As with bodegas in Spain, Quinta wines may come from other properties than the one named.

Racking Racking is the operation to separate the wine from the lees; it is called *soutirage* in French. This method aerates and clarifies wine by moving it from one container to another, leaving the lees and sediment behind in the first container.

Récoltant manipulant A category of vinegrower in Champagne who makes his own Champagne (manipulates the grapes).

Reduction The opposite, or complement, of oxidation. From Jancis Robinson's *Oxford Companion to Wine,* page 781: 'Wines, especially red wines held in the absence of oxygen, may suffer from excess reduction; as a result of the slow polymerisation of tannins and pigments. A wine that is reduced tastes dirty and frequently smells of reduced sulphur compounds such as hydrogen sulphide and mercaptans.' Aeration can sometimes cure it.

Refrigeration The physical process used to clarify wines by precipitation of solid elements.

Remontage For red wine, the operation of pumping the liquid up from the bottom of the vat and spraying the cap. The object is to achieve optimum contact between the liquid and the sediment of skins, pips and stalks floating on the top.

Reserve For wines and spirits, the term used for special *cuvées* put aside for ageing or future use. The term also refers to a minimum ageing period for certain spirits such as Calvados, Cognac and Armagnac.

Residual sugar (RS) The level of sugar that remains in wine after fermentation.

Riddling A spectacular as well as basic operation in the méthode champenoise by which deposits of dead yeasts and mineral salts are collected round the cork so that they can be removed. The French term is *remuage*.

Ripeness A measurement of acid, pH and sugar in the grapes; the term is also important in conjunction with the must, in order to extract more colour and flavour.

Robe Literally means 'dress' in French and refers to the overall visual appearance of the wine, both in colour and general appearance.

Rot, grey Rot caused by the same mould as the noble rot, *Botrytis cinerea*, which affects grapes damaged by hail or grapeworm. High levels of humidity favour its development. Grey rot affects the quantity of the harvest, alters quality, and can lead to a disease in the wine called oxidasic casse.

Rot, noble When conditions are favourable – with a dry, sunny end of autumn – grapes develop a beneficial form of decay thanks to the development of *Botrytis cinerea*, the celebrated mould that roasts the Sauternes grapes, producing a concentrated, different type of juice.

Rôti Meaning 'roasted', a characteristic of sweet wines with aromas of dried grapes resulting from noble rot.

Sec, Secco, Seco Dry in French, Italian and Portuguese or Spanish.

Selection by mass Selection of grape varieties coming not from a single clone, but from a group of plants whose genetic structure is different.

Selection de grains nobles (SGN) This expression, meaning selection of noble grains, is used particularly in Alsace, but may also be used in other regions such as Sauternes, Barsac, Cadillac, Cérons, Loupiac, Ste-Croix-du-Mont, Monbazillac, Bonnezeaux, Quarts de Chaume, Coteaux du Layon, Coteaux de l'Aubance, Jurançon and Graves supérieures. It applies to wines made from late-picked grapes affected by noble rot or from *passerillés* grapes with a natural concentration of sugars.

Sorting In the course of the harvest the sorting, or *triage*, is the stage during which green or rotten grapes are removed. Sorting is also the term used for the successive pickings used in the harvest of *passerillés* grapes or grapes affected by **noble rot**. Also can apply to the process of sorting the healthy grapes from the unhealthy, after harvesting, on the sorting tables.

Sour A fungus (*Mycoderma aceti*) which causes wine to change into vinegar when in contact with air. It develops particularly in inadequately filled vats, giving the wine a sour taste and an extremely unpleasant smell.

Spätlese Late-harvested German wines.

Sparkling There are several ways of making a sparkling wine: méthode champenoise; what is known as the 'rural' method (e.g. Gaillac, Die) when effervescence is the result of a secondary fermentation; and the Charmat or *cuve close* method. Effervescence may also be produced by adding carbon dioxide.

Stemming This process of separating the grapes from the stalks. The stalks contain oils and tannins that tend to make the wine bitter and harsh. There is sometimes a need for this process when the grapes are too soft or lacking acidity and structure, for the stems can provide some of the body and firmness that is missing.

Stemmy An unpleasant aroma and taste of wine fermented with an excess use of grape and stems.

Still wines The opposite of sparkling wines, the term also describes wines that are used as a base in the making of sparkling and semi-sparkling wines.

Sulphur dioxide Winemakers have always used sulphur because of its numerous qualities: it checks premature fermentation in the harvested grapes; destroys undesirable yeasts; eliminates microbes and bacteria; protects oxidation; acts as a dissolving agent; and is a precious ally for sweet white wines inclined to referment in the bottle. Sulphur dioxide is now used either in gaseous form or diluted in water at 5 per cent or 18 per cent. Too much sulphur dioxide can produce a taste of rotten eggs and induce headaches.

Sur lie Allowing the wine to be aged in contact with the lees, the expired yeast cells from fermentation. Usually considered to give the wine more taste and extracts.

Taille The process of pruning the vines' branches in winter in order to control yields, bearing in mind the soil, climate and grape variety.

In Champagne, it indicates the part of the must which is drawn off by pressing after the *cuvée*. There is a distinction between the first and second *taille*.

Tannin In English we tend to speak of 'tannin' in the singular; this is inaccurate, as there are different types of tannin, all derived from vegetable substances such as nuts, wood, bark, berries and, of course, grapes. The stalks, skins and pips contain tannins which are released during the fermentation process and the pressing, giving the wine its specific character and contributing to its capacity for ageing. Storing the wine in new wood allows additional tannin contained in the fibres of the wood to be absorbed by the wine.

Tart A rough and harsh sensation in the mouth caused by excess tannins. These are caused by either a rustic grape variety or excessive fermentation.

Terroir An all-encompassing French term referring to the particular characteristics of a specific piece of vineyard land, including but not limited to the sum total of soil, exposure, drainage, climate, trellising, and grape variety. More poetically, it is the unique and magic trilogy of climate, grape and soil.

Thermoregulation The process of controlling the temperature of vats during fermentation.

Thinning A few days before the harvest, it is often helpful to remove the leaves covering the grapes to make the grapes riper and more healthy.

Ullage The vacant area in a bottle or cask between the wine and the cork or roof of the cask. Bottle ullage increases with time, as the wine breathes through the cork. Always look out for excessive ullage when buying an older wine.

Varietal A varietal, or *vin de cépage* is a wine made from a single grape variety. In France the wine must contain 100 per cent of the same variety; in some other countries small proportions of other varieties are allowed, and in others there is no relevant regulation.

This is also said of wine which has the pronounced aroma and flavour of a grape variety and is the general term for wines labelled with names of grape varieties.

Vat room The vat room, or *cuvier*, is where the vats or *cuves* are kept.

Vendanges Tardives (VT) This means late harvesting, which is done to procure over-ripe grapes for sweet wines.

Viniculture The science or study of grape production for wine and of the making of wine.

Vins sur lattes Wines that have been made into Champagne and are stockpiled on their lees prior to **riddling**.

Vintage Originally meaning the grape harvest, as there is only one per year, the term has come to refer to the wine made from the harvest of a particular year. Each vintage acquires its specific nature from a combination of climatic factors that will determine the wine's quality and potential for ageing.

The differences in quality from one year to another are such that most **négociants** blend wines from different vintages to create a better-balanced product; but the outstanding vintages deserve to stand on their own, so they are kept as single harvest stock to be made available as 'vintages'. In the past such vintages were very rare, and wines were sold as NV (non-vintage) or VSR (very special reserve).

Viticulture The cultivation, science and study of grapes.

Yeast, native *see* **Native yeast**

Suggested Reading

THESE are some of my favourite food and wine reference books from my personal library. I am always looking out for good material, so please do not hesitate to contact me via the publisher with anything you have come across that you find indispensable. For this book, I referred to these, as well as ten years of my tasting notes, excerpts from my previously published articles in *Vintage Magazine*, my first book *The Home Cellar Guide*, countless international and regional cookbooks, my husband's gardening encyclopedias, magazine articles clipped throughout the years, winery brochures, and saved menus from hundreds of wine dinners enjoyed across Europe and other delicious corners of the globe.

Anderson, Burton, *Wines of Italy* (Italian Trade Centre, London, 1992).

Ayrton, Elisabeth, *The Cookery of England* (Purnell Books Services Limited, London, 1975).

Gribourg, G. and Sarfati, C, *La Dégustation* (Edisud, Université du Vin, Suze-la-Rousse, 1989).

Johnson-Bell, Linda, *The Home Cellar Guide* (Cassell Books, London, 1999).

Montagné, Prosper, *Larousse Gastronomique* (English edition by Paul Hamlyn, London, 1961).

Peynaud, Emile, *Knowing and Making Wine*, translated from the French by Alan Spencer (John Wiley and Sons, Chichester, Sussex, 1981).

Robinson, Jancis, *Guide to Wine Grapes* (Oxford University Press, 1996).

Robinson, Jancis (ed), *The Oxford Companion to Wine* (Oxford University Press, 1994).

Wilson, James E., *Terroir* (Mitchell Beazley, Reed Books, London 1998).

Index